The Virtual Campus

IFIP – The International Federation for Information Processing

IFIP was founded in 1960 under the auspices of UNESCO, following the First World Computer Congress held in Paris the previous year. An umbrella organization for societies working in information processing, IFIP's aim is two-fold: to support information processing within its member countries and to encourage technology transfer to developing nations. As its mission statement clearly states,

> IFIP's mission is to be the leading, truly international, apolitical organization which encourages and assists in the development, exploitation and application of information technology for the benefit of all people.

IFIP is a non-profitmaking organization, run almost solely by 2500 volunteers. It operates through a number of technical committees, which organize events and publications. IFIP's events range from an international congress to local seminars, but the most important are:

- the IFIP World Computer Congress, held every second year;
- open conferences;
- working conferences.

The flagship event is the IFIP World Computer Congress, at which both invited and contributed papers are presented. Contributed papers are rigorously refereed and the rejection rate is high.

As with the Congress, participation in the open conferences is open to all and papers may be invited or submitted. Again, submitted papers are stringently refereed.

The working conferences are structured differently. They are usually run by a working group and attendance is small and by invitation only. Their purpose is to create an atmosphere conducive to innovation and development. Refereeing is less rigorous and papers are subjected to extensive group discussion.

Publications arising from IFIP events vary. The papers presented at the IFIP World Computer Congress and at open conferences are published as conference proceedings, while the results of the working conferences are often published as collections of selected and edited papers.

Any national society whose primary activity is in information may apply to become a full member of IFIP, although full membership is restricted to one society per country. Full members are entitled to vote at the annual General Assembly, National societies preferring a less committed involvement may apply for associate or corresponding membership. Associate members enjoy the same benefits as full members, but without voting rights. Corresponding members are not represented in IFIP bodies. Affiliated membership is open to non-national societies, and individual and honorary membership schemes are also offered.

The Virtual Campus
Trends for higher education and training

IFIP TC3/WG3.3 & WG3.6 Joint Working Conference on The Virtual Campus: Trends for higher education and training 27–29 November 1997, Madrid, Spain

Edited by

Felisa Verdejo
Universidad Nacional de Educación a Distancia
Madrid
Spain

and

Gordon Davies
Faculty of Mathematics and Computing
The Open University
Milton Keynes, UK

SPRINGER-SCIENCE+BUSINESS MEDIA, B.V.

First edition 1998

Originally published by Chapman & Hall in 1998

ISBN 978-1-4757-6813-8 ISBN 978-0-387-35352-4 (eBook)
DOI 10.1007/978-0-387-35352-4

A catalogue record for this book is available from the British Library

Printed on acid-free text paper, manufactured in accordance with ANSI/NISO Z39.48-1992 (Permanence of Paper).

CONTENTS

PREFACE

The virtual campus: Trends for higher education and training was the theme of the IFIP Working Conference on which this book is based. It was a joint event of Working Groups 3.3 and 3.6, Research and distance Education respectively, of IFIP Technical Committee 3 for Education.

International dissemination and promotion of cooperation are IFIP aims that we particularly wanted to address. This is why we opened the event to non WG members and have established a virtual forum on the WEB that has been widely visited. The programme for the 27 to 29 November 97 in Madrid included invited speakers from leading institutions in the field, reviewed and selected contributions from an open call for papers, on-site demonstrations of large European projects and discussion sessions involving distant and present participants. The event attracted experts from 23 countries. About a hundred persons were involved, from all over the world.

The spread and accessibility of information and communication technologies are rapidly changing practices in learning and research activities, both in professional and academic settings. The number, variety and scale of experiences reported in recent publications shows a growing international involvement concerning not only small groups of researchers but also institutions fully committed in that direction. To analyze the impact of computer network technologies on the classical role and organization of universities is a complex matter, requiring the perspective of a wide range of actors. This Working Conference intended to provide a forum for experts to contribute and raise awareness on a number of key themes. The Programme Committee selected the following themes, around which to organize presentations and debates:

- Single versus dual-model approaches for Universities
- Evaluation, scaleability and socio-cultural issues
- New perspectives for collaboration between industry and higher education
- Collaborative learning at a distance
- Instructional and learning telecommunications models and tools

The format of the book does not mirror exactly that of the event. Part I includes five papers from keynote speakers, and the rest - Parts II to V- contain contributions presented at the Conference. Three keynote lectures were given at Madrid, and the other two were videoconference events shared with audiences at University of Sunderland (U.K.) and Twente University (The Netherlands) respectively. Papers in each part appear in authors' alphabetical order. A list of authors and a keywords index are provided at the end, to aid the reader in moving directly to particular personal concerns.

In Part I, G.Paquette, from Télé-Université, the Canada's oldest distance education institution focuses his chapter on instructional and learning telecommunications models. First, he establishes orientations and principles for the design of a fully and diversified virtual campus and then he provides a conceptual model allowing the description of actors, processes and tools in an integrated way. E. Stacey's chapter, describes the dual mode implemented from the very beginning in Deakin University, Australia. She discusses the rationale for this choice, detailing how the dual model is been deployed in a variety of educational fields and the issues it raises. B.Collis's work shows through examples, ways in which telecommunications activities are been integrated in Twente University. She analyses the innovative aspects that these technologies bring to current teaching and learning practices in traditional universities, and how from this perspective a classroom setting can evolve to a virtual campus scenario. While all these three chapters mention new opportunities to build bridges between academic institutions and members of the community, either professional at their workplaces or adults at home, the two other keynotes focus on this theme. Thorne and Milner's paper presents a project, carried out in the University of Sunderland, where the core motivation is to promote the openness of the University to members of the community, offering them opportunities for learning in a variety of social scenarios. L.Rodriguez-Roselló, reports on the policies, main goals, and actions to be deployed by the European Commission for Telematics Applications and Services for Education and Training in the future.

As indicated earlier, Part II to V include the set of refereed and selected papers by the Programme Committee. Each part also includes a report written by one of the chairpersons involved in the sessions for that theme. Reports appear in the form of an Introduction for Parts II, IV, and V, and as Comments and Discussions for Part III. Reports identify and highlight ideas discussed at the conference. They also provide the author's personal insights on current open questions in this extremely dynamic field. Papers are grouped according to the following criteria:

- Part II, Global approaches, includes two papers describing either models and/or architectures to implement virtual environments.
- Part III, Evaluation, includes four papers dealing with evaluation studies, social aspects, and new roles for universities.
- Part IV, Collaborative learning, includes four papers describing experiences and the technology to support this approach for distance learning.
- Part V, Web Tools and applications, includes eight papers describing cases and on-going experiences to implement telelearning and teaching in a variety of educational fields. They provide tools and stimulating examples for moving forward in changing and improving current practices.

We had an excellent meeting in Madrid. On behalf of the Programme Committee we wish to thank authors and participants. Special thanks to the Local Organizing Committee for their hard work to ensure the necessary conditions for a successful conference. We extend our acknowledgment to IFIP and the Consejeria de Educación de la Comunidad de Madrid for its sponsorship as well to Universidad Nacional de Educación a Distancia and Consejo de Universidades for providing the infrastructure to run the Conference.
The Editors wish to express their gratitude to the members of the Programme Committee for their help and generous work. Finally, we wish to acknowledge the major contribution of Beatriz Barros in the preparation of both the WEB site and this book.

M. Felisa Verdejo and Gordon Davies
January 1998

Programme Committee:
Beatriz Barros, U.N.E.D, Spain
Betty Collis, Twente University, NL, Vice-Chair
Gordon Davies, Open University, U.K. Co-editor
Sebastian Dormido, U.N.E.D, Spain
Helen Milner, University of Sunderland, U.K.
Gilbert Paquette, Tele-Université, Canada
Encarna Pastor, Universidad Politecnica de Madrid, Spain
Elizabeth Stacey, Deakin University, Australia
M Felisa Verdejo, U.N.E.D, Spain, Chair
Martial Vivet, University of Le Mans, France
Joachim Wedekind, German Institute for Distance Education, Germany
Jan Wibe, University of Trondheim, Norway, Vice-Chair

Organising Committee
Beatriz Barros, U.N.E.D, Spain
Jose Ignacio Mayorga, U.N.E.D, Spain
Miguel Rodriguez Artacho, U.N.E.D, Spain

PART ONE

Keynote Presentations

New Wine and Old Bottles? Tele-Learning, Telematics and the University of Twente

B. Collis
Faculteit Toegepaste Onderwijskunde, (Faculty of Educational Science and Technology)
Universiteit Twente (University of Twente)
e-mail:collis@edte.utwente.nl

Keywords
Tele-learning, Intellectual development, Internationalisation, Implementation strategy

1. AN ANNIVERSARY: THOUGHTS OF NEW AND OLD, OF CELEBRATION AND FINE WINE

Today, November 28th, is an anniversary celebration for the University of Twente. Anniversaries are happy affairs; among their many functions, they bring people together who share some common connection but represent different generations of contact with that common connection. The University of Twente, as our common connection, is not old as universities go, but as an institution it is certainly old enough to have old values, and old ways of going about its business. Today, I want to think about old and new. I want to reflect about the idea of "tele-learning" as something new at the University of Twente, and I want to speculate on what it might mean for our old values, our old ways of doing things at this university. And, because I am thinking in terms of an anniversary and of celebration, I want to use a metaphor that relates to celebrating: I want to frame my thoughts around the idea of wine: old and new, mature or still fermenting, I want to expand upon two apparently contradictory parables about wine, and draw messages from these for the University of Twente, telematics, and tele-learning.

2. BUT FIRST, A DEFINITION IS IMPORTANT

I am using the term "tele-learning" but I am quite sure that if we had a quiz right now, and each of you had to give a definition of what I mean by this term, there would be many different answers. Some of you would say: "distance education",

The Virtual Campus F. Verdejo & G. Davies (Eds.)

and picture a scenario where a teacher, like me, is talking not only to the group in front of her, but also to a group clustered at a remote location, and watching the teacher via a room-sized videoconferencing system or television or even via a computer screen. The teacher pauses and asks a question--a student at the remote location, indicates by some technological procedure that he wishes to answer and then his voice and face come through a network or the ether into the monitor in the teacher's classroom.

But I imagine many others of you have a different idea: you picture a student, by herself, in her home, surrounded by piles of books and notepads, busily studying, perhaps for a course similar to those offered by the traditional open universities. She has the benefit of studying when and where she wants, but with the consequence that she looses the benefits of interacting with a skilled teacher in a class environment.

These were the two most popular images for tele-learning five years ago, but now there are other contenders. Perhaps you are picturing a situation in a basisschool (elementary school) in your own neighbourhood: the teacher has one of the school computers in the classroom, a computer with a modem that connects to the networks needed to access the Internet. Within this classroom, with the teacher and pupils side by side, the class is able to bring in information about an event, such as the Mars landing as happened in the summer of 1997, taking place somewhere far away in the world (or even out of the world, as in the case of Mars and the Sojourner vehicle). The teacher and pupils not only access up-to-date information as it is occurring, but also are busy exchanging information and ideas with other classes, in different places, about the event, learning on the way about the solar system, distances in space, and geology.

Or perhaps you are picturing a secondary school, where students routinely check resources available in local, regional, national, or international collections, without paying much attention to the fact that one click of their mouse brings them to a computer in a library in Amsterdam, and another click brings them to the computer in a school in Australia where other students such as themselves have made available useful resources via a WWW site. Sometimes their teacher comes in the room as they search for appropriate resources, sometimes she doesn't.

But there are even more scenarios you might have thought of: perhaps you thought of someone like yourselves, no longer a student, but still someone involved in life-long learning. Not through taking courses in an institution, but by accessing information you need when you need it, sometimes by contacting appropriate persons, other times by reading journals or studying conference proceedings or accessing other sources of professional information. More and more, you are probably, like me, doing this via different World Wide Web sites, as well as by other means such as e-mail, telephone, and of course, reading printed text.

Each of the above scenarios I have described above, and a number of other scenarios[1], all are part of what I call "tele-learning". To encompass all these possibilities, my definition of tele-learning is:

Using telematics for learning-related purposes

Notice that this definition does not say anything about geographical distance, one way or the other. This is intentional, because with telematics when we make a connection with persons they may be in the next room or the next continent; when we connect to information with telematics tools, we maybe accumulating it from the hard drives of our own computers, from our own local servers or from computers on the other side of the world. The point is that with telematics, the distance between myself and the persons with whom I am communicating or between myself and the information with which I am working is not particularly relevant.

And there is another point to notice in the above scenarios. In all of them, a variety of ways of interacting, of learning, with a variety of media, and with a variety of communication methods, can be found. This is deliberate: in my definition, good "tele-learning" comes from knowing how and if and when telematics can support some aspect related to learning better than we do it without telematics, and how telematics can be combined with good pedagogy, good thinking, good debate, good books, good face-to-face interaction, and good working and learning habits to improve the quality of a learning experience. By "better", I mean more efficient, or more enriched, or more flexible.

Thus in the rest of these remarks, when I use the term "tele-learning" I mean simply, telematics used in some way related to the learning enterprise.

Now, back to the idea of a wine-related metaphor that I mentioned at the beginning of this talk: Is tele-learning our New Wine...? Or only some new packaging?

3. TELE-LEARNING AT THE UT, IS ANYTHING REALLY CHANGING?

Previously I asked you to define "tele-learning" and I guessed that there would be many different definitions, with the "correct answer" being "all of the above". But I also imagine that some of you may have had some other sorts of thoughts. Perhaps when you saw the title "tele-learning" as the theme for this anniversary celebration, your deep-down reaction was that all of this "tele" business is something of a buzzword, a current "hype", similar to buzzwords such as the "information highway" or the "information superhighway" or the "virtual information superhighway" or the "virtual whatever". You may think of the World Wide Web as a fad, a bandwagon, more metaphor than substance, more noise than

[1] I begin my 1996 book, "*Tele-learning in a digital world*", with a discussion of 11 such scenarios, and work these out in the subsequent chapters of the book.

real impact. You may be thinking, "Yes, yes, lots of talk but nothing has really changed" in the university enterprise. In fact, this is the first of the wine-related metaphors that I want to use today, the Dutch phrase:

"Oude wijn in nieuwe zakken" (Old wine in new bottles)

Especially if you have gone through various waves of fascination with other technologies and their possibilities for education, particularly the computer itself, you may feel we should have learned our lessons already, that technologies come and go, but basically don't change the way we teach and learn and how we organise our courses and degree requirements and the way we fund persons to study; or the ways we work with our colleagues and our students. You may well be saying, "Please, no more hype".[2]

But I don't want to let the idea continue that tele-learning is some kind of new packaging, some kind of superficial add-on, to business as usual in the University. I want to turn the metaphor around, and instead argue the following: At the University of Twente, I see tele-learning not as a new packaging, but as new wine. I present a new metaphor:

New Wine and Old Bottles

But wait: Is this good or bad? If telematics is the "new wine" in the metaphor, then what are the "old bottles"?

I am going to look at the "old bottles" in two different ways. In the first way, the connotation of this new turned-around metaphor becomes positive, because the definition of "old bottles" that I will use is "old values". I will argue and demonstrate that telematics as a new wine is enhancing and enriching our old values at the University of Twente. In the second way of looking at the old bottles-metaphor, however, the message is a warning. I discuss this second way in Section 9.

4. "OLD VALUES" AND THE UNIVERSITY

What are some of the old values that I believe most important to universities, not only Twente? There are many, but the ones I will focus upon today are the following four:

Values related to "academische vorming" (or what Prof. Van Vught, in his rede for the opening of the University year two months' previously, calls becoming an "intellectual expert")

Values relating to good teaching

Values related to the interaction of local and global perspectives; and

---

[2] I followed this line, comparing the response of educators and society to the possibilities of computers in education in the late 1970s with the response today with respect to the Internet and the WWW, in an analysis for UNESCO in 1996. An abridged version of this analysis is published in the journal *Educational Technology* (Collis, 1996b).

Values related to the university being a focal point of knowledge and expertise.

For each of these, I will show some examples from today, at the University of Twente, of how these old values are being strengthened and deepened by the use of tele-learning, rather than being diminished or threatened; not replacing what the University does well, but adding new dimensions to these old values. In the short time of this presentation, I will only be able to show a relatively few examples; in the WWW site I have prepared to support the demonstration, there will be links to other examples that those interested can study for as long as they wish. The address of this site is
http://www.to.utwente.nl/prj/diesrede/demo.htm

5. ACADEMISCHE VORMING AND TELE-LEARNING

The term "academische vorming" doesn't have an immediate parallel as a term in English[3] although certainly the idea has. However it is an idea that is increasingly under strain as it comes in association with other ideas about the university experience, such as those related to making the university more and more open. However, I agree with our Rector that *academische vorming* is an important, old value, for our young students. Van Vught (1997) uses the phrase "intellectual expert", which I like as a goal of *academische vorming.* I will expand on his definition by noting the following characteristics of an "intellectual expert": someone who is trained in a discipline at a scientific level; has developed into an independent and critical thinker (including being able to be constructively critical of himself); is an individual who can take responsibility and leadership in a problem situation in practical situations where his discipline is relevant and participate in designing and testing a solution; an individual who can speak the language of his intellectual community, who knows its manners and style, who feels at home in its "branches" where ever they might be geographically.

How does a student mature into an intellectual expert? Certainly by studying, but also by undergoing an intellectual apprenticeship, with certain key components. The intellectual apprentice must know the tools of his trade, must be able to articulate his perceptions in the language of his profession, and must understand when this language is used well and when it is misused. This partially comes from reading books and listening to lectures, but just as a child learns the ways of his family, not only by observing and studying but by a continual process of trying the language out himself and receiving supportive re-enforcement and correction as he comes to define himself by the norms. This is similarly the case with *academische vorming*, or intellectual development. I believe this development requires the opportunity to practice finding one's voice in a professional community, to realise genuine success and failure in getting established in that community, and to have around one some persons who care enough to scaffold this process, giving

[3] This is one of a number of terms that I find the Dutch language handles better than my native English; "vormgeving" is another.

opportunities, encouragement and criticism. For the fortunate student at a good university, this initiation process, scaffolded by a wise mentor, gradually takes place.

How can tele-learning enhance this process? I can see many ways, of which the following are only some examples, taken from my own courses here at the University:[4]

Aspect of Academische Vorming	Example of Tele-Learning Enhancement
Guided collaboration with external experts	Writing chapters collaboratively, via e-mail and the WWW; http://www.to.utwente.nl/ism/online/
Guided communication with an external expert	Asking questions about the expert's work and getting a response; http://www.to.utwente.nl/ism/ism1-96/wwwproj/STUDYCTR/Week40/Fdbk40.htm
Learning to learn; practicing the language	Using "design guidelines" as vocabulary throughout a WWW-based course; http://www.to.utwente.nl/ism/ism1-97/wwwproj/studyctr/lin.htm and http://www.to.utwente.nl/ism/ ism1-97/wwwproj/prodctr/44eval.htm
Moving into a collegial relationship with external experts	Via the instructor's contacts, taking an active role in a professional on-line discussion; http://www.to.utwente.nl/prj/teled97/cwelcome.htm
Working with the instructor on professional projects; mentoring the student's initial public presentations about his work	Via cooperation with instructor on WWW-based projects and scientific writing and presentations about the projects; http://www.to.utwente.nl/ism/ism1-97/Edmedia/home.htmand http://www.utwente.nl/prj/teled97/present/sld001.htm
Maintaining close communication with the supervisor when on an outside final (afstudeer) project	Keeping in regular contact via the WWW; http://www.dipoli.hut.fi/~hquirijn/weekrapport/pages/

These are some of the types of professional experiences that differentiate *academische vorming* from taking a series of courses, in the way that the forest is more than the sum of the trees. Critical in these examples is the way that telematics can make it easier for a mentoring relationship between instructor and student to involve guided forays into real-world professional communities. Tele-learning techniques, used by the instructor interested in developing a mentor relationship with qualified students, can deepen and extend the opportunities for the student to find his voice and identity in a professional community. Thus it is not a matter of *academische vorming* OR tele-learning; it is a matter of both.

---

[4] I am using examples from my own courses simply because I know them best and can conveniently offer them as examples. There are, of course, many other examples of tele-learning in the University besides my own courses. For courses making substantial use of WWW environments in the Faculty of Educational Science and Technology, see http://to-www.to.utwente.nl/TO/project/teletop/examples.html

6. BEING A GOOD TEACHER, AND TELE-LEARNING

Here is perhaps where the greatest misconceptions appear about tele-learning. Many seem to assume that tele-learning means instructors no longer giving lectures, no longer being a "regular teacher", but moving to the background, even as in the Open University model, moving out of the picture entirely. I reject this. I feel the opposite. A good teacher who prepares good lectures and is effective in his class presentations should continue to exercise these skills, this craft, but can be even more effective with the addition of tele-learning techniques. To illustrate this, I will use the idea of the "Extended Lecture" that I use for all my lectures and also presentations.

An extended lecture is a lecture whose benefits begin before the lecture and last after the lecture, and where the actual lecture itself is improved, all through tele-learning techniques. Here are examples:

An Extended Lecture:	**Examples:**
Involves use of a WWW site to present the lecture notes, as interactive pages with links, before the class	Http://www.to.utwente.nl/ism/telearn/schedule/schedul.htm and http://www.to.utwente.nl/ism/telearn/schedule/Week18/virt-uni/inter0.htm
During the lecture, invo'ves using this same WWW site to illustrate points with multimedia examples from other sources. (And students who are not physically present at the lecture can interact with the same WWW site, either while hearing the instructor in real time, or via stored audio or video)	Http://www.to.utwente.nl/user/ism/Collis/presents/Coimbra/index.htm Http://www.to.utwente.nl/toprac1/telearn/www/group4/videosum/video/htm/home.htm
After the lecture, students interact individually with the links and resources in the lecture notes, for deeper study than possible in the lecture and with reflective communication added	Http://www.to.utwente.nl/toprac1/telearn/www/group4/videosum/video/htm/opinion.htm
After the lecture, students can supplement the lecture resources by adding material to the WWW site	Http://www.to.utwente.nl/ism/telearn/schedule/Week18/virt-uni/inter6.htm

All of these examples show how a good teacher, who invests much care in his lectures, can extend those lectures, in depth, in time, and over distance, via tele-learning.

There are many other aspects of being a good teacher, such as communicating personally with one's students, giving personal feedback, and keeping one's courses up to date and stimulating. For each of these points, I can show many examples of how tele-learning enhances good teaching, Here are just a few:

Aspects of being a good teacher:	**Tele-learning support**
Communicating personally with one's students	Via e-mail forms made handy within a course WWW site; http://www.to.utwente.nl/ism/telearn/communic/communic.htm
Providing regular feedback and models of good practice for assignments	Via model answers and links to examples of previous work of students, http://www.to.utwente.nl/ism/ism1-97/wwwproj/studyctr/Week44/Int44.htm
Keeping one's course up-to-date and stimulating	Via external links and new sorts of activities such as working collaboratively with students in another university; http://www.to.utwente.nl/ism/telearn/group/Grpp-wp.htm and http://www.to.utwente.nl/toprac1/telearn/www/Group3/home.htm

7. LIVE LOCALLY, THINK GLOBALLY

Another of the important old values of the university is to provide an environment in which participants not only benefit from proximity to each other, but also are aware of larger issues and patterns, beyond the local boundaries, and even backwards and forward in time. Academics have always been aware of larger boundaries for their ideas than only the local setting, and of course have long nourished their own work and that of their home universities by participating in international activities, such as going to a professional conference or working with colleagues from other institutions and countries on professional activities. Students also benefit from mobility during their study[5]. But until recently, much of this mobility was limited by the realities of costs--time and financial. Going away to an international conference is a special opportunity, perhaps once a year for an academic and never for a student, and often depends on finding adequate funding. Working on cross-border projects presents immediate and costly problems of getting everyone together and maintaining the momentum of work over time and distance. Studying abroad is valuable, but costs time and effort to organise, and sometimes becomes disruptive to the student's mainstream academic career.
Tele-learning is making all of these professional international experiences not only more accessible to staff and student alike, but also adds a new dimension to them. Here are just a few examples:

---

[5] The conference, "Internationalisation and the University", co-sponsored by NUFFIC and the University of Twente in May 1997, provided an extended treatment of these points.

Internationalisation:	**Tele-learning aspects:**
Academics have new opportunities for collaborative projects with colleagues in other locations	Using a shared workspace via the WWW support collaborative research sponsored by the EU; http://bscw.dipoli.hut.fi/bscw/bscw.cgi(please note, this site requires a password to enter, but I will demonstrate it during the Rede)
Academics (and students) have new opportunities to publish and to extend the professional conference experience	WWW-extended conferences and video-conferencing at conferences add to the quality and quantity of participation; http://www.iste.org/conferences/teled97/webex/and http://www.ieec.uned.es/~ifip97/
Guest visitors can be integrated into a lecture or a course or a project, via telematics	The external guest can lecture and interact in real time, and/or can make his work available for further study after the lecture or visit; http://itesm.cstudies.ubc.ca/(please note that this site requires a password to enter, but I will demonstrate it during the Rede)

The opportunities already available to University staff (and students) with respect to moving outside the local situation for stimulation or study or professional interaction are now on another dimension because of tele-learning. One's inner circle of professional colleagues can be scattered throughout the world, and it can be easier to communicate with this circle, using various telematics tools, than to communicate with those in one's own building. Important however, is not only the thinking globally, but the ability to translate the relevance of the global experience to one's local situation. This leads to another of the important old values of the University.

8. AND ANOTHER OLD VALUE: THE UNIVERSITY AS EXPERTISE CENTRE

Finally, the University values very much the service it can give to the community, the region, the country. By being acknowledged as a focal point of knowledge, as a centre of expertise, the University serves as a valuable partner in many different projects. Telematics makes these partnerships, at the very least, more efficient, as partners do not need to always travel to meetings and potential partners can find what the University offers and who to contact with support of different information channels, including those involving telematics and in particular WWW sites. Telematics is not only a channel but also a focal point for the University of Twente in many of its partnership activities. Increasingly, the local, regional, national, and international community look to us as a centre of excellence with respect to telematics and telematics applications (including tele-learning). Some of the many examples are shown below:

Focal Point:	Partnership
Telematics expertise nationally	The *Telematics Institute*; http://www.trc.nl/ttti/indextti.htm; the *MESH Project*, http://www.mesh.nl/extern/english.html
Tele-learning expertise within the University	The *CTIT-IDYLLE Project*; http://wwwctit.cs.utwente.nl/Docs/research/project/idylle/IDYLLE.htm
Tele-learning expertise internationally	The *European School Network (EUN)*, http://www.eun.org/

In all of these, telematics is being used in a learning-related context for responsive service and partnership with many different communities. The University of Twente continues to strengthen its international profile in this area; it has already become a focal point for knowledge and expertise with respect to telematics applications.

9. BUT, THERE IS A SECOND SIDE TO THE METAPHOR

The last examples have focused on a positive message associated with the metaphor "New wine and old bottles". Tele-learning is the new wine, our old values are the old bottles, and the fermenting of the new wine in these old bottles brings a valuable result: the old values are strengthened.

But there is, unfortunately, another way to interpret the metaphor. This way comes as a warning. "New wine in old bottles" can lead to a sorry result. Many years ago a truly great teacher made the following observation:

"..no one pours new wine into old wineskins; else the new wine will burst the skins and will be split itself, and the skins ruined. New wine must be put into new wineskins, and then both will be saved" (Luke 5:37, Chalmers-Rheims Version, translation 1954)

The metaphor here is striking: old wineskins in the Biblical time were brittle; new wine ferments, at a certain point the fermentation causes the old wineskins to burst. Both new and old are lost. There is also a message for us in this side of the metaphor. When the "old bottles" represent old procedures, old ways of doing things, that no longer are a good reflection of our old values, it is those old ways that must be replaced before, or after, the fermentation of the new wine of telematics applications bursts their seams.

10. SOME OLD WINESKINS...

Two "old wineskins" are in particular danger from the fermentation of tele-learning in the university, not only our own university but worldwide[6]. The first of these is

[6] For an on-going debate about the impact of telematics on the future university, the *Vision 2010 University* site maintained at the University of Michigan is a good source (http://www.si.umich.edu/V2010/). Also, the work of Tiffin and

our "assembly line" approach to higher education ("Fordism")[7] and the second is intellectual parochialism.

In gradual response to the very positive motivation of providing quality-controlled and affordable university education to a maximal number of students, we have seen the development of a so-called "Fordism" or assembly line approach[8]. It is now assumed that a quality product will come off the assembly line after a set amount of courses, in a set amount of time, starting directly after secondary school, and this product will be road-ready, presumably forever, after this processing. Presumably forever, in terms of government funding policies, because there is no systematic provision for funding for study at the university after the end of this assembly-line period. Already many universities in other countries, particularly Canada and Australia, are breaking away from this Fordism approach, and investing as much systematic attention to what is often called "Continuing Education", or provision for life-long learning as they do to the first-phase learning[9]. Offering courses and programmes to professionals is not only motivated by a post-Fordist philosophy, but also by strong economic factors: the life-long learning market presents an important new client base for the University.

But re-tooling one's assembly line, to continue this metaphor, needs to be done at many different levels before the University of Twente can say it is truly responding to life-long learning. This will require not only the new wine of tele-learning, but will also inevitably result in the need for new ways, new procedures, new approaches to curriculum and academic programmes and funding and to staff time allocation and facility allocation throughout the University. The old ways will simply split at the seams as this fermentation continues.

And another old way that will split with change is what I call "intellectual parochialism". Self-enclosed thinking and teaching, self-feeding on its own work and ideas, will no longer be acceptable in the future university. The synergy between local and global will become so powerful in society as a whole, and the impact of telematics so pervasive and ubiquitous in all aspects of our commerce

---

Rajasingham in New Zealand (via their 1995 book *In search of the virtual class* and the evolving *Global Virtual University* (http://206.154.197.130:80/VU/) which Tiffin is involved in founding) are useful to study.

[7] Volume 17(2), 1996, of the Austrialasian journal *Distance Education* (http://www.usq.edu.au/dec/decjourn/v17n296/issue.htm) discusses the evolution of Fordism in higher education at a particularly thoughtful level.

[8] I discuss this at some length in the final chapter of my *Tele-learning in a Digital World* book.

[9] See for example, the Life-Long Learning Institute at the Helsinki University of Technology, in Finland (http://www.dipoli.fi/eng/index.htm)

and culture, that the instructor who figuratively and literally lectures from old notes, who sees the world through his own research, who is bound within his own walls, will be as much of an anachronism as the candle, the horse-drawn carriage, the butter churn; nice for romantic occasions or for a sense of history but not tools to be funded by society.

Thus my use of the metaphor of "New Wine and Old Bottles" is deliberate for this rede, because it is a metaphor that captures both sides of tele-learning: When the old bottles are the old values of the University, these old values are not brittle wineskins vulnerable to bursting with the fermentation of the new wine, but elastic and flexible. Extending the University experience beyond the confines of time, place, and person allows us--staff and students--to live locally and globally simultaneously, to magnify the opportunities we can scaffold for the professional initiation and the intellectual development of our students, and to strengthen our profile as a leader with respect to applications of telematics. But when the old bottles are old ways of doing things that no longer parallel the old values, then these are old wineskins such as the Bible warns about.

11. SOME REFLECTIONS ON THE NEW WINE...

In all these comments, I have been talking about tele-learning as a New Wine in a way that has not been very differentiating. It is important to note that just as "old bottles" can be seen in different ways, so can the "new wine" of tele-learning. To extend the wine metaphor even more:

Not every batch of new wine will mature into a great vintage
Not all forms of new wine will be valued over time
Some variants of new wine will achieve no more than local consumption
Some variants of new wine will not last long enough to even ferment
And, not everyone wants to drink wine...

I see much of my own work focused on these points (relating to learning, not wine, of course!). Which tele-learning applications will emerge as those gaining a critical mass of acceptance and impact in practice? Can we predict these now? I think so, but that is a story for another speech...

12. OUR TASK AT THE UNIVERSITY OF TWENTE?

I see it as our job at the University of Twente to lead the way in "spotting the great vintages" in terms of telematics applications in society, and thus with respect to tele-learning. Once we spot these great vintages, we need to identify the ways their fermentation can be used to enhance our old values. But we also need to anticipate and reduce the painful impact of this fermentation on many of our old procedures, our old ways of doing things, even our old securities.

At the University of Twente, we have had a head start in pioneer work with applications of telematics in many different fields, including in education, and to this we owe much to the vision and strategy of our Board. The start of the *Centre for Telematics and Information Technology*, (http://wwwctit.cs.utwente.nl) for example, was an important strategic move for the telematics profile of the University. The decisions taken to supply all our students with good connections to the University network and the Internet was also bold and important to all of our subsequent tele-learning initiatives. The climate of encouragement as well as the real support provided by the Board for telematics initiatives is a critical factor in our success as pioneers in many different telematics-related areas.

But, the rest of the academic world is catching up on many of our pioneering ideas. The course "On-Line Learning" (see http://www.to.utwente.nl/ism/online/) was a pioneer in the use of the WWW as a course environment in early 1994; now every university in the Western world uses the WWW in some way in relation to its courses (even if only for the conceptually simplest form of information dissemination). Our involvement, through CTIT, in multi-partner projects involving high-speed networking and its applications to different areas including education was more unique in 1995 when we began participation in the PLATINUM Project than it is now when many such collaborative explorations of ATM and other forms of high-speed, high bandwidth networking are occurring in countries throughout the world.

I believe we have reached a critical point: Even as we continue to strive for pioneering insights in our research and practice with respect to tele-learning, we need to turn our energy and expertise to a new challenge: implementation, or sustainable use throughout the institution.

There is a critical gap between the vision and energy of pioneers and the institutionalisation of this vision and energy into sustainable practice[10]. Sustainable practice is what I mean by implementation: Once we identify what aspects of tele-learning are potential "great vintages", how do we move to support their growth in as systematic and professional way as possible? There are many, many problems when change occurs in an educational institution; this is well known in the literature and in practice. Here is where I see our real potential for leadership in tele-learning now lies: How can we manage its acceptance into educational practice enough so that the fermentation reaches a critical mass of impact?

---

[10] I have made an analysis of this in a speech to be presented to representatives of all Dutch universities and hogeschools in December (see http://www.to.utwente.nl/user/ism/Collis/papers/suncoo.doc). In this speech, I identify three phases: pioneer, "1.000 flowers blooming", and managed change.

13. THE NEW CHALLENGE: TELETOP AT THE FACULTY OF EDUCATIONAL SCIENCE AND TECHNOLOGY

I believe that my faculty, Toegepaste Onderwijskunde (T.O.), is again embarking on pioneer work with respect to tele-learning, but this time in the implementation aspect. Because of the range and depth of experience with tele-learning in our faculty, our own faculty Board has taken a visionary and strategic step. A major project has begun, called ***TeleTOP*** (the Tele-Learning at TO Project), which has as a concrete goal the systematic adaptation of approximately 15 of our courses, this year, to a more flexible form through the combination of new didactics and WWW-based environments. This more flexible form will be immediately put to test through its application with the many students who now participate in our Master of Science Programme in *Educational and Training Systems Design* (http://www.to.utwente.nl/masters/mscgen.htm) as well as new cohorts of part-time students for whom WWW-based course support can allow full participation in our education while continuing with their work. TeleTOP is both a top-down and bottom-up initiative: from top-down, we offer strong professional and technical support, guidance, and strategy, while from bottom-up we recognise the critical importance of faculty acceptance and buy-in and are seeking for each instructor the particular form and mix of tele-learning techniques with other aspects of instruction that will best fit his or her vision of good teaching. We invite everyone to visit the homesite of TeleTOP to follow our progress:
http://to-www.to.utwente.nl/TO/project/teletop/
Through TeleTOP, as well as other initiatives such as those in other faculties, those being supported by the *OC* (Onderwijskundig Centrum), and those within the framework of the *CTIT* (such as the *IDYLLE Project*) we will, again, move forward at the University of Twente as a leader in tele-learning, in the combination of new wine, old values and new methods that we celebrate today at this anniversary.

So, as we say in English at a birthday or anniversary celebration, "Many Happy Returns!" I suggest we use today as a benchmark, and look together again, in five years' time, to see what those returns, related to tele-learning, have been.

14. REFERENCES

Collis, B. (1996a). *Tele-learning in a digital world: The future of distance learning*. London: International Thomson Publications.

Collis, B. (1996b). The Internet as an educational innovation: Lessons from experience with computer implementation. *Educational Technology, 36*(7), 21-30.

Tiffin, J., & Rajasingham, L. (1995). In search of the virtual class: Education in an information age. London: Routledge.

Van Vught, F. (1997). *Academische vorming: over experts en intellectuelen.* Rede, opening academsich jaar 1997/1998, Universiteit Twente, Enschede, NL.

15. BIOGRAPHY

Betty Collis is an Associate Professor in Educational Instrumentation at the University of Twente. Since 1980, she has been acknowledged internationally as a specialist in computers in education, and since the mid 1980s, in telecommunications in education. Her major activity at the moment is being Chair of the TeleTOP Project , in which the faculty is re-designing its courses through the use of a combination of telematics applications, not only to make the courses themselves more flexible but more than this, to move toward a new model of teaching and learning in higher education.

Virtual Learning Centers for XXIst Century Organizations

G. Paquette
LICEF Research Centre, Télé-université
1001 Sherbrooke est, Montréal, Qc, Canada, H2L 4L5
E-Mail: gpaquett @ teluq.uquebec.ca
Web: http://www.teluq.uquebec.ca/~licef/

Abstract

A model of the Virtual Campus is introduced as a result of course development at Télé-université, as well as a product of the research conducted at its research center, LICEF. The Virtual Campus model is based on the networking of a diversified array of actors and resources. Its aim is to offer an access, in real time and in asynchronous mode, to a variety of learning resources: other learners, trainers and tutors, content experts, managers and designers. These different actors communicate with distant computer-based servers offering multimedia documents, courseware, integrated tools for task achievement and training, individual or group message files, projects and activities. We present here a survey of six different telelearning models describe LICEF's Virtual Campus model, its actors and their functions, the process in which they participate and the role they play, as well as the virtual spaces of resources they use. We also present five different implementations of the model and we outline future research and development in this field.

Résumé

Le concept de campus virtuel est ici exploré et présenté dans le contexte de la Télé-université et de son centre de recherche, le LICEF. Le Campus virtuel proposé repose sur la mise en réseau d'acteurs et de moyens diversifiés. Il vise à offrir un accès, en direct et en différé, à diverses ressources d'apprentissage: autres apprenants, formateurs et tuteurs, experts de contenu, gestionnaires, professeurs-concepteurs. Ces différents acteurs ont accès à des serveurs informatiques leur offrant des documents multimédias, des logiciels, des outils de travail et de formation, des fichiers de messages individuels ou collectifs, des travaux à réaliser. Nous présentons six modèles techno-pédagogiques de formation à distance, puis nous exposons le modèle de Campus Virtuel du LICEF, ses acteurs et leurs fonctions, les processus auxquels ils participent et les rôles qu'ils y jouent, ainsi que les cinq espaces virtuels dans lesquels ils évoluent. Nous faisons aussi état de cinq implantations du modèle, ainsi que des perspectives de recherche et de développement dans ce domaine.

Keywords

Virtual campus, Tele-learning, Roles, Actor, Scenario, Virtual space learning

The Virtual Campus F. Verdejo & G. Davies (Eds.)

1. INTRODUCTION

Télé-université was created shortly after the United Kingdom's Open University, in 1972. It is Canada's oldest distance teaching university. Most of its students (90%) are working adult learners. LICEF is Télé-université's research center. Its mission aims to further knowledge in cognitive informatics, particularly through its applications according to three axes: knowledge modeling of learning transactions, learning systems engineering methods and the development of computerized telelearning systems.

The **Virtual Campus** concept has become LICEF unifying's research project (Paquette 1995). The design of our Virtual Campus is based on the networking of actors and resources that are much more diversified than in most other existing telelearning systems. It aims to offer learners synchronous or asynchronous access to various learning resources such as trainers and tutors (animation, pedagogical assessment, advice, monitoring) contents experts (information resources), managers (organization, coordination, accreditation), professors-designers (continued updating of learning resources). On the information highways, many resources are available to the different actors through servers: multimedia documents, educational software, working and learning tools, individual or teleconferencing message files, individual or group productions.

In this article, we will review the main techno-pedagogical models in distance education in order to establish the orientation principles of a virtual campus. Then, we will present LICEF's model of the Virtual Campus, its actors and their functions, the process in which they participate and the roles they play, as well as the virtual spaces where they evolve. Finally, we will summarize the implementation of this model as experimented at LICEF and Télé-université and we will conclude on the research and development outlook.

2. DISTANCE EDUCATION TECHNO-PEDAGOGICAL MODELS

Distance education covers a multi-facetted techno-pedagogical reality, ranging from the simple decentralization of classroom activities to interactive multimedia models that make learning available whatever the time or the location. We now describe these various models and stress the principles that we have retained to design an integrated model of the Virtual Campus.

2.1 Distance education technological models

The distance education world is bubbling. The rapidly evolving availability of multimedia telecommunication is giving way to a increasing number of techno-pedagogical models. We describe them in terms of six main paradigms:

- The ***enriched classroom*** where technologies are used within a traditional setting in order to do a presentation, a demonstration or an experimentation. It is a networked classroom allowing access to campus resources and external databases and it is sometimes called an " intelligent " campus.

- The ***virtual classroom*** (Wilson and Mosher, 1994 ; Hiltz, 1990) mainly uses videoconferencing to support distant learners and teachers, thereby re-creating a telepresence type of classroom ; many university campus now have their own multimedia production studios so they may decentralize training at satellite locations.

- The ***teaching media*** (Pea and Gomez, 1992 ; Bourdeau et al., 1994) is focused on the learner's workstation. It allows access to prefabricated multimedia course contents on CD ROM, either shipped by mail or available from a distant multimedia server. Instruction and didactic resources are offered in such a way that the learner can individualize his own learning process.

- ***Information highway training*** is also centered on the learner's workstation, which serves as a navigation and research instrument to find all kinds of useful educational information. Essentially, a " Web course " is offered on a central site where instructions and pointers related to didactic resources (other Web sites) are gathered in order to accomplish learning activities.

- The ***communication network*** (Henri et Rigault, 1993; Rigault et Henri, 1990) uses the workstation, not only as a media support or as a way to access information, but also as a synchronous (desktop videoconferencing, screen sharing, etc.) and as an asynchronous communication tool (electronic mail, computer teleconferencing, etc.). In this case, technology is used to support learners and resource people within the context of team work or group discussion.

- The ***performance support system*** (EPSS) (Gery, 1997) concerns task-oriented training modules that are added to an integrated support systems within a workplace. Information has a " just in-time " quality and training is seen as a process that is complementary and incorporated into the work process.

Each of these models has advantages and drawbacks. The first two are very popular at the present time. They rest on the traditional paradigm inherent in live information transmission: the teacher uses computerized and audiovisual equipment to animate a real-time multimedia group presentation, broadcast locally or to several distant locations where learners are gathered. This model requires costly equipment as well as the learners and teacher's physical presence simultaneously. Moreover, too often it reduces the learners' interaction and initiative to a level that is in no way better than that of a traditional course presentation in an auditorium.

This approach appears incapable of meeting the growing training needs in a socio-economic context where lifelong learning, sought by busy and mobile people, involves cognitive abilities of a much higher level than what was required in the past. As pointed out by a recent report produced by Quebec's Higher Council for Education.

- " From now on, the emphasis must bear on higher cognitive abilities (reasoning, problem solving, planning) and social abilities (autonomy, communication and collaboration). These are consistent with the capabilities expected from workers following the impacts of information and communication technology on the very nature of work ".

- Rapport annuel 1993-94 du Conseil supérieur de l'éducation, Gouvernement du Québec, p. 24 (free translation by LICEF).

The availability of Internet and multimedia technologies exposes the learner to numerous sources of information among which he must make choices. The new paradigm (figure 1) where the learner, at the center of his learning process calls on many expertise sources, is better represented by the last four models described above than by the first two.

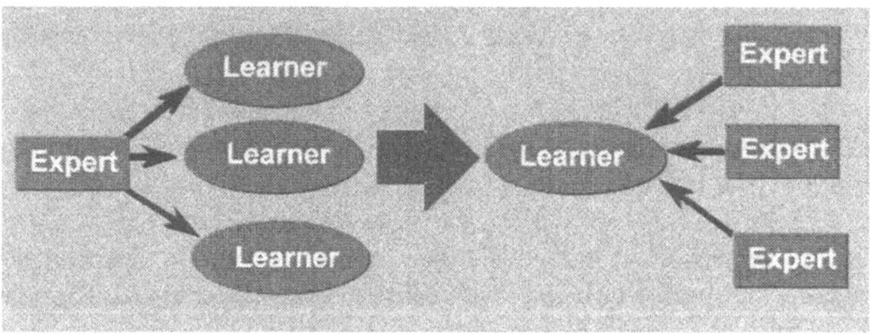

Figure 1. Paradigm shift

In the models of the " teaching media " or the " information highway training " and their application as it is currently, training is personalized but it is also deprived of an important collaborative dimension. However, this dimension can be reinstated if we use the computer as a tool to communicate. As for the EPSS approach, it favors two principles: just-in-time information and learning seen as information processing. The learning scenario concept at the heart of our Virtual Campus proposal is based on these principles.

2.2 Principles that rule the learning systems

The study of these different models and their integration into a constructivist point of view suggest ten principles that should guide the engineering and use of learning systems in the context of the Virtual Campus:

1. A learning system is centered on the learner. The other actors (trainers, managers, informants and designers) activities are defined according to the learners activities.

2. A learning system fully uses the distance as an asset to facilitate lifelong learning. It must be available whenever and wherever the learner may pursue his learning process.

3. A learning system proposes a constructivist pedagogy by bringing forward the learner's pro-activity in building his own knowledge, by taking into account his characteristics and by helping him integrate available information, within a context and usage, that is to say by helping him transform information into knowledge.

4. A learning system is process-oriented in the sense that the learner builds his knowledge by solving problems, by accomplishing tasks and realizing projects.

5. A learning system offers just-in-time learning by making information available at the moment it is required.

6. A learning system must induce the development of knowledge and skills that will enable learners to search, find and process information adequately ; it must facilitate the development of transfer abilities as well as a high level of autonomy in the learning process.

7. A learning system aims to develop social skills and positive attitudes in regard to learning.

8. A learning system offers the different actors various ways of accessing and processing information, such as software environments available for research and communication, for process-related advice, for collaboration among learners as well as among learners and other actors who facilitate the learning process.

9. A learning system supports the learning process through various integrated means within a coherent set of objectives, tools and methods.

10. A learning system is open, that is to say it can be adapted by learners or trainers to the particular needs of learners, teams or groups of learners from different surroundings or cultures. It is modular in order to facilitate its adaptation, updating or its re-engineering.

3. THE VIRTUAL CAMPUS MODEL

Based on the ten principles just stated, we now introduce the model of the Virtual Campus designed by LICEF: Its actors and their roles, the process and the technological tools needed by its actors in order to assume their functions in an integrated telelearning system.

3.1 Actors and process

The learning process is ruled by an actor called " learner " who transforms information into knowledge. " Information " here signifies any data, concrete or abstract, perceptible by the senses and susceptible of being transformed into knowledge. " Knowledge " means that information has been absorbed and integrated by a cognitive entity into its own cognitive system, in a situated context and use.

Transforming information into knowledge by the learner requires the adaptation of pre-existing mental structures or the creation of new ones, which are always integrated to the entire mental system of the learner. Knowledge so created is integrated into a usage as long as it is used in a process that allows the learner to act in his environment.

Information, the starting point of the learning process, is made available to the learner by another actor called " informer ". The informer may be a person or a group of persons that intervene directly, sometimes calles content experts. But it may also be a book, a video, a software or any other material or media that makes part of a knowledge domain available as usable learning information.

" Collective Knowledge " is any socially recognized knowledge. It can be from a general field such as physics or management or a specialized know-how related to the use of a software program or a specific work method in an organization.

We introduced the two indispensable actors in any learning process:

- The LEARNER rules his learning process and transforms information into knowledge.

- The INFORMANT rules the information process, communicates and makes available part of a body of knowledge.

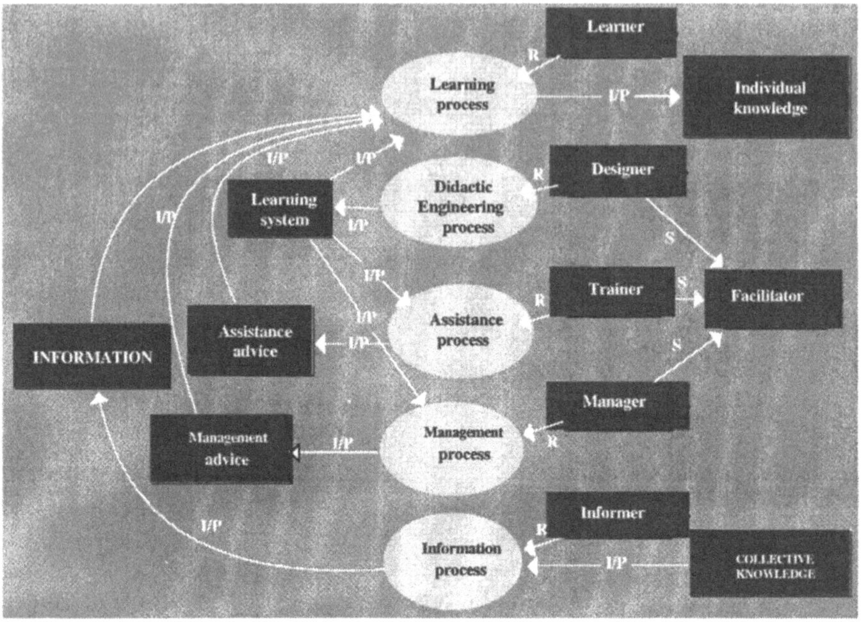

Figure 2. Actors and main telelearning process

- The DESIGNER, rules the didactic engineering process, facilitates learning by building, adapting and maintaining in working order, a learning system (LS) that integrates information sources (human informants or didactic instruments), communication, interaction and collaboration tools intended for the actors, as well as assistance and advice mechanisms (human trainers or computerized help).

- The TRAINER rules the assistance and pedagogical advice process, facilitates learning by giving advice to the learner about his individual process and the interaction that may be useful to him based on the learning scenarios defined by the " designer " actor.

- The MANAGER rules the pedagogical management, facilitates learning by managing actors and events in order to insure the success of the process, based on the scenarios defined by the " designer " actor.

Depending on the specifics of a learning systems, the different actors roles may be filled by a smaller or larger number of people and sub-systems. In traditional class training, for example, the informer and facilitator roles are most often carried out by the same teacher. On the other hand, in the case of autonomous learning through correspondence courses, the learner receives all the learning materials in a kit containing didactic multimedia or multiple media instruments. In performance training, for example, the informer and facilitator roles are most often carried out by the same teacher. On the other hand, in the case of autonomous learning through correspondence courses, the learner receives all the learning materials in a kit containing didactic multimedia or multiple media instruments. In performance support systems, information is available through a computerized environment that is also the learner's work environment.

3.2 Functions and actors roles

Figure 2 shows an overall view of the functions the different actors can take on. We define a function as the process pertaining to an actor and by which he intervenes in a learning situation. There are as many functions as there are actors, each one being associated with its input and product, as well as with the actor that assumes the function.

At this point, each one of the five major functions assumed by one of the actors of the Virtual Campus is described by a " black box ". We know its input and product but not its contents. To determine the contents, we must describe the process through the chain of more or less complex tasks and actions that make up this process, each task's input and product and the principles that rule their execution.

We call " role " any generic process used as a component to define one or the other actors' function in the context of the learning process. A role, then, is a sub-process of the main process which represents the generic function of an actor in a telelearning system.

Table 1 describes, for each actor and his related function, some of the roles or sub-processes that contribute to the function.

We would like to point out that a given role may appear in the function description of more than one actor. For example, the role of explorer of external databases, even though included in the definition of the learner's function, might also be part of another actor's functions.

It must be said that actors are different from typical task functions as defined by a given organization and they must also be distinguished from individuals (participants) that assume the function and the roles. For example, at Télé-université, professor is a task function often covering the roles of the actor " designer " (minus the production of non-printed documents), of the actor " informer " (while training tutors or directly dealing with learners) and the actor " manager " (while supervising tutors). The tutor is another task function who assumes some, but not all, of the roles of the actor " trainer " and the actor " manager " at the same time.

Finally, individuals can be the ultimate incarnation of the actors as well as the task functions. For example, professor X is a participant who acts as the actor " designer " of this course while professor Z is another participant who assumes the function of informer.

ACTOR AND FUNCTION	ROLES OR CORRESPONDING SUB-PROCESS
LEARNER **(Transforms information into knowledge)**	• Navigator in the learning scenario • Explorer of Internal documentation sources • Explorer of external databases • Problem solver • Contracting party in a project • Producer of assessed activities • Self-appraiser of his activities • Social actor • Debater in a telediscussion • Communicator
TRAINER **(Facilitates learning)**	• Diagnostic producer • Advisor • Appraiser of learners assignments • Helper in using the environment • Teams and groups animator • Coach
DESIGNER **(Builds, adapts and maintains a learning system)**	• Training needs analyst • Knowledge model maker • Pedagogical scenario builder • Writer of learning systems plans and cost estimates • Plan simulator • Producer of didactic instruments • Designer of the system's production plan • Producer and director
MANAGER **(Manages actors and events)**	• Planner • Decision maker • Controller • Director of broadcasting operations • Teams and groups organizer • Experimentation and validation organizer • Learning assessment director • Learning system assessment director • Network manager
INFORMER **(Makes information available)**	• Information presenter • Content clarification expert • Manager of mediated knowledge • Trace analyzer • Documents analyzer

Table 1. - Actors in the Virtual Campus and some of their roles

3.3 Specific roles and scenarios

A library of roles that can be played by one or many actors is a central element in our model of the Virtual Campus. These roles are described in a structured way so as to define precisely each actor's function in a given learning system. Considered as a process, each role can be defined by a graph of tasks that comprises procedures (or tasks) to be executed by the actor, the links between them, their input and product as well as the principles that govern them.

We call such a graph a " generic scenario ". Hence, a generic graph of the tasks describes each possible actor's role. By combining generic scenarios, by adapting them and making them more specific to a knowledge domain, we can describe precisely each actor's function in a given learning system (Paquette, Aubin and Crevier, 1997).

Let us take, for example, the role of " problem solver ". Since there are several types of problems, such as classification, diagnostic or design, we can specialize this scenario according to the nature of the problem. Then, a generic diagnostic scenario might become a central element in a more global learning scenario, being followed by a remedial scenario for example. Moreover, since the trainer needs to diagnose the learners progress, a diagnostic scenario can be integrated into the training scenario as well, serving as a basis for the trainer's intervention in the learning process.

A specific actor's scenario results from personalizing the generic scenarios that have been retained as applicable to his function in this particular learning system.

Hence, let us suppose that we intend to build a telelearning system about automobile mechanics. The learner's specific scenario would include tasks such as searching for information in technical guides, followed by a diagnostic process applied to some system in an automobile, then, by a telediscussion session about this type of diagnostic and finally by an self-assessment about automobile mechanics diagnostic. Four generic scenarios will have been combined and specifically adapted according to the field of study in order to generate a specific learning scenario.

Moreover, in the same telelearning system, the trainer will have to play the role of " advisor " according to the learners search about automobile diagnostic, to do so, he will also use the generic diagnostic scenario but will apply it in the hope of identifying the learner's difficulties in solving this type of problem. He will then animate the telediscussion and insure (generic scenario of supervision) that each learner correctly completes his self-assessment. We then obtain, for the same situation, a specific training scenario.

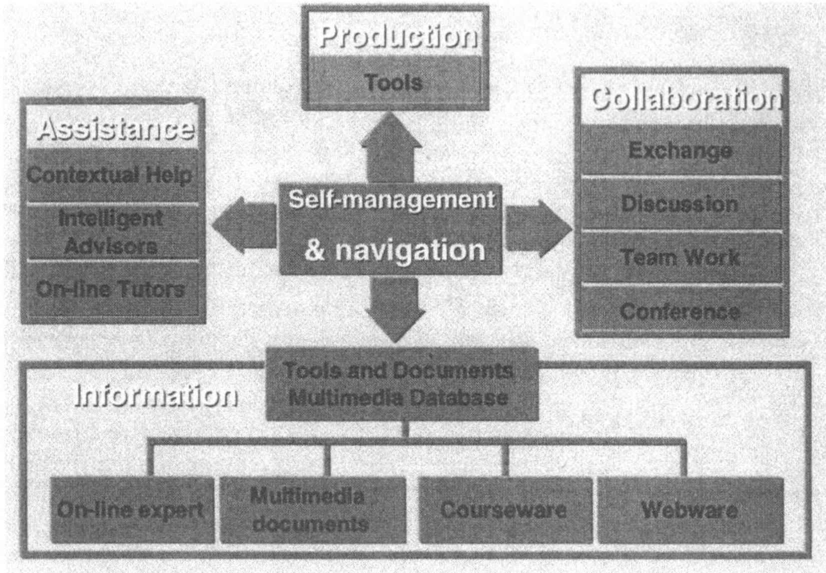

Figure 3. A telelearning system's five virtual spaces

3.4 The actors virtual spaces

In an object-oriented perspective (Rumbaugh et al, 1991), examining the process governed by the different actors allows us to infer technological objects that can be useful to effectively play their roles in a telelearning system. Whatever the actor, we may hence discover five virtual spaces, as described on figure 3, in which each actor evolves in his own fashion.

This telelearning software environment is called an " HyperGuide ". It is composed of five spaces: self-management and navigation, information, production, collaboration and assistance.

On the actor for whom it is intended, each one of these HyperGuide environments provides an access to various services. Among them, the Scenario navigator allows the actor to navigate in his scenario and gives him a way to access other available tools such as self management tools: notes assignments, diary, workplan, or knowledge model navigator.

Each actor also benefits from:

- An information space in which are gathered various types of documents and data needed to fulfill his function, including multimedia documents, web sites and on-line content experts;

- A production space in which are gathered the tools needed to produce assignments or to intervene in the learning system, for example text editors, spreadsheets or simulators;
- A collaboration space in which are gathered the tools needed to exchange files with other participants, to realize team work, to participate in telediscussion or seminar through various forms of synchronous or asynchronous teleconferencing.
- An assistance space where help, advice or an adaptation of his environment are available from a resource person or the computerized system.

The production space is represented by a **work and production workbench** allowing a given actor to accomplish the tasks that have been defined in his scenario. In the case of the actor DESIGNER, it will be, for example, the telelearning systems engineering workbench (AISTA)[11] that enables him to navigate in the scenarios of the telelearning systems engineering method (MISA), so that he can define the plan and specifications of the learning system and specify the other actors HyperGuide environments.

4. IMPLEMENTATIONS OF THE VIRTUAL CAMPUS

One of the advantages of the Virtual Campus model presented here is its adaptability to different technological contexts and the modularity that makes its components reusable. The speed of technological evolution makes it necessary to design such open models so that learning systems can evolve without the need to rebuild from scratch every time a new type of pedagogical material becomes available. This model's versatility is illustrated through five courses developed at Télé-université or prototypes developed at LICEF, implemented during the last six years.

Table 2 summarizes each project according to characteristics such as: the knowledge domain; the pedagogical model, at the heart of which are the learning scenarios defining each actor's role (here only the learner is considered); and finally, the media model including the pedagogical material, the tools and the technological infrastructure needed to deliver the telelearning system.

The first implementation shows that the model is independent of technology. It is a multiple media course that does not use telematic tutoring or on-line collaboration tools. The navigation-management space uses such media as printed guides that describe activities and productions to be realized by the learner as well as text, video and software information sources. The communication and collaboration space is composed of meetings and telephone conversations. The assistance space consists of telephone tutoring and examples of software usage included in a printed technical guide.

---

1. AISTA in an extension actually being developed at LICEF of AGD, a course design performance support system (Paquette et al, 1994).

Components of the LS	Traditional multiple media	HyperGuide 1 (1992)	Internet course (1994)	COVI (1996)	CECO (1997)
Knowledge model (types of knowledge units)	Introduction to artificial intelligence (concepts)	Introduction to instructional design (procedures)	Introduction to Internet (procedures)	Training and competiti-veness (concepts)	Training and competiti-veness (concepts
Learning scenario	Readings in a book, video, problem solving with specialized software	Case study and course design activities	Search on Internet to achieve a project	Virtual colloquium : research, commu-nication, synthesis and presentation	Virtual colloquium : research, commu-nication, synthesis and presentation
Navigation-management space	Printed guide and cross-reference to texts, videos and software	HyperCard to describe interactive scenarios and manage the learning activities	Netscape pages describing the interactive scenarios, giving access to collaboration and assistance tools	Scenario navigator; Metaphorical representation of the virtual colloquium	Scenario navigator; Personal management tools; Generic shell of the Virtual Campus
Information space	Monography grouping the texts, eight 30 minutes videos and 6 software programs	On-line file containing chapters, a printed version of the manual and an off-line video cassette	Netscape pages locally or on Internet giving access to documents and tools	Text documents integrated in the environment; videos on CD ROM or server	Text and video documents integrated in the environment or on a server
Production space	Printed templates; Generic software tools: text editor, spreadsheet,.....; computer printouts using specialized software	Hypercard templates linked to acitivity pages Generic software tools: text editor, spreadsheet,.....	Generic software too^l^s: text editor, spreadsheet,.....	Generic software tools: text editor, spreadsheet,.....	Generic software tools: text editor, spreadsheet,.....; FX-Notes application
Communication and collaboration space	Telephone tutoring; Two meetings with tutor	E-mail; File transfer; Computer textual tele-conferencing	E-mail File transfer Computer textual teleconferen-cing	Asynchronous tools (e-mail, files, computer conferencing) Synchronous (bi-point videocon-ferencing and white board on RNIS)	Asynchronous and synchronous tools multipoint videocon-ferencing, white board on cable modem, ADSL and ATM networks
Assistance space	Telephone tutoring Guide and examples of software use	Telematic tutoring Hypercards for advice & examples linked to each activity	Telematic tutoring & teleconfe-rencing	Tutoring in synchronous and asynchronous modes	Tutoring in synchronous and asynchro-nous modes Learner's trace

Table 2. - Five implementations of the Virtual Campus model

The second implementation of the Virtual Campus model uses simple technological means. This HyperGuide is hypermedia software produced with HyperCard or Toolbook that describes the scenario of available activities through clickable buttons. These lead to an activity summary page that includes instructions, objectives and icons leading to documents to be consulted in order to achieve the activity or serving as assignment templates. The information space is composed of documents (printed and videos) that may be consulted or produced by the learner. Each document is represented by an icon giving access to a text or to the summary of a video. The collaboration space is represented by other icons giving access to electronic mail and computer teleconferences integrated into each module's scenario. The assistance space uses advice or example cards offering help linked to a specific activity. These files are displayed at the learner's demand. The learner can also choose to communicate with his tutor or his team members by using e-mail (Paquette, Bergeron and Bourdeau, 1993).

The third implementation, an introductory course to the Internet, has similar characteristics. However, it uses support on the Internet or locally, with the Netscape browser. Web pages describe the learning activities to be achieved, hyperlinks giving access to documents to be consulted and tools to be used to complete assignments and projects. Asynchronous tools such as e-mail and teleconferencing facilitate collaborative work as well as tele-tutoring.

The last two examples are more advanced prototypes developed at the LICEF Research Centre (Paquette et al, 1995). In both cases, a course in economics was constructed. The intended goal was to facilitate collaborative learning by using contents that had modular qualities. The metaphor was that of a virtual colloquium or conference center. In both cases, students had the necessary means to accomplish research and team production of reports that were then presented to the group within the virtual conference. Various mechanisms were implemented at the workstations to allow access to multimedia production and communication documents and on-line advice by tutors. However, in the second case, the environment was much richer compared to the first example since the course was run within the larger context of a computerized Campus model. Many media, including server-based video were use. Self-management, group management and production tools were also included. Finally, a full network support was provided for desktop video conferencing and white board facilities, as well as asynchronous teleconferencing using cable-modem, ADSL and ATM broadband technology. This last experiment has proven the feasibility of an heterogenous networking of a group a students using different network support, while still being able to undertake various collaborative learning activities.

5. CONCLUSION

The Virtual Campus model just presented offers an advantage in that it facilitates the implementation of functional capabilities that are required by the system's different users. It also makes it possible to verify that all spaces and tools needed by the participants are adequate and designed following a systemic perspective according to each of the five actors points of view in a given learning system. The model also enables us to take into account the various levels in a complex telelearning system and, consequently, to see better each required tool's anchoring point. This is because the model makes a clear distinction between the generic Virtual Campus level and the more specific level of an actual learning system or a course.

Moreover, to facilitate as much as possible the model's generic characteristic as well as its independence from the various means of implementation, the architecture platform that supports the system was designed using a layered approach. In this fashion, the physical networks level is as isolated as possible from the applications level. Between the two, the middle layer supports the computer program intended to enable the implementation and execution of different scenarios by linking them with physical means and software. It is at this particular level that LICEF's actual research and development efforts are focused. It should lead to the production of a new prototype in 1998, enabling designers to build Virtual Campus environments more easily.

At the same time, the model is also the starting point for the huge plan undertaken by Télé-université to re-engineer its technological infrastructure and its 250 courses, taking into account the means available to students at home and in the workplace today, together with their probable evolution. Télé-université expects to put all of its courses in a Virtual Campus environment in the coming four years, using various degrees of technology integration.

The Virtual Campus model presented here was also adapted to help define UQAM's campus-distance model (SAMM project), as a virtual partnership campus with three other universities or superior schools (ETS, INRS and UQAM), as well as to the development of the turnkey computerized school model, supported by Quebec's Education Ministry.

6. ACKNOWLEDGMENTS

The author wishes to underline the contribution of Claude Ricciardi-Rigault, Chantal Paquin, Ileana de la Teja and all the teams who participate in the various Virtual Campus projects at LICEF and have helped these ideas to develop. Also, a special thank to the Quebec Information Highway Fund and the TeleLearning National Network of Centers of Excellence, who have contributed to the funding of these projects.

7. REFERENCES

Bourdeau J., Frihida A., Gecsei J., Paquette G., De la Teja I. (1994). *Accessing distributed multimedia documents for instructional use.* ED-Media International Conference, Vancouver, September 1994.

Gery G. (1997). *Granting Three wishes through Performance-Centered Design* NATO Communications of the ACM, volume 40, number 7, pp.54-59, July 1997.

Henri F., Ricciardi Rigault C. (1994). *Collaborative Learning and Computer Conferencing.* NATO Advanced Workshop, Grenoble, Sept.1993; to be published in T.T. Liao (Ed) Advanced Educational Technology: Research Issues and Future Potential, Springer-Verlag, Berlin.

Hiltz S. (1990). *Evaluating the Virtual Classroom,* in Harasim, L. (ed.) *Online education: perspectives on a new environment.* New-York: Praeger, 133-184.

Paquette G., Aubin C. and Crevier, F. (1997). *Design and Implementation of Interactive TeleLearning Scenarios.* Proceedings of ICDE'97 (International Council for Distance Education), PennState University, USA, June 1997.

Paquette G., Crevier, F. and Aubin C. (1997). *Méthode d'ingénierie d'un système d'apprentissage (MISA).* Revue Informations In Cognito, numéro 8, 1997.

Paquette G., Ricciardi-Rigault C., Paquin C., Liégeois S. and Bleicher E.(1996). *Developing the Virtual Campus Environment,* ED-Media International Conference, Boston, USA, June 1996.

Paquette G., Ricciardi-Rigault C., Bourdeau J., Paquin C., Liégeois S.(1995). *Modeling a Virtual Campus Environment for Interactive Distance Learning,* ED-Media International Conference, Graatz, Austria, June 1995.

Paquette G., *Modeling the Virtual Campus* (1995). In "Innovating Adult Learning with Innovative Technologies (B. Collis and G. Davies Eds) Elsevier Science B.V., Amsterdam, 1995.

Paquette, G., F.Crevier, C. Aubin (1994). Knowledge in a Course Design Workbench. *Educationnal Technology,* USA, volume 34, n. 9, pp. 50-57, November 1994

Paquette G., Bergeron G., Bourdeau (1993). The Virtual Classroom revisited, Conference TeleTeaching'93, Trondheim, Norway, August1993.

Pea R., & Gomez L. (1992). Distributed multimedia environments. *Interactive Learning Environments, 2,* 73-109.

Ricciardi-Rigault, C., Henri, F. (1994). *Developing Tools for Optimizing the Collaborative Learning Process,* Proceedings of the International Distance Education Conference, June, Pennstate.

Rumbaugh J., Blaha M., Premerlani W., Eddy F. & Lorensen W. (1991). *Object-Oriented Modeling and Design.* Engl. Cliffs, NJ : Prentice Hall.

Spector M., Polson M. & Muraida D. (1993). *Automating Instructional Design: Concepts and Issues.* Engl. Cliffs, NJ: Educational Technology Publications.

Wilson J. & Mosher D. (1994). *The Prototype of the Virtual Classroom* Journal of Instructional Delivery Systems, Summer 1994, 28-33.

8. BIOGRAPHY

Gilbert Paquette is director of the LICEF Research Centre of Télé-université, he is involved in instructional design support systems, knowledge modeling techniques and tools, advisor system design and HYPERGUIDES, the main Virtual Campus project in Quebec. He is active in three international research consortia, has published three books and directed a dozen-distance learning multimedia course or courseware development.

3

New Research Avenues on Multimedia based learning in the EU

L. Rodríguez-Roselló
European Commission
Directorate General XIII- Head of Division
Telematics Applications and Sevices for Education and Training and Research Networks

Keywords
World-Wide market, European Action, Education Policy, R&D strategies

The growth of knowledge creation underpinning explosive technological development will increase further in the foreseeable future, and the integration of our economies will continue to entail increased specialisation. This will mean a significant shift in economic activities and therefore of the skills needed to support these activities. The pace and the significance of this technological change is such that industry cannot rely only on new entrants to the job market to match the need for new skills, as was the case in the past. In fact students and the teachers themselves feel uneasy, they are aware of the gap between their training and the needs of society, and want training better suited to their needs.

These macro-economic factors generate a growing and highly diversified demand that the current educational and training system cannot cope with. In addition, there is no prospect of a substantial increase in financial resources, however, the development of new approaches to learning, building on an extensive use of educational technology opens new perpectives to meeting the above challenge. Research and development is therefore needed to prepare for effective, efficient deployment of ICT for learning.

The breadth of research needed cannot be undertaken by small communities of researchers in the Member States working at the point of intersection between education and computer science. A critical mass of research capacity can only be found at the European Union level. It is not enough to bring researchers together, progress will also result from the joint efforts of curriculum developers and the wide range of stakeholders in the education and training system working with the researchers. In addition, thanks to the completion of the internal market and the deregulation of the telecommunications industry, more and more actors are operating at the EU level and are preparing themselves for the world-wide competition.

The Virtual Campus F. Verdejo & G. Davies (Eds.)

operating at the EU level and are preparing themselves for the world-wide competition.

Nowadays there is a broadly shared vision that the success of the information society in the EU is critically dependent on effective delivery of life-long learning to all its citizens and that a large scale European wide action is needed to bring together the expertise available within the Member States. Nowadays, competition is no longer limited to goods, it also includes services that can be delivered at a distance such as education and training. It is of paramount importance that the EU is ready to compete on this key market.

It is also found that one of the main challenges of the planned action is to reduce the time needed to apply research findings at all level of the education and training institution as well as within companies. Research should therefore focus on demonstrating measurable, long lasting gains at affordable costs. This means that technical R&D should be supplemented with relevant, focussed socio-economic research which will help understanding how institutions can best adapt to society's needs and offer new and effective models for learning, how companies will organize training and last, but not least, how the social fabric will integrate those radical changes.

A seamless deployment of the technologies for knowledge and skills acquisition in the information society will result from the convergence of efforts and interest of the different actors: the multimedia industry, the network and telecommunication providers, the users at schools, home, universities and other educational institutions, at companies, as well as on national policies in the member states. Several programmes of the European Commission may stimulate this deployment.

The role of the RTD&D programme in this field is to provide the EU with blueprints for this implementation

This goal can be achieved by testing and showing how innovative systems, methods, and services, if designed for efficiency, scalability and accessibility, can apply downstream the results of basic research to cover the users needs. It should cater then for:

Efficiency

Research is needed to significantly improve the learning process in order to achieve significant lasting and measurable learning gains at a known cost. R&D should address the core of the education process and not just technological add-ons.

Scalability

All important factors, technical, social, or organisational that could impact larger scale, progressive deployment should be investigated and understood.

Accessibility
The solutions selected should allow for a progressive, no disruptive, affordable implementation across the EU catering for a wide diversity of users.

The trends in the education institutions and in companies, the trend in education and training policies and the difficulties encountered in attempts to deploy educational technologies at a reasonable large scale have been analysed in depth and many experimental results are known from previous research and other actions. The Educational Multimedia Task Force report provided a substantial contribution: it identified the needs for the specialisation of universities and the need for networking, enabling cooperation and providing new virtual learning spaces; new industrial training based on on-the-job access meeting the needs of the learning organisation, the move towards a more learner centred approach at the educational system.

A system approach to education and training is needed based on state of the art learning sciences and cognitive science research. An effective action cannot be reduced to pure technical R&D, the efforts should be balanced between the development of tools and methods to support new learning models, advanced content development and their validation in a real life context.

R&D should be based mainly, but not only, on affordable technologies, in other words, based on an intercept strategy with emerging cost-effective technologies and services.

On the basis of the previous achievements of the Telematics Applications Programme and the Task Force on Educational Multimedia, the actions are to tackle all the issues required for the improvement of learning, the learning processes, the content and services and the access infrastructure.

For the improvement of the learning process, sustainable learning gains will be achieved by better supporting more autonomous and more individualised learning, addressing all the components of a modular instructional management system (local learner support, peer learning, remote tutoring, course/curriculum design systems, accreditation systems, knowledge assets management and easy access to learning resources together with new delivery models).

For the development of higher quality learning material three different perspectives are to be considered: the content itself; the embedded pedagogical or didactic approaches; and the adaptability to the learner needs. That means research on new instructional design tools, learner modelling techniques, knowledge modelling and learning ergonomics. The material will range from simple distributed hypermedia to advanced simulation environments such as virtual laboratories.

Providing access to learning resources and services to all learners (e.g. in institutions, on-the-job or at home, including those in remote areas, nomadic or disabled persons) is a key requirement. The development of common platforms will allow full access to services across heterogeneous networks, addressing harmonised identification and retrieval of learning and of other knowledge resources.

All the above will lead to seamless advanced learning services which will harness the technologies in order to be more efficient and accessible to all learners regardless of their location, language and catering for a broad diversity of needs.

The implementation could follow the following lines:

- Establish the scientific base
- RTD on components of learner centred learning systems
- Validate research results in experimental studies

The action should also allow for proposals containing innovative, high risk but also high pay-off ideas that may advance knowledge on the main themes such as proposals that cut-across traditional disciplines. Finally, the action should contribute to the standardisation process by launching pre-standardisation activities aimed at ensuring the reusability of multimedia material and the interoperability at the tools and at the service level.

BIOGRAPHY

Luis Rodríguez-Roselló received his Telecommunications Engineer degree from the Technical University of Madrid. He has worked as Director of the Research and Development Department for the ITE (*Instituto de Tecnologías para la Educacion*) depending of the Spanish Education Ministry and later as Main Advisor for the New Technologies Program of the same Ministry. Since 1989, he is Head of Division within the European Commission, DG-XIII, and also coordinates the Educational and Multimedia Software Task Force.

Learning at a virtual campus: Deakin University's experiences as a dual mode university

E. A. Stacey
Deakin University
221 Burwood Highway
Burwood, Victoria 3125
Australia
e-mail: estacey@deakin.edu.au

Abstract

Deakin University was created as a "dual mode" university when the Australian government rejected the single mode model, yet gave Deakin the role of a national distance education provider as well as a regional campus based university. Deakin used the opportunity to become an innovative institution which has used resource based teaching for on and off campus students. Deakin has continued to develop the concept of flexible learning as it has become a multi campus university and has researched and integrated the use of technologies to develop a virtual campus which serves all of its students, both nationally and internationally.

Keywords

Dual mode, Flexible learning, Virtual campus, Computer mediated communication, Electronic conferencing

The Virtual Campus F. Verdejo & G. Davies (Eds.)

1. INTRODUCTION

1.1 Deakin's virtual campus

Paul is based in Kalgoorlie in the Western Australian desert, the third location to which his mining company employer has relocated him during his 2 years studying for a Masters of Business Administration degree. Dave, one of his fellow small group members, is based on the central Queensland coast but frequently works in the remote Northern parts of Australia in his scientific job. Sarah, Melissa and Judy are based in metropolitan cities in South Eastern Australia and a new member of the group, Doug, who is an expatriate Australian working in San Francisco has just joined the group this semester, claiming that this course is still cheaper than most MBA courses he would be eligible to study in America. The group works together on two weekly tutorial assignments to which each person contributes part of the set task. They post their answers to an electronic conference based at Deakin's Burwood campus, for feedback from the group. After the group have discussed the tutorial answers the group assignment is collated - a task shared equally around the group.

The lecturers who coordinate the units that they are studying are based on Deakin's Warrnambool campus on the southern Victorian coast and the tutors who are interacting with the groups and collecting and assessing their group assignments are based on the Burwood (Melbourne metropolitan) campus. The library they access electronically is situated in regional Geelong and the students' administrative support is coming from both Burwood and Geelong.

The physical location of the students is irrelevant, however, as their central communication is through their computers via small and large group electronic conferencing. They access course notes and databases from a related web server and can share and open html documents and URL's of relevant World Wide Web sites as appropriate. Their reading is a mix of print and easily shared and updated electronic documents.

This is Deakin's virtual campus, a meeting point for its students whether they are on or off campus.

1.2 Deakin's role as a dual mode institution

Deakin is a dual mode university which was incorporated in 1975 at much the same time as many of the single-mode European institutions. The possibility of a single mode university modelled on the UK Open University at Deakin was ended by the Karmel committee of the Federal government who rejected this type of institution as too centralised and inhibiting to the innovative dual mode approaches already accepted in several Australian universities (Karmel, 1975). There was also a commitment to provide regional universities for our widely scattered remote country centres and Deakin was established to provide a regional campus based university at Geelong in country Victoria as well as to be an Australia-wide distance education provider.

The first Vice-Chancellor of Deakin University, Professor Fred Jevons, though inspired by the UK Open University model and wanting to emulate its quality of distance education materials at Deakin, was hindered by the initially small scale of course size at Deakin. The cost factor of producing high quality distance education materials meant that using them with on campus students as well was a feasible way to rationalise costs and Jevons (1986) described this as one of the advantages of the dual mode approach. Other advantages were the greater credibility attached to the courses "if they are seen to come from the same stable as the sort of traditional programs with which people feel comfortably familiar" (Jevons, 1986, p6) as well as the credibility that the research base of the university gave to courses, something which many distance education institutions, at that time, could not provide. Jevons also claimed there were "spillover effects" (p6) of preparing distance education materials which improved the quality of face to face learning and teaching because distance education "brings much of the teaching process out into the open" (p7). Even in Deakin's early days the Vice Chancellor had faith in the convergence theory of technology having the effect of making on and off campus teaching more similar and the distance education institutions more innovative in researching and developing this area.

Deakin has continued to play this role in Australia and to be innovative because of its dual mode role. Though initially driven by a pragmatic rationale as described above, the combination of resource based learning for on and off campus courses has put us at the forefront of the move to flexible learning that has infiltrated the most traditional of our campus based universities with the availability of the technologies of the 1990's. Flexibility of location and circumstance for learning was possible through a student-centred, resource-based approach and Deakin was made University of the Year in 1995, (an award bestowed by external evaluators of the university system, who publish a Good Universities Guide for students (Ashenden & Milligan, 1995) on the basis of the quality of our flexible and innovative approaches to course design and delivery.

We rationalised our number of faculties to five in the early 1990's as we became a larger multicampus university through nationwide government directed mergers of Universities with Colleges of Advanced Education (Calvert, 1992). All campuses of the new Deakin were encouraged to develop a dual mode of course delivery which produced economies of scale, particularly in some of our larger undergraduate degrees. The continuance of the policy of teaching the same course on and off campus with technological means of delivery and interaction mainstreamed where appropriate and achievable, has meant Deakin has continued to be at the forefront of the convergence of distance and on campus teaching and learning.

Currently at Deakin there are 29,070 students enrolled, 17,102 on campus students enrolled and 11,968 off campus students enrolled. A breakdown of these figures show that the on campus full-time student group (12,462) has far greater numbers than the off campus full-time group (1415). Thus the bulk of our off-campus students are part-time, workplace based students, mostly mature age students returning to study for upgrading professional accreditation. The substantial number of our part-time on campus students (4,640) can also benefit from our flexible learning approach by facing less insistence on only face-to-face attendance with a variety of modes of interaction through our virtual campus capabilities. Deakin also has another population of students, as many again as the mainstream university population (approximately 27,650), studying throughout Australia, Europe and Asia through the University's commercial arm, Deakin Australia, and making us one of the largest suppliers of training in Australia.

I will discuss the implementation of our current dual mode approach through a comparative description of several of our university's major course offerings and their modes of delivery. I will provide a commentary gathered from many of the Deakin academic staff involved in teaching and coordinating these courses and will describe their perspectives of dual mode reality and the issues it raises. I will also discuss the way we are planning to explore and implement our progress to a virtual campus (our virtual reality?).

There has been an active and ongoing discussion among distance educators about the continuing directions of single and dual mode universities, particularly as many previously campus based universities have begun to perceive new communication technologies as the means to their global delivery of education. I will conclude with a discussion of some of these issues and our experiences in the context of this discussion, through my own focus as a teacher and researcher at Deakin.

2. DEAKIN'S COURSE DELIVERY

2.1 Overview

Our dual mode reality in 1997 consists of:

• Undergraduate courses taught in a dual mode with on campus students sharing the same print, multimedia materials and assessment processes as off campus students.

• Many postgraduate courses taught largely off campus with few courses sharing a dual mode of on campus teaching.

• A virtual campus created via computer mediated communication which can transcend an on/off campus division but which is still reaching full implementation.

• Many "off shore" courses, particularly in Asia which use electronic communication within their central course provision.

• University-wide projects aimed at implementing and mainstreaming the capablities of technologies in the delivery and support of all courses at the university, seeking to develop the full market advantage of a dual mode university.

2.2 Undergraduate courses

Many undergraduate courses are still taught to large numbers of students studying full time on campus. We are committed to this process, as the continuing socialisation, as well as education, of the school leaver has long been an important role of the university in our community. As the employment structure of society has changed, this student population has changed too. With fewer immediate prospects of employment when leaving school, competition for tertiary places has increased. Students often work in low skilled jobs at a rate of hours which would have previously been considered full time work loads. Many of them support themselves while studying under a government subsidised delayed fee scheme (students pay a part of their education costs or HECS, the Higher Education Contribution Scheme). Therefore a flexible approach to course teaching also helps these students manage their learning time in less traditional ways.

In some of our major undergraduate courses students have been given the opportunity to use computer laboratories or home computers and modems to link to interactive conferences for some of their tutorials. Ideally these conferences would merge groups of on and off campus students, but though all students on a course are using the same print resources and multimedia resources, difficulties providing stable electronic environments have meant that different approaches have been taken by different faculties and courses in our virtual campus provision.

The **Faculty of Business and Law** has provided their off campus Bachelor of Commerce students with electronic conferences as an option, rather than a requirement as some of their students had access problems as they attempted to link electronically. There is 40-50% participation of these off campus students particularly when committed staff have built electronic communication into their course. Currently the on campus students aren't required to use electronic interaction but this is planned for implementation in the next two years as better computer facilities and network provision for on campus students become available.

The Bachelor of Commerce, one of our larger degree courses, has about 1500 students on campus and 500 off campus students who study the same course from the same print guides and the same textbooks. They are assessed in the same way and have the same teaching staff, a dual mode course. The course is also offered in Malaysia with a locally based server enabling electronic communication for course use. The market advantage of such a dual mode is in being able to continue the course in either mode wherever a student may be located. The same resource based course exists in Sydney, Penang, or Western Australia so it can be continued whether a student is moved by their job or for family reasons. The off campus course is well taught and supported often very interactively if electronic conferencing is used. The perception within the market of students and their advisers, of off campus learning being by correspondence only and inferior in interaction and contact, is slowly being changed.

The major undergraduate course of the **Faculty of Education**, the Education Studies Major, has the opposite situation, with on campus students confident with their electronic interaction which is a teaching competency that they are required to develop within their course. The students are able to attend "tutorials" in a flexible electronic environment and discuss issues online each week. However where this would ideally link them to the off campus students, these latter students do not have sufficient access to computers and computer communication to so far make this a viable option. We are attempting new software and electronic access measures to help solve problems but we still have a body of students without computers and modems who we are committed to support. Though all other course material and assessment is the same, the computer based component of the course has had to differ for off campus students until there is equity of electronic access for all students. This means that at present, the on campus students have more modes of interaction and flexibility, with lectures, face-to-face tutorials, print and multimedia resources as well as electronic communication.

Other faculties also teach their undergraduate courses in a parallel mode on and off campus, with off campus students relying more on print and multimedia materials. The **Arts Faculty** were early innovators who developed materials for on and off campus teaching and have continued teaching a single curriculum. In some more practically oriented courses in the Faculties of **Science and Technology** and **Health and Behavioural Science,** face-to-face teaching is seen as more appropriate with 18 year-old school leavers taught on campus. Mature age workplace based students are taught off campus mainly in print mode with some additional computer based delivery.

In the sciences, on campus lectures and classes are still perceived as an integral part of the course, with face-to-face teaching used in teaching the foundational knowledge of maths, physics, biology, building and architecture complemented by practical application. Even in collaborative teaching between Deakin and local institutions in Asia, a face-to- face mode of teaching is supported either by visiting Deakin staff or local lecturers with additional provision of supplementary electronic communication.

However each group is considered in the context of their situation for the most appropriate methods of delivery. Technology is used as a supporting environment, often providing a dialogue for questions and for feedback through news groups and email or electronic conferences. Video teaching between campuses is being trialed in teaching Chemistry and has been used consistently in some cross campus Health Sciences courses. Computer based learning tools are used for enrichment and as replacement for laboratory work for workplace based mature age students. Such technological tools can assist students to link theory with practice, and real world knowledge and can be used with both on and off campus modes, for the students without real world knowledge as well as those in the workplace.

2.3 Postgraduate courses

Except for a core of research students, some of whom are campus based, many of Deakin's postgraduate students are studying professional coursework degrees as part time, off campus students.

Such courses are ideally suited to a virtual campus delivery and this has been established for many of the postgraduate courses

In the **Education Faculty,** a "virtual graduate school" was begun in 1995 with an electronic conference established using FirstClass conferencing software. Students studying in the Education Doctorate piloted the new system through the use of Deakin Interchange, a suite of software that included FirstClass conferencing and also provided a range of software for accessing the Internet, as well as software tools for research such as database searching tools and bibliographic software.

The **Education Doctorate** students were not a group who had used computers extensively for communication, as they were mature age students who mainly used computers for word processing. However, as researchers into learning, they expertly articulated the process of learning to use the online environment and provided us with a rich source of data for understanding the development of an active online discussion and the processes it involved (Stacey, 1997b). Providing these students with a virtual space for discussion of their research, as well as methodology and content issues, has broken down the isolation that many off and on campus research students experience.

The electronic conference has become the main form of communication for the Education Doctorate and with a course requirement to gain electronic access, its use has been mainstreamed which has facilitated an active and essential discussion. Electronic communication use has been built into the course structure with tasks which require students to share written contributions for discussion within small groups. The required electronic communication use and the required integrated tasks are factors which have made the virtual discussion central to the doctoral program. With a committed course team as well as provision for technical and student support in the developmental stages, it has become a valuable virtual campus where students generously share experiences, ideas and information and challenge each others ideas. It has also been possible to set up specialised discussions with guest lecturers from other countries which provides our students with access to experts. This process has a flexibility that means students communicate as a group though they are living in distant locations from New Zealand to Western Australia to Asia.

Students in the Masters of Distance Education course, who had been early electronic communication pioneers at Deakin with an older textbased system, also upgraded to the more user friendly graphical interface of First Class to become part of the virtual graduate school. Students studying the theory and issues of distance education have become active conferencers through coursework that has used an electronic discussion of ongoing tasks and activities to engage students in learning interactively. Conferences are gradually being integrated into course delivery of all the faculty's masters coursework programs as staff become confident of teaching this way and begin to embed the use of CMC into their coursework. There is a need for staff commitment and active use of the electronic conferences to guarantee their success. Ongoing response and facilitation of group interaction by the teacher is an important aspect of CMC use.

A unit focusing on teaching and learning with CMC has also been included in the newly accredited Master of Professional Education and Training in the Faculty of Education in response to students' growing interest in the theory and practice of teaching in a virtual medium. The research study from which this unit was developed was one which researched another electronically pioneering course at Deakin, the Master of Business Administration course.

The **Faculty of Business and Law** has been committed to providing innovative course delivery for their MBA course from its beginnings as the first such course available by distance education in Australia. There is a syndicate group structure which is central to the pedagogy of the course, with students studying and collaborating together in small groups of up to ten students, simulating, a workplace team environment. As students are situated remotely from one another, this grouping process required a central electronic communication system as a way that students could share documents and discuss issues.

From researching the practice of innovative teaching staff within the course, I found that CMC was used effectively when lecturers were able to structure an authentic use for interaction and when the electronic conference was central to the course activity with conference contributions counting towards assessment. The MBA's small groups were also a way of managing electronic conferencing effectively when there were large student numbers who would be an unwieldy and overwhelming large group discussion. By learning collaboratively through structured tasks, students shared the diverse perspectives of the group members, clarified ideas through the group communication and gained feedback to ideas from group members. They could seek group solutions for problems and share resources and provide a supportive social environment for ongoing study (Stacey, 1997a).

The MBA has provided electronic communication for up to 400 students concurrently with the greatest effectiveness in subjects that have built the conference interaction into the assessable tasks and expectations of the subject delivery. Staff commitment to this communication is essential for its successful use especially as the student group use of CMC is the course's main focus.

A new Master of Commerce course offered by this faculty has also made a commitment to the use of electronic interactive groups. As a new full fee paying course directed to the workplace based students, a computer and modem and Internet access are required and the course is being marketed as providing electronic access and interaction. From the beginning of the course, staff are being involved in professional development through an especially established electronic conference and course and there is an executive commitment for staff to teach in an active electronic campus.

2.4 Deakin's Virtual Campus

One of the major barriers to the successful mainstreaming of the virtual campus has been the cultural change required to get staff to become confident online teachers. Many staff have been used to traditional distance education where little interaction with students was required, the main interaction for the student being with the well prepared text for the course. There were often minimal phone calls to students and cost cutting anonymous markers used as ways of reducing costs of courses. The legacy of such a system meant that some staff became comfortable teaching like this and in an environment which rewards research and publication, these could be more easily achieved without the time consuming teaching that electronic conferencing can mean. The professional development required to develop confidence to teach successfully in a virtual mode was often rushed or put off with the ever increasing busy workload of academic staff.

The distance education literature is divided about the issue of changing this focus and direction of distance teaching, particularly with Holmberg's (1989) theoretical support of the notion of the autonomous student interacting with effective text and individualised tutor feedback. Bates (1991) argues that this focus on the importance of interaction to distance education is a function of the involvement of dual mode universities particularly that of Australia and North America (Bates, 1995) and the value they place on traditional interactive on-campus teaching. However the research (Stacey, 1997a) and evaluation (Goodwin et al, 1995) carried out at Deakin has developed a theoretical basis for the value of an interactive virtual campus which uses collaborative group learning to improve the effectiveness of distance learning.

The student and market demand for a virtual campus has also driven Deakin's strategic planning to make this a mainstream possibility. To address the need for staff to become more capable of teaching in such a virtual campus environment, Deakin has recently launched a new range of projects to mainstream flexible learning through electronic delivery of courses. This is in response to the worldwide changes that have occurred in electronic communication and the expectation of students that digital technologies are used in teaching and learning. Deakin's strategic plan defines Deakin's need "to provide learning experiences which are flexible; accessible; technologically advanced; learner centred and customer focused; service oriented; and which recognise the needs of lifelong learners." (Rowlands, 1997, p1) has focused activity at Deakin to provide professional development and support for staff learning to teach electronically.

Deakin's dual mode approach will be enhanced by the capability of a more efficient provision of interactive communications technologies and by developing the capability of staff to teach with theses technologies. The support services in the university, Information Technology Services, Learning Resource Services (print, editorial and graphical design), Academic Development (including software development and professional support) and the Library are all being integrated into the project so that academic staff have time release and access to skilled staff as they develop their courses into appropriate technological media.

Such a strongly coordinated project with active executive involvement and support will be worth watching as it unfolds at Deakin. Strong leadership combined with the involvement of innovative staff, cooperative effort from all branches of the university's support services and resources and efforts pitched at the mainstream course delivery level should take Deakin's dual mode strengths into a virtual campus that combines to better serve the needs of all students.

The virtual campus has the potential to change the dual mode process significantly as groups of students can be taught as one group regardless of their physical location. This possibility is also attractive to the traditional campus based universities who have begun to look at technology as a means of providing them with a global market and could change the process of distance education provision worldwide. In Australia achieving this reality has been a slower process than originally conceived (Hesketh et al, 1996), particularly as our technological infrastructure has only recently been developed to reach many of the locations of the student population who require electronic access. Just as important have been the development of student and staff computer capabilities and skills which are only slowly reaching a point where they make use of a virtual classroom. Only as access is improved and as the teachers' skills in the electronic environment are developed, can there be a true merging of on and off campus student groups.

The virtual campus is very much dependent on the abilities and commitment of its community to interact in this mode. As Daniel (1997) has commented, the virtual university will fail "unless it can evoke the personal commitment from students and staff that is the basis of an academic community." Deakin is seeking through its current projects to translate the current commitment to the dual mode approach into the new technological environments so that its virtual campus can provide a more effective learning environment for all its students.

3. REFERENCES

Ashenden, D., & Milligan, S. (1995). *Good universities guide to Australian universities and other higher institutions.* Port Melbourne: Mandarin Australia.

Bates, A. W. (1991). Third generation distance education: The challenge of new technology. *Research in Distance Education_3(2), 10-14.*

Bates, A. W. (1995). Technology, open learning and distance education. London: Routledge.

Calvert, J. (1992). Deakin University. In Mugridge, I. (Ed.*), Perspectives on distance education: distance education in single and dual mode universities.* (pp. 19-31). Vancouver: Commonwealth of Learning.

Daniel, J. (1997). *The mega-university: The academy for the new millennium?* Proceedings of ICDE Conference, The New Learning Environment: A global perspective. Pennsylvania State University.

Hesketh, B., Gosper, M., Andrews, J. & Sabaz, M. (1996).*Computer-mediated communication in university teaching.* Canberra: Australian Government Publishing Service.

Holmberg, B. (1989). *Theory and practice of distance education.* London: Routledge.

Jevons, F. (1986). *Dual mode institutions - the way forward.* Open campus n12, Deakin University: Geelong.

Goodwin, C., Rice, M., Stacey, E. & Thompson, L. (1995). *An evaluation of Deakin Interchange pilot program*. Deakin University: Geelong.

Karmel, P. (1975). Open tertiary education in Australia. *Report of the Committee on the Future of Tertiary Education Australia to the Australian Universities Commission.* Canberra: Commonwealth Government Printer.

Rowlands, J. (1997). *Deakin's flexible teaching and learning initiatives*. Paper presented to the Academic Development and Support Committee, Deakin University.

Stacey, E. (1997a). Collaborative Learning at a Distance. In Evans, T., Jakupec, V., & Thompson, D. (Eds.), *Research in Distance Education 4* Geelong: Deakin University Press.

Stacey, E. (1997b). *A virtual campus: the experiences of postgraduate students studying through electronic communication and resource access.* http://ultibase.rmit.edu.au/Articles/stace1.html

An acknowledgement to those at Deakin who contributed their time and ideas to the preparation of this paper: Professor Jocelyn Calvert, Dr Trevor Hutchins, Mr Ray Bantow, Ms Heather Briggs, Ms Anne Ingram.

4. BIOGRAPHY

Elizabeth Stacey is a lecturer in the Education Faculty at Deakin University in Melbourne Australia. She teaches educational computing courses particularly those incorporating the use of computers and communication technologies into curriculum. Her research and publications are focused on these areas. She has researched and published about school age learning with computers, and the use of interactive technologies, particularly audiographics and computer conferencing. Her doctoral research has explored collaborative group learning through computer mediated communication with adult learners.

She is currently coordinating the Master of Distance Education Course while teaching units about flexible teaching and learning which explore the integration of new technologies and supervising students studying student support issues which focus on this area. She is also part of the Education Doctorate team and is supervising students who are exploring flexible learning and the use of communication technologies in a range of settings.

The University for Industry Pilot Project

M. Thorne
Vice Principal and UfI Pilot Project Director
Napier University
Edinburgh
UK
e-mail: mp.thorne@napier.ac.uk

H. Milner
Project Manager for the University for Industry
and Assistant Director of Learning Development Services
University of Sunderland
Sunderland
SR1 3SD
UK
e-mail: helen@ufi.org.uk or helen.milner@sunderland.ac.uk

Abstract

The new UK Government of 1st May 1997 stressed their commitment to a skills revolution featuring a University for Industry (UfI) aimed at increasing the competitiveness and the employability of the UK workforce. A pilot project was established in early 1997, in the North East of England, to prototype the UfI and test some of the techniques which a national implementation might use. Its model is one of private-public partnership, where the UfI is not a new provider but a broker of new and existing courses and a catalyst to create a culture, which will embrace lifelong learning.

Keywords

Education policy, Lifelong learning, Private-public partnership

The Virtual Campus F. Verdejo & G. Davies (Eds.)

1. INTRODUCTION

The UK needs a skills revolution, if it is not to slip down the international league table of competitiveness. This revolution requires step-changes in people's demand for learning and in their ease of access to education and training opportunities. The new UK Government of 1st May 1997 stressed their commitment to education and training; one element of their new education policy is proposed to be a University for Industry. The UfI will increase the competitiveness and the employability of the UK workforce.

In the UK, each time there is an educational transition - people moving from school to college, or from college to university - individuals are lost from the educational system and they never return to learning. This is relevant at all levels from basic skills, through university and into post-graduate study. At the basic levels, literacy is a problem for those both in and out of work, at the highest level doctors and engineers need to update their skills every 8 to 10 years. In some professions the need for lifelong learning commitment is recognised, in most it is not.

In December 1996 the Institute of Public Policy Research (IPPR) published a report *The University for Industry: creating a National Learning Network.* It was the culmination of over two years research by IPPR's Josh Hillman which had included work with key figures, in particular working with the University of Sunderland. The research was based on approaches made by prominent members of the (at that time) Labour Party in opposition, Gordon Brown and David Blunkett (now Chancellor of the Exchequer and Minister of State for Education respectively), and was supported by them.

The University for Industry (UfI) model as set out in the report (Hillman, 1996) describes a new type of organisation which would not be another provider, but would rather be a broker, connecting individuals and companies to learning programmes that best met their needs.

The University for Industry will move learning out of the institutions and nearer to where people are, culturally as well as geographically. By bringing together oganisations which already exist into a network it will enable education to be sold to millions of people across the UK rather than in small isolated pockets. The University of Sunderland has been working on this agenda for the past seven years.

The IPPR model has the following key elements:

- The UfI as one gateway to education and training: an impartial broker.
- The UfI must increase the demand for learning.
- The UfI must increase participation.

- It needs to be user led, not provider led.
- It will stimulate lifelong learning.
- It will commission courses or materials.

A pilot project was established in early 1997 to prototype the UfI and test some of the techniques which a national implementation might use. The project is led jointly by IPPR and the University of Sunderland and is based in the North East of England. There is a strong, strategic collaboration between regional and national partners, including companies, TECs, local authorities, colleges, universities and voluntary agencies. Funding is based on major sponsorship from Sunderland City Training and Enterprise Council, Sunderland City Council and the NatWest Bank Group, but highlights a public private partnership with many other companies and organisations providing substantial benefits "in kind" including the National Extension College and the BBC. The evaluation of the pilot is funded by the Department for Education and Employment (DfEE).

2. THE UFI IS A BROKER

The UfI is drawing on existing provision into a framework based on a computer network; using this people can choose between difference course being offered by different providers. All of the courses are delivered by provider organisations and the role of the UfI is to broker these opportunities and not to deliver them.

The pilot has established a one-stop-shop for education and training. There is a freephone line which is available 14 hours a day, 7 days a week providing easy and efficient access to information and advice as well as to telephone booking for a range of tasters and courses. Over 800 calls were made to 0800 26 26 39 during October (1997) indicating an instant response to this mode of information provision.

At the heart of the University for Industry pilot is innovative use of the Internet. Wherever someone is in the region they can use the Internet to browse information, course details, opening hours of learning centres, make a request for a full pack or book onto a free taster or a course. In the home, the workplace, and at all of the learning centres people have access to the online UfI system.

The system includes an online database of courses which can be searched by staff in the call centre as well as by anyone on the Internet. It includes online booking for courses and online learning for those who want it.

The Internet is the medium-tech approach for the UfI pilot project. A sophisticated online system has been designed for the pilot by two small companies: The Leighton Group, in Sunderland, and Telematica in Swindon.

The pilot is embracing the benefits of here-and-now technology. There have been no new cables put into the ground. Some centres have high-speed links to the Internet others have modem links with standard telephone lines. If UfI is to be egalitarian, it must rely on a range of access points with a range of types of interaction. The pilot has chosen the Internet as the common channel as it is the only cost effective solution to carry the service. It is also scaleable to include more learners and more partners with an affordable level of investment at a future date if required.

One of the most innovative aspects of the project is that the providers are able to add, modify and delete course details directly onto the database over the Internet from work or from home. This allows them to take responsibility and control for their own course listings rather than having to channel all information through a central administration.

3. LEARNING CENTRES

The University for Industry is based around a network of learning centres (in November 1998 there were 34). These centres are closely matched to people's lifestyles. Of course there are centres in the University, colleges and schools, they are also in resource or training centres in companies and big organisations, and in leisure locations such as the Sunderland Football Club stadium and Learning World, a joint University of Sunderland and Gateshead College learning centre at the MetroCentre shopping complex (the biggest indoor shopping centre in Europe). There are learning centres in the communities in which people live, recognising learners' loyalty to their local environment.

The minimum requirements for a UfI pilot learning centre are one computer linked via the Internet to the University for Industry project computer system - the virtual engine for the UfI - a named contact person and advertised open access times. Some centres have one computer, others have over 250.

4. THE UNIVERSITY OF INDUSTRY IS NOT A PROVIDER

The University for Industry pilot has established a brokerage between the potential learners and the providers who can support their learning.

The brokerage provides information about courses. All of the contents of the courses on offer via the UfI pilot project are the responsibility of the providers involved. These providers are the University of Sunderland, the colleges of Gateshead, Newcastle and the City of Sunderland and some school and community provision, as well as commercial providers such as distance learning offered by the National Extension College.

The pilot is focused on what might be called "skills for work". Courses fit into areas such as IT and the Internet, communication, using number and finance, the business environment and skills for small businesses.

Free tasters are being used as one of the elements in the marketing armoury. They can allow those nervous, disinterested in or out of the habit of formal learning to develop, or regain, confidence in their ability to learn. There are five tasters currently on offer - *IT for the Terrified*, *Internet for All*, *Time Management*, *Writing Successful Job Applications* and *Communicating in the Electronic Office*. These are all offered free of charge and are available at all 34 learning centres - content is based within workbooks which are sent to the learners at home and can be used in the centres; tutor support is available face-to-face at the centres or via telephone. These are not courses, they are not assessed or examined (all concepts which are barriers to participation) but they are a first step towards a course - and progression is a key factor to the pilot project.

As Learning Works (Kennedy, 1997) addresses: "The inequality of the current arrangements is the most compelling reason for change. Those who have already succeeded are now most likely to take part in further learning."

One of the pilot Ufl success stories is a young man, 17 years old, who left school with no qualifications and was unemployed; he was outside an education system which had failed him. He was attracted to the *Internet for All* taster and then progressed onto another taster, *Communicating in the Electronic Office*, these were free and interesting. He spent time in the learning centre in the local library with support from a tutor, but has spent more time on his own with the workbooks using the computer in independent study. He has now registered on a course and is working; he has developed confidence as well as essential employability skills.

A fundamental idea behind the pilot is to allow learners to start learning as soon as possible rather than wait until the start of the next academic term. A face-to-face course will start just as soon as the minimum number required for a cohort have been registered.

For those who wish to start immediately or are forced by circumstance to study on their own the pilot offers a number of distance learning courses. These are from many providers including the National Extension College (largely paper based) and Cambridge Training and Development (multimedia and online learning).

The pilot Ufl project is removing barriers to learning - there is one simple access point for all information, there is a range of subjects, at a range of levels and using a range of delivery mechanisms. The Ufl as broker begins with the marketing and ends when the learner is booked onto a full course with a provider; it is at that moment that the provider takes over as contact point.

5. EFFECTIVE MARKETING

Money must be spent to tackle under-participation. As Learning Works (Kennedy, 1997) says: "A society which is so expert in selling goods should be able to find ways of selling education."

Education must compete with business in selling. The marketing of learning must be very professional and needs to consider the marketing messages as well as the media used.

Tele-access, via the pilot project's free phone telephone number, offers truly innovative ways of selling educational opportunities, monitoring learners and providing information about the next appropriate step. Follow-up calls to all those who have previously enquired maintains contact and enables further direct selling.

The backbone of the pilot project is telemarketing, leaflets through household doors, a poster campaign on buses and at a range of lifestyle locations, as well as events which includes family learning. We are working with partners in newspapers, radio and television to raise the local profile of the unique access to learning opportunities the pilot is bringing to the region.

A range of messages are being tested - all aimed at making people currently not engaged in learning to pick up the telephone and ring. Messages such as "Earn More, Learn More" and "No More Excuses" highlight the benefits that learning will bring as well as find answers for all the reasons people give for not wanting or not needing courses. These are aimed both at employed and unemployed people.

The initial marketing effort is directed at achieving one single key response - dial 0800 26 26 39 for more information. The telematic management tools gather details for market research as well as market intelligence, indicating marketing successes and information regarding important gaps in provision.

The UK needs to affect a change in attitude to learning. Society needs to value learning and to appreciate the necessity of the lifelong nature of it. The BBC are working closely with the pilot to discover ways in which a national broadcaster can support this shift in social beliefs. Senior managers in companies are also involved in demonstrating the value, which they place on training.

6. COMPANIES

Improving competitiveness and performance of individuals and of companies is important for UfI. The project involves a number of companies in the region. The strategy includes working alongside current training plans and in-house provision to ensure that employees have access to the opportunities that the pilot offers as well as integration with existing development.

Lite-On, an electronics firm in Ashington Northumberland, has opened up their training room to all employees, employees friends and family, and parents and staff of a local school. All the Ufl tasters are on offer there as well as access to the online system to book onto further courses that might interest them.

Vaux, a Sunderland-based brewery, and Sainsbury's, a supermarket, both see that there is a dual benefit in providing opportunities to the general public at the same time as involving their staff.

Roadshows in the canteen at lunchtime is one way in which the pilot is directly interacting with employees - discussing the ways in which the pilot can interest them as well as listening to ways in which the pilot does not meet their needs.

The nature of a provider is changing during the project. Companies such as Siemens, and Black and Decker, are offering places on their own training courses to other companies and to the long-term unemployed. This helps to increase both the competitiveness of the supply-chain (Siemens) and the skills of their future workforce (Black and Decker). The role of Ufl is to broker the courses to the individuals interested in taking part. Unions too are running courses and supporting learning centres within factories.

7. SUMMARY

The pilot will be completed in July 1998. It is attempting to allow potential learners to be active not passive, making active choices about their learning from realistic and relevant information which the pilot Ufl manages.

The DfEE will be formally evaluating the pilot project enabling all of the key elements and issues to be discussed and analysed. Other important issues such as funding and quality have been debated locally and a working model put into practice. The Further Education Funding Council is working closely with the pilot and is keen to explore ways in which the current funding methodology does and does not match the learning support in the project.

The project puts learning right at the centre of people's lives - using commercial marketing techniques to sell learning and to link individuals into new and existing educational opportunities. The one-stop-shop approach provides flexible access to hundreds of courses. People can learn when and where it suits them. In the first four months of operation over 1000 registrations have been made using the Ufl project brokerage. The University for Industry will continue to evolve until it is embedded as an essential plank in the lifelong learning culture of the UK.

8. REFERENCES

Hillman J, The University for Industry: creating a National Learning Network IPPR 1996 ISBN 1860300510

Kennedy H, Learning Works - widening participation in further education Widening Participation Committee Report, FEFC 1997, p. 50

Kennedy H, Learning Works - widening participation in further education Widening Participation Committee Report, FEFC 1997, p. 102

9. BIOGRAPHIES

Michael Thorne is currently Vice Principal at Napier University in Edinburgh. Until December 1997 he was the Pro Vice-Chancellor at the University of Sunderland where his responsibilities were for Learning and Student support, recruitment, the Student Charter, and IT strategy. He is the author or co-author of 11 books and a large number of academic papers and articles.

Helen Milner is Assistant Director of Learning Development Services and Project Manager of the University for Industry Pilot Project. Helen has worked at the University of Sunderland since 1992. She has worked for over eleven years in online and interactive communications networks within education including for The Times and in Australia. Her University role includes managing EU funded projects, developing flexible learning materials and developing and implementing learning strategies for teaching and learning.

PART TWO

Global Approaches

Introduction to the Global Approaches

E. A. Stacey
Deakin University
221 Burwood Highway
Burwood, Victoria 3125
Australia
e-mail: estacey@deakin.edu.au

Keywords
Virtual classrom, Web applications

The papers in this section investigate a range of technology-enabled virtual classrooms and discuss the issues these raise and the solutions that have been initiated. One paper focus particularly on World Wide Web based systems while the other describe projects using other technologies as well, including ISDN networked tools for synchronous classroom approaches. All of the writers describe a changing view of education and learning, with technology enabling and initiating new approaches to learning and teaching, often from a more constructivist perspective. Such a perspective does not consider learning as acquiring an unchanging body of knowledge which is disseminated with the use of technology, but perceives learning as a process that requires an innovative interactive environment through the available technologies. This environment allows the learner to develop or construct their own understanding of concepts as they interact with the ideas of their teachers and other learners.

Nicola Henze and W Nejdl of the University of Hannover also look to the World Wide Web as a learning environment for applying innovative teaching and learning approaches from a constructivist perspective. Rather than use the web as a lecturing environment, they use constructivist theory to frame their use of a web based environment for the teaching of computer courses.

They describe their development of a learning environment on the web which can provide authentic activities in real world situations with responsibility for performance with the student. Students work in collaborative groups with access to tutor feedback and through project-based learning and goal-based scenarios which emulate real world applications, they are developing an accessible database of student computing projects all managed in a web environment. Their adaptive hyperbook learning environment is available to students in remote locations and is the basis of their virtual learning environment.

The Virtual Campus F. Verdejo & G. Davies (Eds.)

The UNED experience of a gradual developing virtual campus is described by Clara Pérez-Molina, J. A. Rodriguez-Criado, C. de Mora, J. Carpio, M. Castro and J. Peire. The importance of using a technology that integrates into their existing Study Centre Network with its successful local support centres where students can use technological facilities, has made the use of synchronous technologies from radio broadcasts to videoconferencing appropriate to their organisation and style of learning and teaching. UNED's electronically networked centres have enabled their involvement in the DEMOS project which combines access to asynchronous resource and administrative use and communication with synchronous teaching in multimedia environments through ISDN lines and LANs. Students and teachers can share screens and computer applications and can have a visual and audio presence through their shared multimedia computers .

They describe the possibilities that the new technologies provide for group learning and more interactive distance learning which also influences approaches to course and material development. The new technologies again changing the teaching and learning approaches of the virtual learning environment.

A Web-Based Learning Environment: Applying Constructivist Teaching Concepts in Virtual Learning Environments

N. Henze and W. Nejdl
University of Hannover, Lange Laube 3
30159 Hannover, Germany
e-mail: {henze, nejdl}@kbs.uni-hannover.de

Abstract

Internet-based teaching and learning has been the topic of many recent projects and research work. While it is relatively easy to use the Internet to transport conventional types of lectures and course notes, it is more difficult to utilize the full power of Internet-based techniques to advance teaching and learning conceptually. In this paper we will discuss the KBS Virtual Learning Environment built within our group, its theoretical background in the form of constructivist models of learning and teaching, its use for our courses and its implementation.

Keywords

Distributed Learning Environments, Constructivist model, Hypermedia, HTML

The Virtual Campus F. Verdejo & G. Davies (Eds.)

1. INTRODUCTION

Within the KBS Virtual Classroom Project, we have been working on virtual learning environments based on the Internet and the World Wide Web since 1996. One main goal for this project has always been to utilize the full power of these techniques to innovate teaching and learning for our courses, instead of just transplanting ordinary lectures onto the Internet. In this paper we will discuss the educational issues motivating our approach and the concepts and technical issues to implement such a learning environment.

We start by discussing our approach of goal-based scenarios within this framework. We analyze the concepts and properties necessary to use goal-based scenarios in our teaching environment and how we apply them for our courses and exercises. We will discuss the techniques to support such an environment and how we implement them on top of the Internet and World Wide Web. We conclude with a preliminary evaluation of recent courses.

2. CONSTRUCTIVISTIC MODELS OF LEARNING

Computational learning environments benefit from a strong background from educational theory. Simply reproducing conventional teaching and learning concepts in a computational environment does not utilize these new technologies. Educational models, which show particularly interesting features for many parts of academic education are constructivist models of learning and teaching (see also the discussion of the relationship between such models and the field of instructional technology in (Duffy, 1992).

Critical elements in the design of constructivist learning environments are the specification and use of authentic and complex activities during the learning process (Fishman, 1991). Authentic activities shift part of the ownership for learning and performance from the teacher to the student. While working on their tasks in real-world situations, students have to learn and apply the required skills at least partly by themselves. This does not allow learners to passively consume a lecture without critical reflection, learned knowledge and skills are needed to perform the task which stimulates the students to think about the arising problems and techniques. The teacher's role is to coach the students and to describe the initial concepts necessary for their task.

Real-world examples are characterized by the complex context in which they arise: few applications of techniques and concepts occur in the simplified forms used for highly abstracted exercise problems often presented to learners (see also the discussion in (Duffy, 1992). While abstraction is of course necessary and small exercises can be used to discuss specific issues, project-based learning has to be used to rebuild real-world complexity. The global project context determines the learners perspective on a given task, while subtasks in a smaller context provide guidance of the learning process.

The ability to develop multiple and alternative perspectives on a problem is also a central skill for performing tasks. Collaborative learning promotes the exchange and reflection on different views. As project work is often done in teams, learners train their capabilities for team-work and collaboration.

2.1 Project-Based Learning Approaches

Constructive learning models and project-based learning can be supported by different approaches and can be viewed from different perspectives. We will sketch some of these starting from the concepts discussed in (Schank, 1994).

Simulation-Based Learning By Doing: Acquisition of knowledge is guided by goals or projects actively pursued by the students. Knowledge and techniques are learned and used to fulfil specific tasks which are needed to reach the project goals. Teachers have to give help when needed. To support learning by doing, simulations of all kinds of tasks can be built.

Incidental Learning: Projects and goals of a course have to be selected by the teacher in such a way that skills and knowledge needed to pursue these goals correspond to the (conventional) course content. Obviously, in a task oriented learning environment not only a single set of techniques leads to project success. So, although the base set of knowledge and skills that will be learnt is set, students can individually control their learning, depending on their previous knowledge and their individual preferences.

Learning by Reflection: Students are encouraged to reflect on given problems and on different solutions found by themselves or other student groups. Continuous discussion of teachers and students leads to original solutions and new insights.

Case-Based Teaching: Presentation of knowledge by the teaching staff depends to a certain extent on the progress students make in solving the given problems. Support is oriented mainly around cases with attached related knowledge, facts and problem solving methods. These cases can be continuously added to the knowledge base of the learning environment and represent an increasing knowledge and support base for the students.

Learning by Exploring: Communication between teachers and students is a very important aspect in this approach. Topics of the course are discussed in study groups or with the teacher. Small learning units contain the basic knowledge needed. Learning units are presented in the knowledge base which is extended by students and teachers. Students are engaged to study and to find out facts, skills, and research results on their own.

2.2 Goal-Based Scenarios

To pursue the different approaches discussed in the previous section, we use the idea of goal-based scenarios, also discussed in (Schank, 1994). Goal-based scenarios are used as a framework for our learning environment and provide both

the scenario context which models real-world applications as well as the scenario structure which settles the features of an adaptive learning environment.
Within the goal-based scenario framework we provide the context, motivation and material needed to work on specific projects. These projects are chosen such that a basic set of knowledge and techniques is needed to solve them plus additional in-depth knowledge about specific issues related to this basic set. Tutorial help is given by the teachers who answer the questions of their students, if possible at the moment the questions arise (just in time). Students are encouraged to discuss approaches and solutions in small working groups. Additionally, students have access to a knowledge base about the subject. This knowledge base contains studying material, ideally centered around cases, complete with solutions, additional information and knowledge and problem solving strategies. Both teachers and students extend the knowledge base, which therefore also contains a repository of former projects. This serves to connect new problems and already solved cases and provides easy access to needed materials.

The role of teachers as coaches and mentors implies that students have access to teachers besides fixed lessons during the week. Similarly a knowledge base will not be effective, if access to it is restricted to a few hours during the week. Team-work on real-world problems cannot be interrupted by missing communication. All these points are critical to constructivistic learning environments but can usually not be sufficiently realized in a traditional environment.

To support such a goal-based scenario approach, Internet and World Wide Web technologies as well as various database, artificial intelligence and hypermedia techniques allow us to build learning environments offering the following facilities:

Availability of working environment and communication facilities.
Students and teachers have anytime-access to the working environment which is needed to solve their tasks. Communication and discussion facilities also have to be continuously available for discussing course related topics.

Team-oriented learning.
Small learning groups working on specific projects allow collaborative learning, increasing learning efficiency and team working capabilities.

Personal mentoring.
Students need to have a mentor that can supervise and help them individually during their projects. Discussion within working groups is similarly encouraged. The learning environment has to enable flexible and time-independent communication between mentors and their students.

Distributed time-independent access to the course knowledge base.
Students should have anytime-access to the knowledge base, both for reference as well as for extension.

Adaptive course knowledge bases.
Students have to use the knowledge base in different ways, depending on project progress and previous knowledge. The knowledge base therefore should have adaptive capability, offering additional help for beginners and in-depth knowledge for experts, as well as different routes and indices for different purposes and readers.

Extensible course knowledge bases.
As the knowledge base can be extended both by teachers and students, its structure, navigation paths, visualization and user adaptivity has to be modeled explicitly to allow easy extension by simple instantiation of models (similar in purpose to database schemas).

3. OUR CURRENT VIRTUAL LEARNING ENVIRONMENT

In this section, we will discuss the main features of our current learning environment, following the requirements introduced in the previous section. The learning environment is being continuously enhanced for all our courses and laboratories. We will start with features available for all our courses, and then describe specific course instances.

3.1 Availability of the Working Environment

In order to make the working environment continuously available, access to all parts of the working environment (in this case background and project information as well as the necessary software tools) are available over the Internet. Access to the Internet for students is either from campus computers, over phone lines and terminal servers (administrated by the university computing centre and the students themselves), and by way of Internet providers.

All necessary tools are available for most current operating systems, so students can use them locally at every computer they have access to, including of course their home computers. If license restrictions make this impossible (as in the case of a large software engineering tool), at least anytime access over the internet is available (currently with X11 interface). Locally used tools are always internet-based, so access to central servers, repository and communication facilities is always possible.

3.2 Project-Based Learning

Most current courses and laboratories have specific large-scale projects, tailored specifically to the course contents. The current programming laboratory for undergraduates for example consists of two programming projects within one semester, the software engineering course focuses on one larger project spanning two semesters (using the development of an e-mail client to illustrate practically the whole software process), a second course in artificial intelligence and an advanced programming laboratory focus on intelligent agents (architectures, possibilities, and development of specific agents).

All project results are presented on the World Wide Web, where they are available for other groups as well as for students in future semesters. This motivates students to not only solve larger real-world problems, but also elaborate them in a way suitable for external presentation. Results for the various parts of the projects are usually published as soon as they are available, to encourage discussion of intermediate results between student groups.

3.3 Team-Oriented Learning and Mentoring

Project-based learning is done in groups of two to four students. Groups are formed at the beginning of each semester. Students in such a group work on a common project and present their results together. Collaborative learning and working is encouraged. For each group we assign a personal mentor, who can either be a graduate student, a Ph.D. student or the professor. This mentor is available personally at specific hours during the week, or anytime by electronic communication facilities. Group meetings and discussions are possible in person, or electronically. Documents can be managed on a central repository with version management facilities (with distribution and update to local computers managed over the Internet) as well as on our WWW server.

3.4 Electronic Communication Facilities

Each student group has a group communication centred, which includes e-mail lists to all students within this group (plus another one including the group mentor), a communication room on the WWW (read and write access restricted to members of the group), a presentation room on the WWW (which is readable by everyone), and a central repository (based on a client/server version of CVS) with configuration and version management.

Each course includes three discussion groups (implemented as newsgroups), one for official announcements (Announcements), one for general discussion and questions as well as course oriented exercises plus student answers (Discussion Forum), and one for free communication not directly related to the course (Cyber Cafe). The Announcements and Discussion Forum are also automatically archived, indexed and made available over the WWW. Synchronous communication at present can take place over a text based chat tool, the KBS Online Chat Forum.

All facilities / client programs are available on all supported operating systems and computers connected to the Internet.

4. NETWORK ENVIRONMENT

Figure 1 shows the hardware/networking environment underlying our solution. The central server located at our institute serves as the central repository for all course-related material like lecture slides, tutorials, web pages, hyperbook, programs etc. All central repositories (CVS, WWW communication and presentation area etc.) are also stored at the institute's server. A variety of working environments for accessing the data are supported: classically working on a client at the institute and accessing the data through Ethernet/NFS; accessing data from home PC's via a modem connection to a dedicated machine in the institute's network; accessing data from the university computer pool or from the (student's) home PC connecting via modem to a dedicated student server (configured to support a large number of parallel modem and ISDN connections).

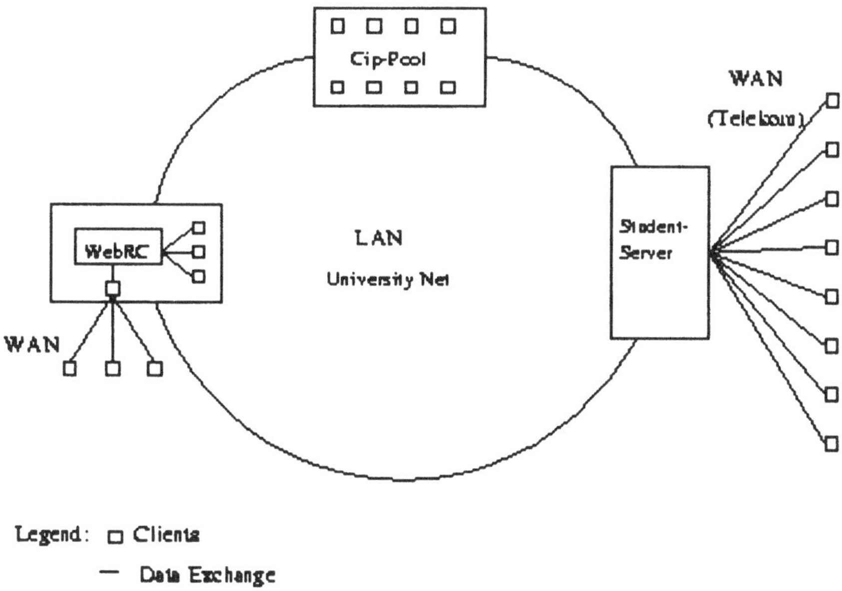

Figure 1. Hardware and Networking Environment

5. ADAPTIVE HYPERBOOK

In this section we present the initial design of a hyperbook for the courses Introduction to Computer Programming and Software Engineering. In contrast to the rest of this paper, the hyperbook system described in this chapter is not yet in production use, but is currently being written and implemented. We hope to be able

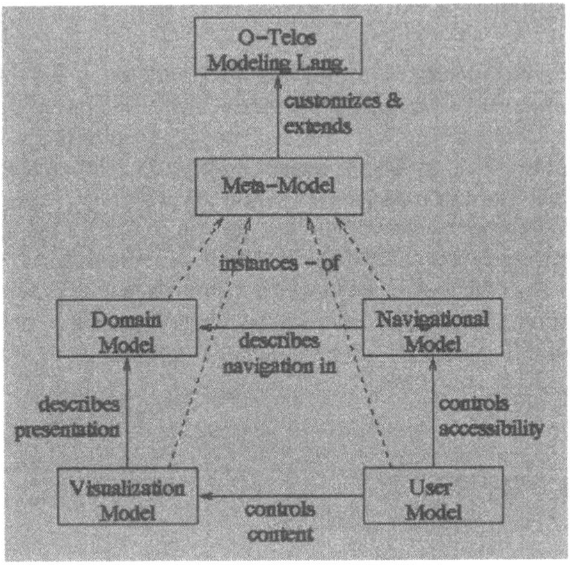

Figure 2. Hyperbook Modeling in Telos

to use it starting next semester. The modelling language and methodology as well as the underlying system is described in more detail in (Fröhlich, 1997a, 1997b, 1997c). In this section, we will discuss the general principles and the use of the hyperbook within our learning environment.

The goal of the hyperbook system is to provide an adaptive extendable environment/hyperbook, centred around projects and cases, which tightly integrates case descriptions and solutions, concept descriptions and more conventional tutorial notes etc. and contains all material needed for the courses and the projects. As the hyperbook has to be extensible by different authors as well as by students, a systematic model of all aspects of the hyperbook (domain structure, navigation, visualization and adaptation) is necessary. All these details are declaratively defined in the various models (including navigation through links, indices etc).

In the last years, several methodologies for hypermedia modelling have been developed, among which the Hypertext Design Method (HDM) (Garzotto, 1993), the Relationship Management Methodology (RMM) (Isakowitz, 1995), and the Object-Oriented Hypermedia Design Model (OOHDM) (Schwabe, 1996) are the most prominent examples. These methods provide primitives for modelling a hypermedia application domain. Based on this domain model the possibilities for navigation are described. As pointed out in (Isakowitz, 1995), such methods are best suited for designing front ends to loosely structured data. The navigational concepts proposed in these methods are geared towards indexing a large amount of relatively simple information pieces. On the other hand, educational hyperbooks

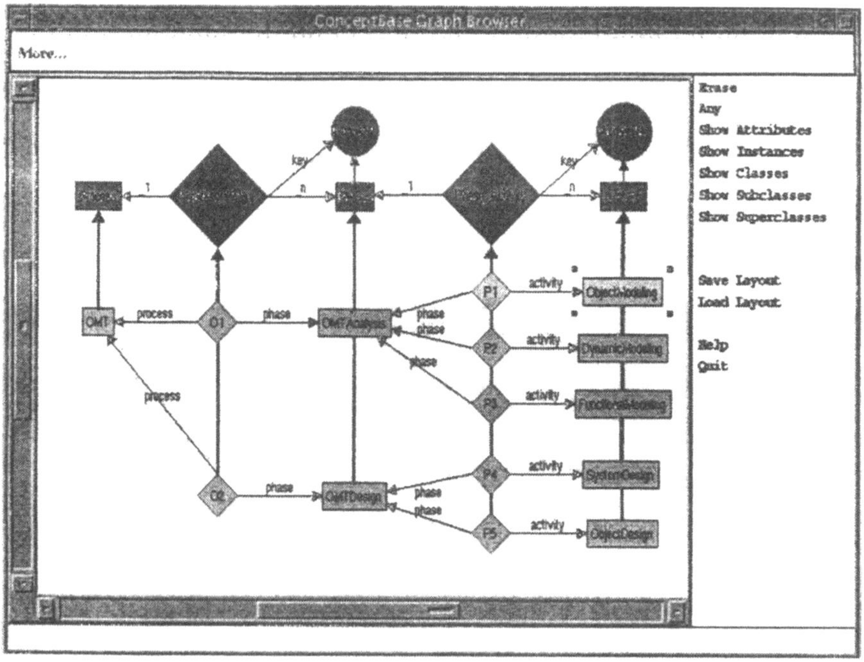

Figure 3. Part of the Software Engineering Domain Model.

have to include various forms of (sequential) tours, user models to adapt to the user's experience and visualization models.

On the other hand, current work in adaptive hypermedia textbooks (such as (Kay, 1994), (Brusilovsky, 1994a, 1996a, 1996b)) concentrates on building domain models and user models for adaptive hyperbooks, using semantic nets to describe these domain models and to index the hyperbook with the corresponding domain nodes. Our work builds on these concepts and focuses on the modeling language and meta-language for building domain models, explicit navigation and visualization models and user models.

For the declarative representation of the hyperbook data models we use a dialect of the object-oriented conceptual modelling language Telos (Mylopoulos, 1990), which is implemented in the ConceptBase system (Jarke, 1995). This language combines object-oriented concepts with deductive rules and constraints. Due to its representational power Telos is suitable for meta modeling, i.e. for describing domain-specific modelling languages (Nissen, 1996). In this spirit, we have used a Telos meta model to define the primitives used for domain modelling, navigational modeling, user modeling and visualization modeling, as shown in figure 2.

The domain model describes the concepts of the application domain, in our case centred around the setting of a task. A small part of the domain model of the software engineering section is shown in figure 3. It shows the definition of a Software Process consisting of several Phases, (1:n relationship between Software

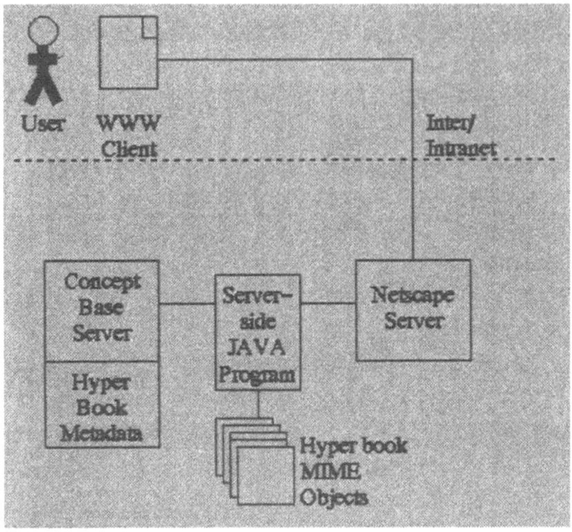

Figure 4. System Architecture

Process and Phase). This relationship is indexed by the key attribute PhaseNr (Phase Number). This key attribute specifies the order in which the Phases are presented. Each Phase in turn has several Activities. The bottom part of the figure shows specific instantiations for the OMT software process.

The relationships defined in the domain model are the basis for systematic semantic-based navigation in the hyperbook. The navigational model specifies the details of navigating the book, using a set of predefined concepts. All hyperlinks in the hyperbook document are generated automatically from the description of the hyperbook in the database.

The visualization model is built upon WWW pages, page fragments and mime objects, and defines how the material in the hyperbook is presented. The user model is based on a description of prerequisite knowledge (describing the relationship between initial and more advanced concepts) and a simple overlay model like the one used in (Brusilovsky, 1994b). Therefore the presentation can adapt to different knowledge levels of the learner, as well as different preferences.

Figure 4 shows the basic system architecture, which is based on standard components complemented by a server-side applet and the ConceptBase database manager. After logging into the system by activating the login applet a user-specific starting page is displayed. The user navigates the hyperbook by activating links. Whenever a hyperlink is activated the name of the corresponding domain object plus the name of the user are passed to a server-side applet. The applet queries the data base for the fragments of the page representing the domain object and for the domain object's navigational possibilities. From this information it constructs a user specific page. It does so by combining the visible fragments in a HTML page. Then it updates the user model by marking this page as read and uploads the page to the client, where it is displayed in an ordinary WWW browser.

6. SPECIFIC COURSES

6.1 Introduction to Computer Programming

This introductory course for undergraduates particularly emphasized the working environment (complete working environment available locally for each student computer as well as for university computers), communication and discussion over the Internet (with weekly questions/exercises and student answers in the Discussion Forum), and group work (four students in each group). Projects in this course were quite small, but will be larger in the next semester.

The accompanying programming laboratory during the summer semester focused on larger projects (two during the semester, with five alternative projects), and was run completely over the Internet (including electronic group communication and presentation facilities), with personal student mentors for each group (and personal meetings of groups and mentors as well). All project information as well as additional information about Ada 95 (taught during the winter semester and used for the first project) and Java and C++ (learned during the programming lab and used for the second project) was available online.

6.2 Introduction to Software Engineering

This set of courses covers two semesters, and includes lecture and exercise hours. Presentation of course contents is focused on the basic knowledge needed for a software engineering project, and is experienced within a specific project context, namely developing an e-mail client. The first semester focuses on analysis and design issues, the second on implementation, testing and some more advanced issues. The project is done in student groups of three to four people, with a Ph.D. student and the professor as personal mentors. Discussion of solution possibilities, alternatives and results is done as needed, presentation of results in the WWW is done weekly, the semester finishes with an evaluation of the different projects by the student groups.

6.3 Introduction to Artificial Intelligence

This set of courses also covers two semesters, the first one centred around general AI techniques, the current one and a graduate laboratory focus on the in-depth analysis of intelligent agents in form of a student projects (from the theoretical analysis of agents, agent architectures and frameworks to specific implementations). Again, students work in groups of two to three, with a personal mentor and regular discussion of results. While the last AI course (taught for the first time and only for a few students) was hampered by a very inhomogeneous student group, the project results within the lab were very encouraging and will be used in further courses.

7. EVALUATION

So far, we have formally evaluated part of our environment within the course Introduction to Computer Science and Programming, which stretches over two semesters. This course is taken by about 100 students mainly studying electrical engineering and technical computer science. The first semester includes a two-hour lecture and one hour of exercises, the second semester includes another two hours of exercises in the form of a programming laboratory.

In winter 96/97 we supported a course and exercises with our virtual learning environment. A questionnaire (Henze, 1997) in this semester showed that our concept was mostly accepted by the students and improved the student's learning progress.

One part of the questionnaire was concerned with the structure of the groups, their working processes and communication flow. The investigation showed the different knowledge of the students at the beginning of the course. More than 40% of the students already had good or very good programming skills, about 30% said they had only little experience while the others had no programming experience at all. All but one of the groups consisted of students with different programming skills.

Students in the course liked the possibility to reach their mentor anytime during the week and contacted them very frequently. About 20% of the groups used only email to contact their mentor while 50% of the groups wanted additional personal meetings with their mentor. However, communication between the members of the group themselves was done in different ways. About 70% of the groups did their exercises mainly on the basis of personal meetings, no group exclusively used email, 10% worked by phone.

Another part of the questionnaire was aimed at the comparison of the groups, their performance and interest. The mentor's opinion about their groups performance together with the results the group members reached in the examinations during the course showed that about 10% of the groups could be described as very good, 45% as good, 35% as average and 10% as only poorly interested. The attempt to characterize good groups led to only one significant difference in comparison to the other groups belonging to the course: Good groups are good at teamwork. This further shows the necessity of encouraging collaborative working and project-based work among the students.

In summer 97 we supported the subsequent programming laboratory within the Virtual Learning Environment. Students who took part in the programming laboratory were involved in two large programming projects which each covered a half semester. It was the students responsibility to divide and delegate the project into single tasks among their group. 59% of the students told that they had no problems in managing their projects, 23% had more or less difficulties in organizing their common work. In a few cases collaboration within the group was very difficult as team members stopped working and left the group completely. We are currently discussing several alternatives for helping students work better within groups, as we see this as an important testing ground for their further professional work after graduation.

On the other hand about 71% of the students told about good and very good teamwork. During the whole programming laboratory students usually used email to contact their mentors, only a quarter of the student groups had regular meetings besides email discussions (which contrasted to their behavior during the programming lecture in the preceding semester).

The version control system CVS (included in the summer semester) was not used as much as expected. Two main reasons may explain this behavior. First, CVS was not introduced during the winter lecture, so students had already installed their own ways to control the program versions, e.g. by using email for sending the current version to other group members or by using a dedicated location in one user's directory with free access for the group. Second, although the projects covered half a semester they were probably still too small to really need advanced configuration and version management.

A few groups documented the project progress among their group using the Communication Room. The final presentation of the projects in the group's Presentation Room (public access) was very successful: About 88% of the students liked the possibility of presenting their work on the World Wide Web (the results can be seen at http://www.kbs.uni-hannover.de/praktikum/praktikum97 /teilnehmer.html). The projects presented there are fully documented: a (readable) implementation together with a complete documentation (README, INSTALL, description of the program structure and of used algorithms, a short user's manual) as well as test protocols can be found there. While we had introduced the basic structure (documentation, sources, etc.) the student groups showed great enthusiasm in presenting their work and their group.

8. CONCLUSION AND FUTURE WORK

In this paper we have discussed the KBS Virtual Learning environment developed at our institute. We have analyzed the requirements for the design of this environment, resulting from constructivistic models of teaching and learning, and their implementation within our Internet-based Virtual Learning Environment has been shown. We also discussed the use of our environment and a preliminary evaluation of its use for our courses.

Future work will mainly concentrate on improving the overall concepts, and on continuing the design and implementation of our hyperbook environment to build really adaptive and extensible course knowledge bases. Especially within the area of hyperbook design a lot of research questions are still open and need to be addressed.

9. REFERENCES

Brusilovsky, P. and Pesin, L.(1994a) ISIS-Tutor: An Intelligent Learning Environment for CDS/ISIS Users. In *Proc. of CLCE'94*, Joensuu, Finland.Brusilovsky, P. (1994b) Adaptive hypermedia: an attempt to analise and generalize. In *Workshop on Adaptive hypertext and hypermedia at UM'94*, Hyannis, Cape Cod, MA, USA.

Brusilovsky, P., Schwarz, E. and Weber, G. (1996a) ELM-ART: An intelligent tutoring system on world wide web. In C. Frasson, G. Gauthier, and A. Lesgold, editors, *Intelligent Tutoring Systems* (Lecture Notes in Computer Science, Vol. 1086), pages 261-269, Berlín, Springer.

Brusilovsky, P., Schwarz, E. and Weber, G.(1996b) A Tool for Developing Adaptive Electronic Textbooks on WWW. *In Proceedings of WebNet'96 - World Conference of the Web Society*, Boston, MA, USA.

Duffy,T. and Jonassen, D. (1992) Constructivism and the Technology of Instruction. Lawrence Erlbaum Associates, Hillsdale, New Jersey.

Fröhlich, P., Henze, N. and Nejdl, W. (1997a). Conceptual modeling for educational hyperbooks. In *The 4th International Conference on Multimdedia Modelling*, November 17 - 20, Singapore.

Fröhlich, P., Henze, N. and Nejdl, W. (1997b) Meta-modeling for hypermedia design. In *Proc. of Second IEEE Metadata Conference*, Maryland.

Fröhlich, P. and Nejdl, W.(1997c). A Database-Oriented Approach to the Design of Educational Hyperbooks. In *Proceedings of the AIED'97 Workshop on Intelligent Educational Systems on the World Wide Web*, Kobe, Japan.

Garzotto, F., Schwabe, D. and Paolini, P. (1993) HDM - A Model Based A pproach to Hypermedia Application Design. *ACM Transactions on Information Systems*, 11(1).

Henze, N. (1997) Auswertung der Befragung der Teilnehmer der Vorlesung Grundzüge der Informatik, Technical Report, University of Hannover.

Isakowitz, T., Stohr, E.A. and Balasubrahmanian, P. (1995) RMM: A methodology for structured hypermedia design. *Communications of the ACM*, 38(8).

Jarke, M., Gallersdörfer, R., Jeusfeld, M., Staudt, M. and Eherer,S. (1995) Conceptbase - a deductive object base for meta data management. *Journal on Intelligent Information Systems*, 4(2):167 - 192.

Kay, J. and Kummerfeld, R.J. (1994) An individualised course for the C programming language. *In Proc. of the 2nd International World Wide Web Conference*, Chicago, USA.

Mylopoulos, J., Borgida, A., Jarke, M. and Koubarakis, M. (1990) Telos: A language for representing knowledge about information systems. *ACM Transactions on Information Systems*, 8(4).

Nissen, H.W., Jeusfeld, M.A., Jarke, M., Zemanek, G.V., and Huber, H. (1996) Requirements analysis from multiple perspectives: Experiences with conceptual modeling technology. *IEEE Software*, 13(2).

Fishman, B.J., Honebein, P.C., Duffy, T.M. (1991) Constructivism and the design of learning enivronments: Context and authentic activities for learning. In *NATO Advanced Workshop on the Design of Constructivist Learning Environments.*
Schank, R. and Cleary, C. (1994) Engines for Education. Lawrence Erlbaum Associates, Hillsdale, New Jersey.
Schwabe, D., Rossi, G. and Barbosa, S.D.J. (1996) Systematic hypermedia application design with OOHDM. In *Proceedings of the Seventh ACM Conference on Hypertext*, Washington DC.

10. BIOGRAPHIES

Nicola Henze has received her masters degree in mathematics from the University of Hannover. As a member of the knowledge-based systems group at the University of Hannover, she is working on adaptable and adaptive hypertext systems and user-adapted learning environments.

Wolfgang Nejdl has graduated from the Technical University of Vienna in computer science, and is currently full professor for computer science at the University of Hannover, and head of the knowledge-based systems group. He has worked in the areas of databases, artificial intelligence and hypermedia for education, and has published more than 90 articles in conference proceedings and journals on these subjects.

8

An experience in UNED on building up a Virtual Campus

C. M. Pérez-Molina, J. A. Rodríguez, C. de Mora, J. Carpio, M. Castro and J. Peire
Dpto. Ing. Eléctrica, Electrónica y de Control, ETSII, (UNED)
Ciudad Universitaria s/n, 28040 Madrid, Spain,
e-mail: clarapm@ieec.uned.es

Abstract

The paper describes how the DEMOS project (funded by the European Commission, 4th Framework Programme 1996) will be implanted at UNED. The proposal was born as an initiative of UNED as part of its plan to cover the needs of new distance learning applications to be used in the current and future telecommunication networks. DEMOS intends to design and develop a distributed learning environment for distance education scenarios shaping a Virtual Campus, where co-operation among teachers, learners, tutors and experts is supported in a very flexible way. It is focused on the development of multimedia applications for education over heterogeneous telematics environments. The applications may be adapted to the different kinds of users and the different infrastructures available to facilitate the demonstration and exploitation phases.

Keywords

Distributed learning systems, Virtual campus, Learning scenarios, ISDN lines

The Virtual Campus F. Verdejo & G. Davies (Eds.)

1. INTRODUCTION: OVERVIEW OF UNED

UNED is the most important distance learning university of Spain and according to the number of enrolled students is the largest University of the country. Almost twenty-four years of steady, consistent growth in all areas, using its own particular administrative, academic and educational system, have led to many international educational forums referring to the "Spanish higher distance educational model". Initially set up as a "second chance" university, its subsequent development, led UNED to play a far more significant role in Spain than was originally expected.

UNED is nowadays especially committed to continuing education and professional improvement, and to the development of a teaching methodology based on the latest communication and information technologies. The nation-wide nature of UNED is also worth mentioning, as this is an extraordinary feature which has withstood the Spanish decentralisation process, and which is undoubtedly the key to a large part of UNED's potential (Moreno,1993).

In the academic year 1996-1997, UNED's overall enrolments reached 160,000 students; the number of full-time teaching staff at the Central Headquarters in Madrid is now 1,000. There are approximately 4,000 part-time tutors, working in 60 Study Centres spread throughout the Spanish territory, and nine more so-called "support" Centres located in some European and Latin American countries. UNED offers degree courses in fifteen different fields, including the Humanities and Social Sciences, Mathematics, Physics, Chemistry, Industrial Engineering and Computer Science. Apart from these traditional courses -which in most cases also comprise Ph. D. programmes -, UNED offers Continuing education and "pure" Open courses at different levels and in a wide range.

1.1 Study Centre Network: methods and technology

Two main features of UNED are relevant for the purpose of this paper and the project as a whole: UNED's Study Centre Network and the methodological model that is being used in the teaching-learning process of the University.

The student support system of UNED relies on the Study Centre Network; students make their enrolment there, take care of all administrative issues, have their tutorials, and have access to all other services provided by the Central Headquarters university and by the Centre itself. UNED's Study Centres are autonomous in all areas except in strictly academic matters (for which they depend on the Professors and academic departments of the Headquarters). The fact that Study Centres were set up as a result of both public and private local initiative in medium-sized towns where no traditional university studies were available has enabled them to grow into highly dynamic institutions involved in the local community and its progress. The traditional effects of university education (the exodus of graduates to large urban areas) are thus reversed: the small and medium-sized towns benefit from the improved academic and professional qualifications of their citizens and workers (García-Aretio, 1994).

As far as distance teaching methodology is concerned, UNED is introducing new technologies in a very gradual and careful way, looking to obtain maximum benefit from and development of "old" technologies, such as printed materials of different kinds, rather than rushing prematurely towards any methodological panacea, the results of which are as yet unclear. Thus, the original UNED methods based on the production and distribution of printed matter, individual attention from the Study Centre and its tutors, and radio broadcasts, have been maintained and developed as the methodological core of the University. To this, have been progressively added the following: the production of audio-visual material, direct attention to students from the Central Headquarters via telephone, daily television broadcasts, distribution of computer-based teaching programmes, and the introduction of a large telematic network using the new electronic technologies -wideband network linking all campus buildings, videotext, electronic mail, videoconference system, etc. UNED has set up an Educational Videoconferencing Network which comprises thirty-eight videoconferencing rooms, three of them at the Central Headquarters in Madrid, and the rest installed at thirty-five Study Centres (Carpio, 1994).

All the above-mentioned means are now used simultaneously at our University, so that methodological plurality has become one of the most peculiar features of our system. This means that the tool to be developed and tried out with the DEMOS project will be taken as one more element to be added to our list; our objective is to increase in number - and in quality - all possible means to give support (administrative and academic) to our students. The number of students, their geographical dispersion, and their tremendously different interests and capacities, do not allow for a single way of providing services and support, no matter how effective that way could be. In short, we are aiming at integrating this DEMOS tool in our system, and probably not so much to overhaul our system around this tool.

2. DESCRIPTION OF DEMOS PROJECT AT UNED

2.1 Different kinds of users

There are a wide variety of students at UNED. Some time ago UNED's average student was a man or a woman in his or her thirties, with a full time job and a family, who just wanted to improve his/her qualifications in order to look for professional promotion or just professional development in general. At the moment, there are many young students coming out fresh from secondary school, and that kind of student represents the majority, but on the other hand, there are also many mature students who are looking for a second university degree.

Many students have other responsibilities apart from their career, so they have little time to study. Students always want to make the most of their learning activities and experiences; at UNED they are used to studying by themselves. However, when they live in periphery areas, even in remote ones, isolation, the feeling of loneliness and the consequent lack of feedback from teachers or other students can be the reason for many dropouts. This is the kind of student we want to deal with in this project; we hope that through this new technology the distance learning methodology at our university will improve.

We have identified three different types of potential users in the DEMOS project:

1. **The home-based student (type A).** Many students have other responsibilities apart from their career, so that they have little time to study. Although he or she lives close to one of the Study Centre, work and family pressures do not allow many visits to the Centre. Therefore s/he works at home and has a computer with average technical characteristics and access to the standard telephone service (PSTN).
2. **The home-based student (type B).** This is just a variation from the previous type. The student is again working alone at home but he or she has more sophisticated computer equipment including multimedia equipment, high-speed modem and, of course, access to PSTN. Considering the evolution of prices for ISDN, this is a student who could have access to ISDN in the very near future.
3. **The Study Centre-based student.** Even though attending tutorials is not compulsory in our University, many students go quite frequently to the Study Centre, especially students living in medium-size towns for whom it is easy and fast to get there. Most Study Centres offer many facilities, including computer equipment, access to ISDN and LAN, etc. Students taking the same course have the opportunity to meet and work together, and to have the support of a tutor at least once a week throughout the academic year.

2.2 Walking down a Virtual Campus

The services provided by DEMOS include a set of tools integrated in a Windows application, so it is easy to use and furthermore it gives an integrated look. DEMOS has been developed taking into account *what* our students need and *how* we can cover these needs with a telematic environment.

Each user will be able to use one or more DEMOS applications with the same basic and cost-effective hardware platforms: PC clients running MS-Windows 95 and UNIX servers. There is an integrated HTML welcome page for accessing the DEMOS applications so only one user authentication will be done.

Next let's specify the way our DEMOS system works in order to achieve the students' requirements. It is like 'walking' through a Virtual Campus, and it could be described as follows:

Information and Administration

Information is provided through Internet access to a centralised information system. Students can visualise and recover information by means of common web browsers. Topics covered are namely personal data, DEMOS information, public announcements and participants' news space.

Administration involves registration of students and control of activities. Some administration tasks can be performed via the Internet, but not all because of security. In this last case, a special purpose application, the administration manager utility, is developed allowing secure information handling from well-defined client sites, namely local computers belonging to system administrators.

The Information and Administration facilities are supported by a centralised client/server database management system which implements data storage and security control on database access. Stored information may consist of users' data, both students and teachers, as well as system usage such as session attendance and library or bookstore usage. Database edition and updating is performed transparently with the interactive support provided by the user interface, either web browsers or the administration manager utility.

Students can submit registration information via the Internet, which should be confirmed by the administration service. Once confirmed the registration, permissions are granted for the different services. See Figure 1.

Figure 1. Entrance to the Virtual Campus.

Virtual Library and Asynchronous Study

This facility is very similar to a common Library, in which the user can search and use the didactic materials provided by the teachers and where the student is able to practice self-study. The student is allowed to consult any hypermedia document, navigating through it as well as following stored classes off-line, not only the teaching material but the teaching process itself, including the actions, video image and voice of the teacher.

Virtual Bookstore

This service allows the electronic distribution of didactic material, where it is important to control and register the kind of information distributed (free, restricted) and who it is distributed to, especially if there are copyrights. The solution that has been adopted is an ftp-like asynchronous tool managing a documents database for security permission and accounting, allowing the DEMOS students to search/retrieve multimedia documents from it.

Learning Scenarios

Here we describe a set of applications that simulates the most common learning and training situations between a group of users (teachers and learners). A classroom metaphor is used to develop these situations.

1. **Tele-Teaching:** This will take place at the Distributed Virtual Classroom, where the teacher and the students are connected on-line through their terminals. This facility is the main core of DEMOS and it allows applications, tools and material in all kind of formats (text, programs, images, audio and video) including multipoint videoconferencing to be shared. The teacher's terminal is allowed to play the role of the session's director. See Figure 2.

Figure 2. Tele-Teaching scenario.

2. **Tele-Tutoring:** Through this facility the teacher is accessible to the learners during some time previously agreed (normally 4 hours a week). To handle several requests a queuing mechanism has been required. When a learner has a problem he can call the teacher to put it to him. This tool allows the personal communication (point-to-point) between the teacher and the student: in an asynchronous way (like the electronic mail but with multimedia features) or on-line between both (then, it can be considered as an individual or point-to-point use of the Virtual Classroom). See Figure 3.

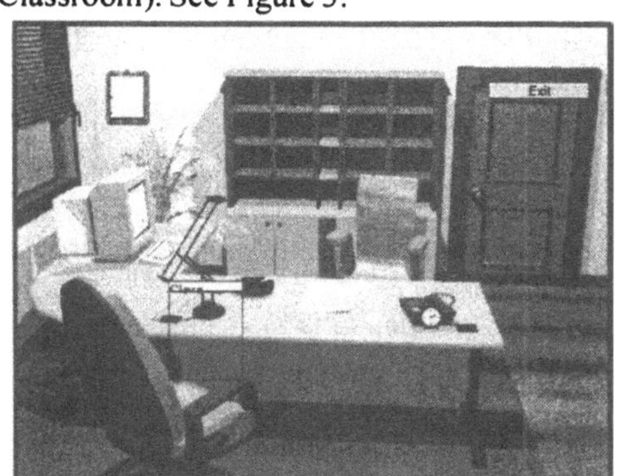

Figure 3. Tele-Tutoring scenario.

3. **Meeting sessions:** This is where a discussion among groups of learners about any question is carried out. They are always able to share windows applications and the blackboard system for working collaboratively on them. In this application all the users have the same role, it is possible to have a chairman but it is not necessary. See Figure 4.

Figure 4. Meeting sessions scenario.

Café Room

This tool is the discussion forum for the students, there the students can get in touch by multimedia electronic mail and create discussion news groups (similar to the ones of the Internet).

3. TECHNICAL ASPECTS OF THE VIRTUAL CAMPUS

From a technical point of view DEMOS is an advanced telematic environment that includes synchronous (on-line) and asynchronous (off-line) applications. It runs on different hardware platforms, based on multimedia PC servers, using point-to-point and multipoint modes.

Demos Distributed Virtual Classroom is very flexible in terms of communication configurations. The only important requirement is to have the TCP/IP protocol. The following configurations are sustained:

- Over LAN: Different users connected to a LAN.
- One ISDN line: One to one or multipoint communication through a basic ISDN line.
- Two ISDN lines: One to one or multipoint communication trough two basic ISDN lines.
- The two above configurations plus LAN: In the student side can be a LAN, sustaining not only one but many students.
- PTC connection via modem.

Obviously the quality of transmission depends on the bandwidth of the channel. For high quality in video and audio transmission the two ISDN lines configuration is recommended. For very high audio transmission, an audio codec can be used which allows mono CD audio quality. Other configurations are however supported allowing a balance between the investment and the available features. In sum the system is affordable to most students.

With DVC the number of simultaneous connections depends on the instructor's router capability. See Figure 5. For the most frequent scenario, which is the distance tutoring activity, eight simultaneous connections are more than enough, which makes the system highly versatile.

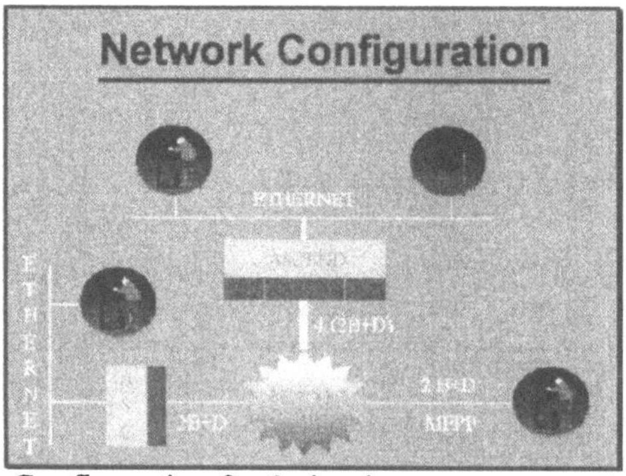

Figure 5. Network Configuration for 2 simultaneous connections through ISDN.

DVC can integrate different market videoconferencing systems since it is almost independent of such systems. Features such as application sharing or application control, do not depend on the videoconferencing system used.

Communication cost is one of the most important criteria of acceptance by users of DEMOS. PSTN can be used as a low cost public access network (mainly by users located in rural areas), but in the majority of cases ISDN access (128 kbps) is used in order to use all video-conferencing and multimedia capabilities without any constraint. See Figure 6.

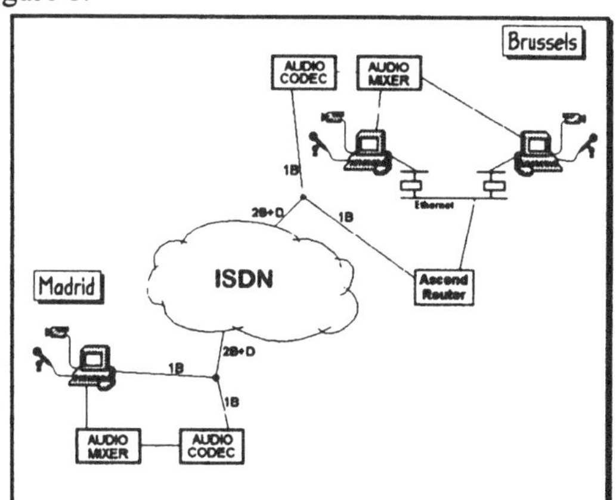

Figure 6. Detailed Configuration for an ISDN connection.

When a connection is opened, the user can send information to all the users of the group, to a single one or to any subset of them. Because of the actual limitations of PCs only one video-window can be displayed, so the user who has the turn (the teacher or the student depending on the case) sends his video/audio signal to all the others and can choose one of them. Basically there are two different modes of transmission: the control data flow requires a protocol like TCP that ensures the correct transmission of the information, however video and audio use UDP because the loss of some information is not too important (Sánchez-Dueñas, 1994).

4. IMPACT AND LAUNCHING

DEMOS could mean a great innovation in distance learning, since through this new system it is possible to allay the feeling of loneliness of every distance student, improving his/her motivation and consequently the benefits from study time. Students are able to meet their teachers as well as their classmates and to establish a personal communication like is carried out in a traditional university.

Owing to the wide diversification of students in our university, all the applications offered by DEMOS have been adapted to the heterogeneous network infrastructure available in each user's site, so flexibility increases the number of potential beneficiaries (Carpio, Pérez, 1996). Also these applications have a friendly interface, using metaphors for minimising the interface learning period, and for helping the user in concentrating on the material used in the learning process instead of on the way of using the application itself. All the actions that a user can do in each moment have been represented with intuitive icons.

We believe that, given the peculiar features of UNED, the Study Centre is the more rational "unit" for validation and demonstration of any new learning programme, at least during the first stage. This is because, even if the students do not attend tutorials regularly or do not benefit from the services of the Centre, they still "belong" to it in an administrative sense and have to go there for examinations and, if necessary, for practical seminars. The first prototype of DEMOS is ready at this moment. Then the validation phase will start with students in four Study Centres, mainly belonging to the UNED's European EuroStudy Centers Network, next academic year.

From a pedagogical point of view, this represents a big challenge. DEMOS pays special attention to the preparation of materials. There is a facility that lets the authors create materials (in an easy and friendly way) which will be used in the application, especially in the virtual classroom. A collaborative hypermedia editor has been used which allows creating those courseware multimedia materials including also files and objects made with many different standard-authoring tools.

5. REFERENCES

Carpio, J and Ramos, E. (1994). UNED-EVCN: UNED Educational Videoconferencing Network. *DELTA Conference for Education and Training*. Düsseldorf, 1994.

Carpio, J. and Pérez, C. (1996) Enseñanza a Distancia utilizando las Nuevas Tecnologías Telemáticas. *Jornadas Las Tecnologías de la Información como instrumento para la Formación Permanente: Nuevas perspectivas para la Formación Abierta y a Distancia.* Universitat de Valencia, 1996.

García-Aretio, L. (1994). *La Educación a Distancia Hoy* (in Spanish). Ed. UNED.

Moreno, J.M. (1993). UNED: The first twenty years. *EADTU Newsletters*. No 13, April.

Sánchez-Dueñas, G. (1994). EDUBA: Applications for Education on Wide Band Communication Networks. *DELTA Conference for Education and Training*. Düsseldorf, 1994.

6. BIOGRAPHIES

Clara M. Pérez-Molina received a degree in Physics from the Complutense University, Madrid, in 1995. She has been working as researcher last two years at the Department of Electronic Engineering and Computer Science in the Spanish distance learning University (UNED). She is one of the members of the DEMOS project team of UNED. Her research interests include object-oriented programing, information and databases management systems, and neural networks.

Carlos de Mora is an Industrial Engineer. He holds an Associate Professor at Department of Electrical, Electronic and Control Engineering. His research interest is focused on Control Theory, Artificial Intelligence and Telematics.

José Carpio received the MS Electrical Engineering in 1985 and the Ph. D. in 1988, both from Technical University of Madrid. He joined the "Ingeniería Eléctrica, Electrónica y de Control" department at UNED in 1989 as Associate Professor. In 1993, he was visiting researcher in the "Department of Operation Research" at Stanford University. From 1994 to 1996, he was director of the Telematic Services Center in UNED. His research interest focuses in Optimization Power Systems and Technology for Distance Learning.

Manuel Castro, Electrical and Computer engineering educator in the Spanish University for Distance Education (UNED), has an industrial engineering degree from the ETSII / Madrid Polytechnic University and a doctoral engineering degree too. He worked during 5 years in Digital Equipment Corporation as senior system engineer. He works as researcher in different projects, ranging from solar system and advanced microprocessor system simulation to telematics and distance learning systems, acting now as and senior technical coordinator. He is now serving as UNED's Information Services Center Director. He has published different technical books and articles for journals and conferences. He is senior member of IEEE and board member of the Spanish ISES committee.

Juan Peire received the MS Industrial Engineering in 1976 and the Ph. D. in 1979, both from University Politechnic of Madrid. He worked as R&D Director in GAMESA for five years. He is author or coauthor of books and more than eighty international papers. Currently, he is the Director of the "Ingeniería Eléctrica, Electrónica y de Control" Department at UNED. His research interest focuses in Distance Learning applications.

PART THREE

Evaluation Studies

9

The impact of the Internet on academic research practices

C. Dowling
Australian Catholic University
412 Mt Alexander Rd, Ascot Vale, Victoria 3032, Australia,
e-mail: c.dowling@mercy.acu.edu.au

Abstract

This paper discusses some aspects of the use of the Internet which have the capacity to impact significantly upon research practices within universities. These include changing patterns of collaboration, challenges to accepted notions of intellectual property and copyright, concerns regarding the validation of electronically based information, changes to the time-frames associated with scholarly research, and the respective roles of electronic and hard copy publishing. Each of these areas is of considerable importance in terms of the role of universities in the future.

Special reference is made to a longitudinal study currently being conducted at Australian Catholic University concerning the impact of Internet access on the research practices of academic staff. The study places particular emphasis on identifying and examining possible changes to patterns of collaboration in research and academic writing both within this geographically dispersed, multi-campus institution and with colleagues from elsewhere. Of special interest is the degree to which traditional concepts of 'distance' remain relevant to the activities of the Virtual Campus.

Keywords

Academic writing, Collaboration, Copyright, Communication technology, Research, Virtual campus

The Virtual Campus F. Verdejo & G. Davies (Eds.)

1. INTRODUCTION

Recent developments in computing technology, in particular those associated with the Internet, are calling into question a number of the traditions of academic practice. This paper discusses some aspects of the use of the Internet which have the capacity to impact significantly upon research practices within universities. While focussing principally on changing patterns of collaboration, it acknowledges a number of related issues which impinge on the practicalities and consequences of such collaboration within academic contexts, including challenges to accepted notions of intellectual property and copyright, concerns regarding the validation of electronically based information, changes to the time-frames associated with scholarly research, and the respective roles of electronic and hard copy publishing. Each of these areas is significant not simply within the context of particular examples of academic collaboration, but more broadly in terms of the ongoing credibility and authority of universities in relation to the creation, representation and transmission of knowledge, with concomitant implications for the maintenance of the structures which currently support those activities.

In most developed and indeed in many less developed countries across the globe, academics who have access to the technology have embraced with enthusiasm the various facilities and capabilities of the Internet. Email, newsgroups, listservs, MUDs, MOOs, user friendly search engines and the multimedia capacities of the World Wide Web have enticed educators and researchers across most disciplines to engage in a range of new and in many cases significantly different practices. While some of these might be seen as enabling traditional activities to be undertaken with greater ease and efficiency, others actually possess the potential to undermine some of the basic foundations upon which our academic endeavours have traditionally been based. These dimensions are acknowledged already in a range of publications from chapters and articles in volumes such as *Changes in Scholarly Communication Patterns* (Mulvaney and Steele (eds), 1993), *The Cultures of Computing* (Star (ed.), 1995) and *Work and Technology in Higher Education: the Social Construction of Academic Computing* (Shiels (ed.), 1995) through journal articles and conference papers initially emanating from a range of discipline areas, but more recently tending to be concentrated under the conceptual umbrella of the Virtual University or Campus.

2. THE RESEARCH PROJECT

In considering these issues, reference is made within this paper to a longitudinal study currently being conducted at Australian Catholic University concerning the impact of Internet access on the research practices of academic staff. The study, currently in its second year, places particular emphasis on identifying and examining possible changes to patterns of collaboration in research and academic writing both within this geographically dispersed, multi-campus institution and with colleagues from other institutions both within Australia and overseas.

In common with many tertiary institutions, Australian Catholic University is devoting considerable resources to facilitating staff access to the Internet. The benefits are generally presumed to include significantly enhanced opportunities for communication and collaboration with colleagues both within and outside the University in addition to improved access to a range of information sources for research purposes. Communication within the University is of particular interest in that the institution comprises eight campuses, several quite small in size, distributed across three states and one territory of Australia. While the number of staff associated with any one discipline area on a single campus may be extremely small, in some extreme cases consisting of a single individual, these groups are actively encouraged to perceive themselves as colleagues within a single institution, clearly "virtual" in regard to its unity and to a significant extent electronically based, with joint responsibility for the content and in some cases for the teaching of units and courses. Within each of the Faculties of the University, national discipline based networks fulfill many of the functions of traditional academic departments in nurturing and developing intellectual content. Collaboration in research activities is an obvious component of this type of cooperation. The resource implications alone, but also, very importantly, the potential for changes to established practice, suggest the importance of monitoring the extent to which the expectations associated with the implementation of this technology are in fact being met (Dowling, 1996). Of special interest is the degree to which traditional concepts of "distance" can be overcome through a strengthening of electronic infrastructures facilitating virtuality.

The research is being conducted through a series of questionnaires and follow-up interviews. An initial survey directed to all permanent members of the academic staff of the University was used to identify those who had made use of the Internet over the previous 12 months (1995), and who were willing to participate further in the project. Of the 167 responses received by the due date, 103 indicated a willingness to continue their participation. At that stage (mid 1996), 62% of the 167 respondents were making use of the Internet to communicate with colleagues in relation to academic matters, 42% specifically in relation to research, while 22% had used the Internet to write collaboratively with colleagues. When considered in the light of the fact that at that time not all academic staff of the University had computers on their desks, a University based training program in the use of the Internet had been offered only on some campuses, the capacity of the network was inadequate leading to access being somewhat sporadic and there was a dearth of technical support, these figures suggest a considerable willingness to use the technology albeit under less than ideal circumstances.

In relation to the other focus of the project, namely using the Internet to access information, 70% of the initial respondents had made use of these facilities to look for information related to their teaching, and 68% for information related specifically to their research activities. While this preliminary questionnaire did not address the issue of overlap between these areas, it is clear that considerable use was being made of the technology for information retrieval for academic purposes. In conversation with a number of respondents it is clear that the fact that these percentages were higher than those making use of the Internet for communication and collaboration with colleagues relates to the transparency of the retrieval mechanisms available on the World Wide Web through programs such as Netscape, the University's browser-of-choice.

Of particular influence in developing a rationale and methodology for this project has been a longitudinal investigation undertaken by researchers from the School of Education, Kings College London. This research, funded by the British Library Research and Development Department, has been in progress since 1992. Associated publications to date include Squires (1993), Squires, Barry and Funston (1994), Barry (1995) and Barry and Squires (1995). The Australian Catholic University project is providing a valuable counterpoint to this research, in that the technology which has been provided to staff is significantly more sophisticated and 'user friendly' than that which was initially available to participants in the British study.

3. COMMUNICATION AND COLLABORATION

It is undeniable that computer networks have the capacity to encourage and facilitate collaborative research and writing. With the current popular focus on the broader social and economic applications and implications of the Internet, the fact that this was, in fact, one of the primary purposes of its early manifestations, can easily be overlooked. The value of today's enriched communications environment encompassing home pages, email, listservs, discussion groups, MUDs and MOOs, in multiplying the possibilities for communication with colleagues should not be underestimated. However, while applauding the potential for interaction within these environments, it should not be assumed that they are the simple equivalents of more traditional forums including exchanges conducted through the medium of refereed journals, attendance at face to face conferences or other forms of presentation, collaboration within a physically and intellectually delineated context such as a laboratory, communication by telephone or conventional mail or, very importantly, those snatched moments and chance remarks in a corridor or over the coffee dispenser, which may provide a sharply focussed impetus for new research directions or understandings. Each of these situations has its own social complexities which are important in determining outcomes. These are well addressed in relation to electronic environments by writings and research addressing broader aspects of computer mediated interpersonal relationships (Rheingold, 1994; Spender, 1995; Turkle, 1995). Nor should it be assumed that it is necessarily advantageous to replace traditional opportunities for collaboration entirely by the newly available modes of communications. While ongoing developments both in the technology itself and in the use to which it is made by academics render the situation extremely fluid, it might well be that a judicious mix of forms of communication would maximise the benefits to be gained. It has been suggested by several staff interviewed in connection with the Australian Catholic University project that chance encounters of the "coffee dispenser" type as distinct from the more purposeful interactions which are initiated on the Internet often have a particularly serendipitous effect on the thinking associated with research activity.

What form does the collaboration of this group of academics take? While the results of the interviews on this subject have not yet been formally analysed, it appears that research related communications cover a range of matters which would be familiar to the traditional academic - namely feedback on ideas for research projects or on written reports and papers, exchanges of information concerning sources of funding and possible outlets for publications, information related to conferences, discussion of the relative merits of other academics as potential supervisors, referees or collaborators, lists of resources pertaining to particular areas of interest and of course the collaborative writing of books, reports, conference papers and the like.

In relation to the search for possible collaborators, it is of interest that several subjects, all younger academics who would not at this stage have had many opportunities for face to face interaction with established researchers in their areas whether in their own country or overseas, alluded to making regular and systematic searches of the home pages of other universities in search of details relating to staff working in the same or allied fields. Having located such people, several of the academics interviewed had gone on to make some form of contact electronically, all of them agreeing that this was less intimidating than the prospect of approaching unknown individuals either in person, on the telephone or by conventional mail.

A further point of interest which has been noted in interviews with the staff at Australian Catholic University with regard to collaboration is the speed with which the cyberspace within which these interactions take place becomes genuinely divorced from geographical space. While a number of participants in the early interviews expressed special excitement at their new ability to communicate with colleagues overseas, in interviews which occurred only six months later these same academics discussed their interactions, primarily through email, in terms which did not discriminate between the local and the geographically distant. Colleagues at other local campuses, even in offices within the same building, clearly occupied the same notional 'space' as contacts on the other side of the world. This is in keeping with earlier findings (Dowling, 1987) in which the implementation of electronic mail in office buildings of large, dispersed organisations, led to electronic communication taking place indiscriminately between physically distant locations, between adjoining offices, and even between adjoining desks. It is particularly interesting in this context in relation to the conscious goal of the University that it should be both perceived externally and experienced internally as a single, integrated institution. (Other initiatives supporting this aim include extensive use of video conferencing for small group teaching and seminars, and the beginnings of Internet based course offerings between campuses as well as for external students.)

4. ACADEMIC WRITING AND THE INTERNET

Internet access brings with it an enormously enhanced potential for collaborative writing. The ease with which textual material can be exchanged and modified by writers interacting through a range of software types and, if so desired, within a virtually instantaneous timeframe, has for many researchers enabled the realisation of the hitherto somewhat abstract concept of the social construction of knowledge. It also contributes to a possible need to rethink for the future certain issues related to the ownership and distribution of textual material.

Even prior to the widespread availability of networked communication, it could be said that the use of the computer as a writing medium weakened from a number of points of view our usual conceptions concerning the sovereignty of the individual author over text (Dowling, 1995). While many of the psychological and phenomenological subtleties relating to the differences between computer based and other forms of writing are beyond the scope of this paper, there are some obvious considerations which pertain to the electronic composition and dissemination of academic writing.

The very ease with which electronically textual material can be assembled and seamlessly integrated into a single document may raise generalised doubts concerning the source, the originality and the uniqueness of a particular piece of work or of its component parts. The possibilities for such involuntary 'collaboration' are exacerbated by the extent to which current developments in communications technology, particularly those related to the Internet, facilitate the uncontrolled dissemination of material previously subject to processes of distribution which enabled the source to be acknowledged and validated. For the academic community, dependent as it has traditionally been on the notion of the authoritative text for which an identifiable individual author or authors may be held responsible, such developments raise a number some dilemmas. A recurrent theme in discussion of this issue with participants in the Australian Catholic University study has been the need to balance the advantages of electronic dissemination of research related discussion and findings with the increased risks that such readily accessible material may be taken and re-used without due acknowledgment. Many academics, including this author, can already provide instances of such practice. While plagiarism is not, of course, a new problem, the ready availability of large amounts of material in “useable” form greatly facilitates its occurrence. In addition, the sheer volume of information available on the Internet decreases the likelihood of detection in that few academics can now claim intimate knowledge of all, or even most of the texts available in their field. Indeed in both the King’s College (Barry and Squires, 1995) and the Australian Catholic University studies, researchers have expressed an ongoing need for training in techniques of information retrieval in order to cope with the ever increasing amount of material available electronically.

5. ACADEMIC PUBLISHING AND THE LEGITIMACY OF ACADEMIC KNOWLEDGE

Within academic contexts, the contrast between the potential for rapid electronic dissemination and the painstaking but often frustratingly slow process of publishing in refereed academic journals has led in many disciplines to a mixture of publishing media becoming legitimised by default, for different purposes. Where speed of dissemination of research findings is seen as important, particularly in the more "practically" oriented disciplines such as many of the sciences, it is now widely accepted that the "real" exchanges of ideas and results takes place through electronic media, with publication in traditional paper based journals increasingly becoming a retrospective event, having more to do with the formal recognition of achievements and credentials associated with funding and promotion processes than with the actual process of the creation and dissemination of knowledge. It is interesting to note in this regard the recent burgeoning of electronic 'journals' subject to refereeing processes which compare favourably with those associated with traditional paper based journals endorsed by the academic hierarchies. In some instances the hard copy and electronic versions of the same publication complement one another while fulfilling different needs.

Traditional understandings of the legitimacy of academic knowledge depend heavily on processes of validation through which sources of information may be established and their 'legitimacy' assessed. In the realms of traditional publishing, methods of ascertaining and evaluating the source of textual material included the reputation of the publishing body, particularly in regard to the processes by which a manuscript was accepted for publication, a clear understanding of the extent to which the purported author was in fact responsible for both the content and the presentation of the text and so on. In the case of electronic publishing, the 'provenance' of information is less apparent, putting far more of the onus of evaluation on the individual reader. While this is very much more in keeping with the processes which apply outside academia, it lies at a considerable remove from the well established scaffolding of citation and counter citation which has traditionally supported the structures of 'legitimate' academic knowledge. The extent to which this is perceived as a problem is in part a function of our philosophical beliefs concerning the nature of 'knowledge', in particular the extent to which we are comfortable with the notion of a degree of 'social' construction which includes participants who may be situated well outside the boundaries delineating those traditionally accepted as 'knowledgeable'.

Understandably much of the academic hierarchy, including funding bodies, approaches the issue of non-traditional forms of publication with considerable caution. There is certainly wide variation in the processes which govern electronic publication, ranging from the totally unregulated output of an individual to stringent systems of quality control which equate quite reasonably with traditional practice. With time, the differences between these should become more widely understood. However while in some fields there is an obvious need for recognised means of attesting to the accuracy of published material, in other areas it might be suspected that the anxieties have more to do with such issues as the establishment of status both within and between disciplines, or the maintenance of existing systems of promotion, than with concerns about knowledge *per se*.

This is an area which currently generates heated debate among the Australian Catholic University staff interviewed, both in relation to their own research and to the standards which should govern the use and citation of electronically based sources by students. There is clear variation between disciplines and between individuals within disciplines. Within this University there is pressure from individual staff in a range of areas, including both the sciences and the humanities, for a cautious acceptance of the new publishing media - including the Internet and CD ROM or disk based publications. Considerable resentment is expressed at the perceived intransigence of some elements in the academic hierarchy which do not as yet afford great value to such publications.

Of course the sheer availability of academic resources via the Internet creates other consequences in relation to knowledge creation, including concerns as to whether the timeframes traditionally associated with research degrees should be shortened in acknowledgment of the benefits both of more efficient information retrieval and of the efficacious effects of word processing on academic writing. While acceleration of the research process might be perceived as having benefits in terms of efficiency and economic considerations, some of the Australian Catholic University academics have expressed concern that this could result in insufficient "thinking" time being available to researchers, with deleterious consequences for research outcomes. Similar concerns were voiced by researchers interviewed during the Kings College study (Barry and Squires, 1995).

6. COPYRIGHT

Matters related to the definition and regulation of intellectual property, including basic copyright law, are obviously of special interest to academics. Within the context of Internet based research and publication, questions relating to the ownership of electronically mediated textual material are particularly important.

In addressing these issues we tend to assume that, for the majority of people who may be involved, traditional understandings of individual ownership and of property rights related to the control of intellectual assets remain basically unchanged. While the widely touted concept of the computer based information society has undoubtedly strengthened public acceptance of the notion of intangible products such as "information" as tradable commodities, it is possible that the extraordinary burgeoning of a proliferation of alternative network 'cultures' might stimulate broader adherence to a number of contrary points of view upon which ethical or moral decision making could conceivably be based in the future, including the idea that information should be freely accessible to all. Such beliefs are clearly at odds both with traditional understandings and with the growing emphasis on the commodification of abstract information.

Both individual academics and their institutions require clarity in relation to the ownership of the products of research activity. While patent law is obviously of great importance in many fields, the potential for change wrought by computing technology pertains most strongly to questions of copyright. Much of the discussion concerning the legal aspects of ownership of computer based material centers around the abstract or ephemeral form of the electronically stored product as compared with the fixed and tangible nature of a paper based document. As a consequence of such qualities, identification of 'original' text or of subsequent alterations may not be possible. Further, the new ease of distribution through computer networks, allied with ideological positions supporting so-called 'free' access to computer based information, introduces complexities which may not be adequately addressed through piecemeal modifications to existing law. It is undeniable that the supreme ease with which electronically based material may be copied, modified and disseminated without the consent of the original author creates significant challenges to existing copyright regulations, a number of which are currently under debate around the world.

This uncertainty is an obvious factor in the hesitation felt at both an individual and a systemic level regarding the status of electronic publications.

7. CONCLUSION

The embracing of the Internet and associated technologies by academics is inevitable and clearly has many benefits to offer, particularly in relation to the ability to access information and to communicate with colleagues. Nevertheless, as argued in this paper, there are a number of issues associated with the use of this technology of which researchers themselves and those responsible for the encouragement and management of research should be aware. There is currently a great deal of interest, at both a theoretical and a practical level, in the use of the Internet for teaching and learning. However there is also a strong sense in which the research enterprise underpins the whole notion of a university, whether virtual or otherwise. This aspect should not be neglected in our consideration of the impact of computing and communications technology on tertiary institutions.

8. REFERENCES

Barry, C. (1995) Critical issues in evaluating the impact of IT on information activity in academic research: developing a qualitative research solution, in *Library and Information Science Research*, 17 (2), pp. 107 - 134.

Barry, C. and Squires, D. (1995) Why the move from traditional information-seeking to the electronic library is not straightforward for academic users: some surprising findings, in *Online Information 95*, Meckler Press, London, pp. 177 - 187.

Dowling, C. (1987) Mind Your Language: Computers and Communication, in *Proceedings of the Australian Computers in Education Conference,* Hancock, J. (ed.), Adelaide 1987, pp. 39 - 43.

Dowling, C. (1995) Quills to keyboards: the impact of computing technology on academic writing, in *Proceedings of the 1995 Annual Conference of the Higher Education and Research Development Society of Australasia (HERDSA)*, Rockhampton, July 1995, pp. 270 - 276.

Dowling, C. (1996) Whose words are they? Some aspects of the ownership of textual material in electronic environments, in *Proceedings of the Australian Computers in Education Conference*, (disk format) Canberra, April 1996.

Dowling, C. (1996) Academia Online: the impact of the Internet on academic research practices, in *Proceedings of the 1996 Annual Conference of the Higher Education and Research Development Society of Australasia (HERDSA)*, Perth, July 1996.

Fraser, M. (1993) Intellectual Property in Australia: Libraries and Copyright, in Mulvaney, J. and Steele, C (eds) (1993), *Changes in Scholarly Communication Patterns*, Canberra: Australian Academy of the Humanities, Occasional Paper No. 15.

Lyman, P. (1993) Libraries, Publishing and Higher Education, in Mulvaney, J. and Steele, C (eds) (1993), *Changes in Scholarly Communication Patterns*, Australian Academy of the Humanities, Canberra, Occasional Paper No. 15.

Mulvaney, J. and Steele, C (eds) (1993) *Changes in Scholarly Communication Patterns*, Australian Academy of the Humanities, Canberra, Occasional Paper No. 15.

Rheingold, H. (1994) *The Virtual Community*. Secker and Warburg, London.

Shiels, M. (ed.) (1995), *Work and Technology in Higher Education: the Social Construction of Academic Computing*. Lawrence Erlbaum, New Jersey.

Spender, D. (1995) *Nattering on the Net: Women, Power and Cyberspace*. Spinifex Press, North Melbourne.

Squires, D. (1993) The Use of Information Technology to Support Information Access in Research, in D. Johnson and B. Samways (eds), *Informatics and Changes in Learning*, Elsevier Science Publishers B.V., Amsterdam, pp. 183 - 185.

Squires, D., Barry, C. and Funston, T. (1994) *The Use of IT-Assisted Information Systems in Academic Research*. British Library Research and Development Department, London, Report No. 6215.

Star, S.L. (ed.) (1995) *The Cultures of Computing*. Sociological Review Monograph, Blackwell, Oxford.

Turkle, S. (1995) Life on the Screen: Identity in the Age of the Internet. Simon and Schuster, New York.

9. BIOGRAPHY

Carolyn Dowling received a PhD from Monash University, Melbourne, Australia in 1994. A lecturer in computing since 1984, she is currently an Associate Professor at the Australian Catholic University. She is Head of the School of Arts and Sciences, which encompasses the Department of Mathematics, Science and Information Technology, the Department of Humanities and the Department of Visual and Performing Arts. Her research interests include a range of HCI issues, the impact of the Internet on academic research practices, 'virtual' environments for learning, and computer based writing.

Comparison of students' thinking processes when studying with WWW, IMM, and text based materials

L. Henderson, I. Putt, D. Ainge, and G. Coombs
School of Education
James Cook University of North Queensland
Townsville, Queensland, Australia
e-mail: Lynette.Henderson@jcu.edu.au

Abstract

This paper reports data obtained on the thinking of Bachelor of Education students as they interacted with World Wide Web (WWW) subject lecture material. The data were obtained from eight participating preservice teachers via stimulated recall interviews. The thinking (or mediating) processes engaged in during study sessions that related to the academic content of the WWW subject are detailed and discussed. The data are also compared with that obtained from an earlier comparative study of the thinking processes of two cohorts of inservice and preservice teachers: one group interacted with a professional development interactive multimedia (IMM) courseware package and the other with text based materials.

Keywords

Student thinking, WWW, Interactive multimedia, Stimulated recall interviews

The Virtual Campus F. Verdejo & G. Davies (Eds.)

1. INTRODUCTION

A recent development in distributed learning environments involves the use of the WWW to deliver tertiary courses. Jacobson and Spiro (1995) and Oliver, Herrington, and Omari (1996) suggest that, because the Web allows browsing and thematic exploration, it facilitates higher order cognitive processes. However, despite the Web's ability to link learners instantaneously with its expanding and dynamic information base, the extent to which it promotes thinking skills and strategies is unknown. It is readily recognised that learning does not automatically occur as a direct result of the ever-increasing sophistication of computers and other educational technologies used for transmitting information. Rather, learning is related to the quality and quantity of thinking undertaken by learners (Litchfield, 1992) as they interact with computers as (un)intelligent tools (Jonassen and Reeves, 1996; Wild, 1995). That is, learning outcomes are a function of the thinking processes activated by instructional tasks and other learning activities.

Much existing research data regarding the efficacy of distributed learning environments is anchored in the process-product paradigm. The paradigm is based on the assumption that instructional stimuli give rise to learning outcomes and that students are mostly passive recipients of instructional strategies (Shulman, 1986). Recognition of the simplistic nature of this general cause effect paradigm when applied in the social sciences led to a fundamental reconceptualisation of research into teaching and learning materials used in flexible (or open) learning environments (Gibbs, Lockwood, Morgan, and Taylor, 1982; Marland, Patching, Putt, and Store, 1984; Parer, 1988). One such reconceptualisation favoured the adoption of the mediating process paradigm which focuses on student thought processes that mediate, or come between, instructional stimuli and learning outcomes. Mediating processes can be viewed as the fine grained elements of cognition through which, and by which, learning outcomes are realised.

A recent Australian study based on the mediating process paradigm focussed on mediating or thinking processes used by learners studying hard copy text (Marland, Patching, and Putt, 1992). Another investigation, that extended this work, was concerned with identifying the thinking processes activated by learners as they studied interactive multimedia (IMM) courseware materials (Putt, Henderson, and Patching, 1996). The current study builds on this previous work by identifying the thinking processes utilised by first year university students as they studied Web materials, and compares the data with that from the previous two studies. All three studies involved teacher education participants studying in a flexible learning mode.

2. METHODOLOGY

Salomon (1991) describes the contrast between analytic research that is focused on isolating effective instructional treatments and systemic research focused on understanding how instructional treatments work in practice. This study embraced systemic research focussing on the sorts of thinking that tertiary students engaged in during study sessions with the WWW. As occurred with the IMM and text based materials investigations, the WWW study was guided by Reeves' (1995) and Salomon's (1991) pleas that the research context and methodology 'capitalize on authenticity' (Salomon, 1991, p. 16). The students' thinking processes were obtained in realistic, ecologically valid situations as the data were collected from students working in their regular study environment. Thus for the current study, data were gathered in a university setting on the eleventh WWW topic in week 12 of a 13 week semester. Conducting the research after the students had had numerous hours experience with the Web materials permitted minimalisation of any novelty effect. As well, even though the individual videotaped research sessions were of one half hour duration, the researchers felt that authenticity was kept because the subjects indicated that this was about the time that they would normally spend at one WWW study session anyway.

Context and Participants

A volunteer sample of eight preservice teachers was obtained from the cohort studying a compulsory first year education subject ED1441: *Information Technologies in Education.* This subject provides an introduction to the educational significance of current and future developments in information technologies. It includes the social and cognitive effects of information technologies and their relation to schooling; an analysis and design of various media texts; and applications and evaluation of media and computer technologies in education. The topic content studied during the videotaped study session covered social issues relating to technologies. It explored the effects of the Web, Internet, television, and video games on how we think and structure our world as well as the various ways in which these media are being dealt with in our changing world. The specific subsections that the Bachelor of Education students covered in their videotaped stimulated recall session were concerned with computer addiction, group interaction around computers, restricting access to unwanted material and to minors, software solutions, sexually explicit material on the internet, anonymity, privacy and security issues, and video game and television violence issues. There were five females and three males with ages ranging from 18 to 43 years. One was a recent graduate from high school, five had undertaken post secondary study, and two had been away from study for 20+ years. Their computer experience ranged from that of complete novice to one possessing a technical qualification and substantial years of experience in the field of computers. They were in either their first or second semester of a four year Bachelor of Education degree.

Data Collection

Data were collected on two categories of participants' thinking: (a) mediating processes generated as a result of interacting with the content of the WWW courseware and (b) evaluative thoughts about the instructional design features of the WWW materials. The focus in this paper is on a comparison of the results for category (a) with those reported in previous studies by Marland et al. (1992) and Putt et al. (1996).

In the WWW study the design parameters reflected those associated with the previous investigation of mediating processes used by learners studying from IMM courseware (Putt et al., 1996). A process-tracing approach was adopted and followed the strict guidelines developed over long experience with the stimulated recall technique (see guidelines in Marland, 1984; Marland et al., 1992). The interviewer and each participant together viewed a videotape of the study session. The split screen video records of the student's non verbal behaviours and the computer screen contained cues that stimulated each participant's recall of their mediating processes. Based on what occurred in the video, it was the interviewer's role to facilitate the participant's recall and verbalization of their thinking while studying the content of the mixed intranet/internet WWW courseware. The eight stimulated recall interviews, each of about one and a half hours duration, were conducted immediately following each video session and were audio taped for later transcription and analysis.

3. DATA ANALYSIS AND RESULTS

The interview transcripts from which the participants' mediating processes were identified were analyzed by pairs of the authors. Data from each pair were then compared, and, where disagreements occurred, consensus was achieved through group discussion. Data analysis proceeded according to the following steps.

1. Transcript data that were considered invalid (for example, thoughts that occurred during the interview but not during the study session or as a result of a leading question from the interviewer) were identified and discarded so that they would receive no further consideration.
2. The remaining transcript data were analyzed to identify reported instances of student thinking that occurred while studying the WWW course content.
3. These instances of individual mediating processes reported by participants were classified according to the definitions used by Marland et al. (1992) and Henderson (1997). Table 1 contains mediating processes found in the current study together with descriptions from the Marland et al. (1992) and Henderson (1997) studies and examples taken from the present study.

Type	*Description* *Mental activity in which a student:*	*Example*
Affect	reports feelings aroused by content during study	'This is really quite frustrating 'cause I want to know so much more quickly than I do.'
Anticipation	predicts or states expectations that problem, question, or textual feature will be encountered; looks forward to new unit, material; wonders about: the possibility of an event, occurrence in text, relevance of material, content	'I thought, oh, we'll probably touch on some of the material in previous tutes particularly, and might enlighten me about a few issues that weren't covered in the readings.'
Categorisation	sorts items, ideas, skills into different groups, classes	'It was similar to everything I've learned so far. White, middle class domination as per usual.'
Comparison	identifies similarities, differences between two statements, concepts, models, situations, ideas, theories, points of view, etc.	'This satanic impulse sort of thing I was relating to my own Christian views.'
Confirmation	judges that ideas in text support one's own beliefs, practices, tactics	'I agree with parents having a lot of control over what their children have access to.'
Deduction	reasoning process by which a specific conclusion necessarily follows from a set of general premises; uses a logical progression of thought	'... I was thinking they've really constructed that and culturally defined it because ... what is erotic in one culture is very different from what is erotic or unacceptable in another.'
Deliberation	engages in 'thinking' about a topic, prose segment, etc. (type of thinking not disclosed)	'How the graphics seemed to be virtually aimed at children.'
Diagnosis	identifies strengths and weaknesses in idea, strategies, points of view	'It's great that they're doing this, but it needs to be more effective.'
Evaluation	makes judgments about the value, worthwhileness of textual materials, activities, in-text questions, own position or point of view	'I didn't agree with him.' 'Well, it's probably one of the more controversial things; that's what I was thinking about.'
Generating	formulates one's own questions, examples, ideas, or problems; interpolating; going beyond the data	'How in the hell, like, it's not going to be like the club or anything. It's not going to be as personal so I can't see how people can get the kicks out it, it's just a screen; it's a glass screen.'
Imaging	creates a mental image of an idea in text in order to gain a fuller understanding	'What I was reading I was visualising.'
Justification	tries to prove that a proposed action/idea is reasonable or correct through argument	'I was only coming from my own personal experience. I've got lots of cousins and nephews and nieces.'
Linking	associates or brings together two or more ideas, topics, contexts, headings, personal experiences, materials, tasks	'Well the fact that even with my own wife, I believe she has very much the norm attitude.'
Metacognition	thinks about, reflects on, evaluates or directs own thinking	'I had to keep going back over because I didn't understand the definition' 'I haven't got a sort of concept map of how it all works.'
Recall	brings back into working memory an idea, opinion, fact previously stored in long term memory	'That reminded me about something that I had read.'
Reflection	general indication of careful consideration or thought over past action and response; tries to establish the reason or causal link between the action and its response; often stimulates considered action	'I was feeling really uncomfortable. Not so much from the content of the material ... If I hadn't seen it my whole attitude to this may have been very different.'
Selection	identifies key material, gist material, or that which is relevant to assessment	'I thought what I was reading there might be pertinent to the topic so I just took it down.'
Strategy Planning	plans ways of processing or handling content material during study sessions	'I thought I'd read basic text chunk first and go from the top.'
Translation	expresses segments of text in one's own words	'They've put down what children at various ages get from the television and then they talk about toddlers imitating what they see.'

Note: Descriptions are adapted from Marland et al.(1992) and Henderson (1997).

Table 1 Mediating processes identified in the present study

Examples are from the current study

Data on mediating processes while studying the WWW courseware
Mediating processes data resulting from the eight stimulated recall interviews were coded according to the procedure outlined above and frequencies for each type of mediating process reported by the participants were tallied (Table 2). A total of 287 mediating processes were identified from the interactive data in the transcripts. The mean number of reported mediating processes per person was 36. This provides an interesting comparison with the other two studies where only 13 reported mediating processes per person were identified for students studying with the IMM materials but 28 for those learning with the text based materials.

The data in Table 2 indicate a wide variation in the frequency of occurrence of the 19 identified mediating processes. These ranged from 0.03% for 'reflection' to 26.5% for 'evaluation.' This variation in occurrence of the 19 mediating processes is displayed in Table 3. The frequency of occurrence is divided into four levels, namely, very high, high, low, very low which are the same frequency bands used in the Marland et al. (1992) and Putt et al. (1996) studies. In these studies, the 3% and 10% cutoff figures were arbitrarily chosen, whereas 5.3% (100÷19) was the average percentage frequency across all 19 categories found in the Marland et al. (1992) study.

Table 2 Frequency of mediating processes relating to academic content

[a]*Mediating Process*	*Total (n = 8)*	*(%)*
Evaluation	76	(26.5)
Linking	33	(11.5)
Generating	29	(10.1)
Metacognition	27	(9.4)
Affective	27	(9.4)
Strategy Planning	22	(7.7)
Confirming	13	(4.5)
Diagnosis	9	(3.1)
Justification	9	(3.1)
Deliberation	8	(2.8)
Imaging	7	(2.4)
Comparing	6	(2.1)
Selection	5	(1.7)
Anticipation	4	(1.4)
Deducing	4	(1.4)
Recalling	3	(1.0)
Categorisation	3	(1.0)
Translation	1	(0.03)
Reflection	1	(0.03)
Total	287	(100.0)
Mean number of mediating processes per person	36	

[a] based on responses from 8 participants

In Table 3, three mediating processes, namely, evaluation, linking, and generating, have the highest frequencies in the WWW study. Two of these, evaluation and linking, also rated as very high in the IMM and text based studies. While generating rated as very high in the current study, it rated as high in the IMM study and low in the text based study. Three additional comparisons are worthy of note. Metacognition was high in the WWW study but very high in the other two. Whereas strategy planning rated as high in the present study, it rated low in the IMM study and very high in the text based study. On the other hand, 'anticipation' was very low in the present study but high in both of the other studies.

Table 3 Mediating processes grouped according to frequency range

Freq. *(f) %*	*Mediating Processes* *WWW*		*Mediating Processes* *IMM*		*Mediating Processes* *Text-based*	
Very high (f> 10)	evaluation	[a](26.5)	evaluation	[b](18.0)	Evaluation	[c](18.6)
	linking	(11.5)	linking	(11.4)	Linking	(10.4)
	generating	(10.1)				
			metacognition	(19.8)	Metacognition	(12.4)
			affective	(14.4)		
					Strategy plan	(16.8)
High (5.3 < f < 10)	metacognition	(9.4)				
	affective	(9.4)			Affective	(7.8)
	strategy plan	(7.7)				
			generating	(8.4)		
			anticipation	(7.8)	Anticipation	(5.9)
			recalling	(6.6)		
					Deliberation	(8.1)
Low (3 < f < 5.3)	confirming	(4.5)				
	diagnosing	(3.1)	diagnosing	(0.0)	Diagnosing	(0.26)
	justification[d]	(3.1)				
			comparing	(4.8)		
					Generating	(3.6)
					Selection	(4.5)
					Recalling	(4.1)
Very low (f < 3)	deliberation	(2.8)	deliberation	(1.8)		
	imaging	(2.4)	imaging	(0.6)	Imaging	(0.0)
	comparing	(2.1)			Comparing	(1.5)
	selection	(1.7)	selection	(0.0)		
	anticipation	(1.4)				
	deducing[d]	(1.4)				
	recalling	(1.0)				
	categorisation	(1.0)	categorisation	(0.0)	Categorisation	(0.005)
	translation	(0.003)	translation	(0.0)	Translation	(0.005)
	reflection[d]	(0.003)				
	analysis	(0.0)	analysis	(2.9)	Analysis	(1.1)
			strategy plan	(1.8)		
			confirming	(1.8)	Confirming	(2.8)

[a]The number in parentheses is the percentage frequency.

[b]The percentage frequency is based on the 13 mediating processes identified in the study.

[c]The percentage frequency is based on the 19 mediating processes identified in the study.

dThese mediating processes were identified in the Henderson (1997) study.

4. DISCUSSION

This section involves an interpretation of the data on the thinking processes elicited and discusses those mediating processes that displayed significant variation between the three studies.

Mediating Processes

On the surface Clark's (1994) contention that the medium is not the crucial variable in learning outcomes seems to be under challenge by the differences in the mean number of reported mediating process per student between the three studies: 36, 13, and 28 for students studying with the WWW, IMM, and text based materials, respectively. However, this does not seem to be the reason in this particular case. The data in the WWW and text based studies were collected from participants working individually but the IMM participants studied, and were interviewed, in their self-selected groups of two, three or four. It appears that the group situation could have allowed a participant to disengage from thoughtful participation in both, or either of, the study session and the stimulated recall interview. As well it may have suppressed the verbalisation of a participant's thoughts.

The very high percentage (26.5%) of reported evaluative thoughts about the content of the WWW topic is more than twice that of the next highest ranking mediating process, linking (11.5%). It is also a third higher than the evaluative thoughts tabulated for the IMM and text based studies (Table 3). Evaluation is defined as the mental process in which a judgement is made about the value or worth of some aspect of the content of the instructional material. All three studies contained material that was contentious and challenged the students' current practices, thus suggesting that all three studies should have had similar percentages. The IMM study concerned with social justice issues asked the learners to question their own attitudes and classroom practices with respect to racism and other inequities. The text based content presented factors influencing curriculum design that seriously questioned the status quo by offering seemingly radical ideas. A major focus of the WWW topic problematized the access and effect issues concerning gender, equity, rights, and morality in the censorship-violence-pornography debate about Web content material. It seems plausible to argue that it was the nature of this type of content in the WWW topic that produced the percentage discrepancy. It also challenged many of the students' current perceptions by exposure to the research literature. For instance, most students believed there is a direct correlation between television and video game violence and child and adult violence in society, and found it difficult to rework their simplistic cause effect views.

Linking is defined as the process of associating, or bringing together in the mind, two or more ideas, topics, contexts, personal experiences, words, and so forth. Linking usually occurred when an item (e.g., text, graphic, or cartoon that illustrated a concept) prompted recall of an associated item in a participant's memory. It is noteworthy that linking had similar percentage frequencies in all three studies. This is not surprising given that all three sets of materials challenged participants to consider how the information related to their own and peers' beliefs, values and experiences.

Generating encompasses one or more of the following: (a) formulation of one's own questions, examples, ideas, opinions, problems, and answers; (b) interpolation by adding new knowledge through the elaboration of existing knowledge within a given framework; and (c) extrapolation which adds new knowledge by extending an existing framework and going beyond the data (Marland et al., 1992). Why then, given the characteristics of the participants and the nature of the content in the three studies, did the percentage frequency of generating mediating processes increase from text based (3.6%), to IMM (8.4%), to WWW (10.1%)? The most likely reason for the comparatively low percentage for learning with texts is that these participants were identified as assessment driven (Marland et al., 1992). They therefore allocated little time to going beyond what they deemed necessary to accomplish their assessment goals. The comparability of the percentages for the WWW and IMM studies could be attributed to the lack of embedded assessment in the materials and the provocative nature of the content. The latter reason would also help explain why the figure was slightly higher for the WWW.

Mediating processes classified as 'metacognition' are those in which students reported awareness of, reflecting on, evaluating, or directing their own thinking. This definition reflects a widely accepted view of metacognition as referring to students' knowledge about, and control over, their cognitive processes (Weinstein and Mayer, 1986). Even though metacognitive processes were high in the WWW study, they were approximately 50% of those reported for the IMM and 75% for the text based studies. This is a significant comparative difference given the importance of metacognitive strategies in successful tertiary study. This could be due to the quantity of information processed in the WWW study which was considerably larger than that covered in IMM or text for the equivalent half hour videotaped sessions. This suggests that information overload was probably a contributing factor. As well, it left fewer cognitive resources for monitoring their own thinking. These results reflect the fact that as novice tertiary students, the WWW participants had not yet fully learnt the strategies of, and necessity for, metacognitive practices.

Strategy planning refers to thought processes in which students plan ways of processing or handling instructional material or activities during study sessions. The percentage frequency in the present study is approximately four times that in the IMM study but only 46% of that for the text based study. One explanation given by Putt et al. (1996) for the very low frequency in the IMM study was the linear sequence suggested by the instructional designer for studying the five units in the IMM package - *Social Justice Explored* (White, 1993). Students did not appear to negotiate individual pathways through the materials and therefore did not spend time thinking about how they would process the materials but instead just followed the sequence. Furthermore, this IMM package did not include any assessment which might otherwise be likely to lead students to plan carefully how they would process the content.

In contrast, both the WWW and text based materials, while still having linear content menus, allowed students more scope to choose different ways to navigate through the material. Nevertheless, the frequency for the WWW material is less than half that for the text based material; this is in spite of the fact that the WWW subject had a hypertext/hypermedia environment which was conducive to maximum choice of processing. A close look at the particular participants involved in the two studies gives some insight into the reasons for this marked difference in strategy planning between the two. One possible explanation is that the inservice teachers in the text based study were all experienced learners whilst the preservice teachers in the WWW study could be regarded as novice tertiary learners. A second explanation is that the text based materials had embedded assessment items which influenced the way the students processed the materials (Marland et al., 1992). These students generally viewed the objectives of the unit, then looked at the assessment for the unit and determined which materials were necessary to complete that assessment. They next planned to cover this essential material in the most time efficient way. In comparison, there was no embedded assessment within the WWW topic which may have functioned as a similar focussing device.

Anticipation is synonymous with prediction, looking forward to, speculation about, and expectations concerning the likelihood of encountering problems, types of content, and features of the medium. The very low rating for anticipation in the WWW study is arresting in light of its high rated frequency in the other two studies. Indeed, there were 5.5 times and 4.5 times more anticipatory thought processes reported in the IMM and text based studies, respectively. A possible explanation for this disparity is linked to the volume of content covered in the distributed learning environment of the WWW where students could continue exploring live links ad nauseam. Subsequently, they may have found it difficult and/or of little consequence to anticipate what content might emerge.

5. CONCLUSION

The authors argue that the Web should be used as a cognitive tool to enhance thinking, problem solving, and learning. To attain this goal, the study highlights two major implications for the instructional design of WWW materials.

First, it draws attention of instructional designers to the existence, types, and relative frequencies of mediating processes in which students engage while interacting with the WWW distributed learning environment (and that of IMM and text based materials). Second, there is a need for instructional designers to plan educational materials that will activate desired mediating processes as part of student learning. This is related to initial evidence that suggests instructional designers can actually engineer presentations to increase or decrease rates of occurrence of selected mediating processes. (See previous comments about the different rates of occurrence of strategy planning between the three studies.)

One approach that could be incorporated in WWW design is to make explicit the thinking processes the students could use to engage with the content satisfactorily.

For example, Henderson, Patching, and Putt (1994) have been able to activate metacognition by the use of embedded prompts and interactions in university level IMM materials. We argue that this is an area that requires more attention by instructional designers and researchers.

6. REFERENCES

Clark, R. E. (1994) Media will never influence learning. *Educational Technology Research and Technology*, **42**(2), 21-29.

Gibbs, G., Lockwood, F., Morgan, A., and Taylor, E. (1982) *Student learning and course design 1: In-text teaching devices in Open University texts* (Study Methods Group Report No. 12). Open University, Milton Keynes.

Henderson, L., Patching, W., and Putt, I. (1994) The impact of metacognitive interactive strategies and prompts embedded in interactive multimedia in a cross-cultural context: An exploratory investigation. In *OPEN LEARNING '94, Proceedings of the 1st International Conference on Open Learning*, (pp. 181-186). Queensland Open Learning Network and The University of Queensland, Brisbane, Australia.

Henderson, M. (1997) Multimedia Interactivity: An investigation into learners' mediating processes during click-drag activities. B.Ed. (Hons) thesis. James Cook University, Townsville.

Jacobson, M., and Spiro, R. (1995) Hypertext learning environments, cognitive flexibility and the transfer of complex knowledge. *Journal of Educational Computing Research*, **12**(4), 301-333.

Jonassen, D. H., and Reeves, T. C. (1996) Learning with technology: Using computers as cognitive tools. In *Handbook of research for educational communications and technology* (ed. D. H. Jonassen), (pp. 693-719). Macmillan, New York.

Litchfield, B. C.(1992) Evaluation of inquiry-based science software and interactive multimedia programs. *Computing Teacher*, **19**(6), 41-43.

Marland, P. W. (1984) Stimulated recall from video: Its use in research on the thought processes of classroom participants. In *Video in higher education* (ed. O. Zuber-Skerrit), (pp. 156-165). Kogan Page, London.

Marland, P. W., Patching. W. G., and Putt, I. J. (1992) *Learning from text: Glimpses inside the minds of distance learners*. James Cook University of North Queensland, Townsville.

Marland, P. W., Patching, W. G., Putt, I. J., and Store, R. E. (1984) Learning from distance-teaching materials: A study of students' mediating responses. *Distance Education*, **5**(2), 71-91.

Oliver, R., Herrington, J., and Omari, A. (1996) Creating effective instructional materials for the World Wide Web. In *Proceedings of AusWeb96: The second Australian World Wide Web Conference* (ed. M. Nott), Southern Cross University, Gold Coast, Australia.

Parer, M. S. (1988) *Textual design and student learning*. Gippsland Institute of Advanced Education, Churchill, Victoria.

Putt, I., Henderson, L., and Patching, W. (1996) Teachers' Thinking Elicited from Interactive Multimedia Professional Development Courseware. *Educational Technology Research and Development*, **44**(4), 7-22.

Reeves, T. C. (1995) Questioning the questions of instructional technology research. *Proceedings of the Annual Conference of the Association for Educational Communications and Technology, Research and Theory Division* (pp. 459-470). Association for Educational Communications and Technology, Research and Theory Division, Anaheim 9, CA.

Salomon, G. (1991) Transcending the qualitative-quantitative debate: The analytic and systemic approaches to educational research. *Educational Researcher*, **20**(6), 10-18.

Shulman, L. S. (1986) Paradigms and research programs in the study of teaching: A contemporary perspective. In *Handbook of research on teaching* (ed. M. C. Wittrock), (3rd ed.), (pp. 3-36). Macmillan, New York.

Wild, M. (1995) Empowering learners: Using computers as cognitive tools. In *Changes in the learning environment* (ed. D. Thiele), (CD–ROM), (pp. 59-70). Open Learning Technology Corporation, Adelaide. Also available on-line at: [http://www.oltc.edu.au/oltpd/docs/inv01.html].

White, B. (1993) Social justice explored [CD-ROM]. Townsville: Queensland State Education Department.

7. BIOGRAPHIES

Lyn Henderson is senior lecturer at James Cook University of North Queensland, Australia. Her fields of teaching and research interests concern the cultural contextualization of instructional design of interactive multimedia (IMM) and the world wide web (WWW) offered in various flexible learning modes. Other research interests focus on the mental models, thinking processes, and teaching-learning strategies used by teachers and learners (from early childhood through tertiary in Australia and the United States) when interacting with each other and/or electronic databases, IMM, and the WWW.

Ian Putt is a senior lecturer in mathematics education at James Cook University, Townsville, Australia. He has been involved in teaching mathematics education courses at a distance via printed text to inservice teachers and through interactive multimedia (IMM) courseware to Aboriginal and Torres Strait Islander teacher education students in their home communities. His current research interests focus on tertiary students' thinking while studying with IMM and WWW materials and their usage patterns of such courseware. He also supervises post graduate students in the area of teaching problem solving in upper primary and lower secondary school.

David Ainge is senior lecturer at James Cook University, Townsville, Australia. His current research interest, besides tertiary students' thinking processes of learning with the WWW, is on uses of virtual reality in schools. Virtual reality appears to have great potential for education, and my current research in primary schools is investigating its capacity to enhance: (a) active learning, particularly in hard-to-motivate students; (b) individual construction of learning; and (c) learning across a range of ability levels.

Geoff Coombs is a lecturer in social and cultural studies in education and the acting director of the Professional Experience Unit at James Cook University, Townsville, Australia. His current research and teaching interests include the ethnographic study of education and schooling and WWW instructional design. He also conducts professional development courses in creating WWW sites and developing effective web search strategies for school-based educators.

11

Collaboration between universities and enterprises in the Knowledge Age

R. Lewis
Professor of Knowledge Technology
Information Systems and Services - Lancaster University
Lancaster LA1 4YW UK
r.lewis@lancaster.ac.uk

C. Vizcarro
Profesora Titular
Facultad de Psicología - Universidad Autonoma de Madrid
Campus de Cantoblanco
28049 Madrid
carmen.vizcarro@uam.es

Abstract

This paper suggests that a radical review is required of the way in which universities carry out their research and teaching roles. Political and economic factors are forcing change and the classical role of universities for delivering knowledge to customers is being challenged both in research and in the way teaching and learning take place.

In this new context, information and communication technologies allow an alternative approach to be taken. In this approach it is argued that the delivery of content should no longer play a major role; remote access to digital libraries and learning support through tele-tutoring are becoming increasingly common. The new role relates to supporting the *process* of knowledge exchange and acquisition rather than the delivery of *content*.

This paper is not concerned with creating virtual campuses to support traditional courses based on formal knowledge. Rather it reports on some experimental activities in which students learn through participation in research in naturalistic settings. It is further suggested that enterprises can come to see universities as partners in learning and research activities to the benefit of both parties. The use of information and communication technologies play a key role in making it possible to support the exchange of informal, context-related knowledge.

Keywords

Collaboration universities-enterprises, Knowledge, Communication technology

The Virtual Campus F. Verdejo & G. Davies (Eds.)

1. INTRODUCTION

Opportunities which are offered by new information and communication technologies, among other factors, are stimulating a re-analysis of the role and operation of many organisations as well as in making adaptation to new demands easier. Universities are not uninvolved in this process and could/should be at the forefront of innovations which have their origin in changing perceptions on the nature of knowledge. Classically, universities have been centres for the creation and diffusion of knowledge through their prime functions as institutions for research and teaching. However, it is becoming necessary to review that role, and particularly the processes involved, as the way in which 'knowledge' is viewed is changing and new forms of knowledge become tradable commodities.

New perspectives are emerging from psychological and linguistics research which place increasing attention on the socio-historic, cultural, distributed and contextual nature of cognition (Nardi, 1996). Without being pedantic it is helpful to be reminded of the definitions of data and information which played an important part in defining computer science in the 1960's (IFIP, 1970). To build upon and extend those definitions, one may view:

- *data*: as the syntactic codes on which machines operate;
- *information*: as the addition of semantics which humans apply to (processed) data in context;
- *knowledge*: as the ability to apply information to solve particular problems; and
- *intelligence*: as the experience which allows the appropriate choice of knowledge to invoke at a particular time.

It is important to realise that, once past the level of data, *context* is a critical factor in the processes central to those concepts.

The primary form of 'knowledge' with which universities have been engaged is what might be termed formal or scientific; this is the 'knowledge' which they themselves have played a big part in creating and it is that *content* on which they have built the curricula which are currently being taught. The use of telecommunications to create virtual campuses for the diffusion of such content with access to various sources world-wide and a certain amount of assistance and tutoring through the same networks, is being explored in many universities. But is this the whole future?

As suggested above, context is critical to considerations of information and knowledge. It is even suggested that all knowledge is socially-shared and cannot exist within an individual person. These notions lead to a belief that it is *knowledge in context* which is taking on increasing importance and that apprenticeship should come back to take a leading part in education and training*. The key point is that

---

*For example, in France some universities are engaged in serious debate with communities outside their doors about 'alternance' (courses split between university and industry) and the publications of Céreq (whose quarterly newsletter has an English version) are heavily biased towards continuous training in

this demand for education and training is not only for formal knowledge but for the tacit, experiential, often pragmatic knowledge of the workplace - professional and artisan.

The point of great importance to realise is that universities have no *ownership* of this form of knowledge; it cannot be 'taught' in the traditional way. This paper explores an alternative role for universities which involves both their teaching and research activities and their increasing reliance on industry and other outside communities. But, first it is important to review the nature of the professional knowledge which is becoming increasingly valued.

2. PROFESSIONAL KNOWLEDGE

In the natural course of work, knowledge is used and exchanged in formal settings and in chance encounters. Its focus is the identification and resolution of practical problems and it draws on both scientific, established knowledge and that which is derived from working practices and experience. The problems are often ill-defined and yet decisions have to be made.

This knowledge is part of the practices of large numbers of people working in a wide variety of contexts. Solutions to problems are not always clear-cut and the consequences of actions may have broad implications and side-effects. Context is central to a large proportion of the knowledge which is used and optimal solutions are required since there may not be a unique 'correct' solution.

Extensive applied knowledge of this type, together with flexible and efficient ways to exchange this knowledge within communities of practice, are crucial in successful organisations. Clearly, the most effective organisations are those which capitalise upon the knowledge which resides within them, that is, within the workforce of that organisation. Each person may need the knowledge of others in order to work effectively and the way that knowledge can be accessed and shared becomes a critical factor in operational efficiency. In the same way, this type of knowledge and practice, and the processes of its exchange or sharing, should also be an important part of the education of future professionals. For this reason universities should have a goal of facilitating the acquisition of these processes.

In the workplace, exchanges of knowledge relate to the task in hand and problems to be solved. Face-to-face communications are very rich both in terms of the knowledge exchanged and in the potential for social cohesion. But, such encounters are not always possible or easy and, what is more, little or no trace of the interaction is left behind for future reference - even the records of formal meetings are scant in depth and rationale. This is often referred to as a lack of organisational memory:

---

companies (see http://www.cereq.fr). Also, in Germany formal knowledge provided by educational institutions greatly emphasises learning in applied fields during specific periods of time, especially in professional training and in universities.

> " . . . The problem is not a scarcity of documents and artefacts for organizational memory, but rather the quality, content, and organization of this material. For example, an effective organizational memory would be able to answer such often asked questions as 'Why did we do this?' and 'How did such and such come to be the case?' Rarely is this possible now." (Conklin, 1992, p. 133)

Conklin goes on to suggest the need for a process-orientation which has three technological elements: hypertext, groupware and rhetorical method. *The key to making good use of such tools is that they should not require extra, specific effort but must 'tap into' the existing flow of information in the organisation.* There is a requirement for organisational change but also there is a synergy between this memory requirement and other emphases on quality, customer service and other process-orientated approaches which are already gaining ground in the organisation of enterprises.

This section has tried to illustrate the nature of knowledge which is important in enterprises who increasingly believe that their competitiveness depends upon ways in which they can capitalise on the knowledge held by individuals in their organisation* and which needs to be made accessible to others. An important distiction is made in this paper between:

- *scientifically validated information* which is made available through somewhat restricted though well-recognised channels of education, training and professional practice;
- *information of a less formal nature,* which is often tacit, the validity of which is less clear but which is needed and used within communities of practice.

and, further, there is a need for:

- the *flexible, timely sharing of knowledge*, from both an academic and a professional perspective.

It is on the last two points that this paper focuses in examining new roles for universities both in the processes of research and the processes which can support learning.

3. RESEARCH

While universities have traditionally seen research as an activity aimed at the creation of knowledge 'for its own sake', there are some signs (for better or worse) that two major trends are influencing the nature and processes of university research. One of these is political/financial as governments (in Europe and the UK, at least) are seeking ways to reduce public funding of research and engender an enterprise or free-market culture into university research as has been encouraged in

---

*An interesting review of organisational memory with extensive references is given in a paper by Bannon and Kuutti (1996).

industry with the removal of barriers to transnational trading (for example, in the telecommunications and civil airline markets) and globalisation (Sigurdson & Tallving, 1997). In parallel with this, there has been a move towards government support for 'strategic' research. One example of this occurs in a UK Government paper (HMSO, 1986) where a strategic research area is defined in terms of social, economic and scientific timeliness as being "an area which promises significant advances in the medium term and will generate new knowledge . . . which must offer clear opportunities for economic exploitation." More recently such a position was restated when Newby (1992) introduced the Corporate Plan (1992-97) of the Economic and Social Research Council (ESRC) in the UK.

The (implied) outcome of such a policy is that industry should fund applied research and universities themselves need to generate their own funds for basic research. This seems also to be the policy of the European Commission. In order that universities meet this challenge, collaboration with industry and other 'users' of research outcomes is essential. In this context:

> "A critical role in defining the agenda for research is held by those whose professional work could be influenced by the outcomes of research. Such stakeholders are the practitioners who carry the professional responsibility of advancing their field by the adoption or adaptation of the outcomes of research and the products of development.
>
> Once research moves beyond the quest for basic knowledge, that is it moves towards the applicable, even the medium term strategic, its value lies in the exploitation [by those affected by research] of its outcomes. It will usually be the case that such outcomes bring about pressure for change; but there is a natural human reaction to oppose change as the *status quo* is usually less threatening than the unknown.
>
> If this premiss is accepted, the fear of the unknown needs to be minimised and one way to achieve this is to ensure that those implicated are a part of the rationale for undertaking the research, that is for defining the research agenda and for being full participants in the research process itself. . . . Furthermore, they also become stakeholders in the process of research - they come to 'own' the outcomes and, hence, are more likely to be willing and able to capitalise upon them."
>
> (Lewis, 1992, p. 159)

All of these directions of research point to the increasing importance of closer partnerships between universities and enterprises. Of course, there has been much collaboration in the past but now the links are essential - at least from the perspective of universities. So, if this is a major need, what role might communication technology play in satisfying that need, at least in some part?

The core action in a university-enterprise partnership is undertaken by a number of individuals who form a distributed community. This community has its rationale and coherence through the set of *common intentions* (goals) which have been established through negotiation. The subsequent, specific activities may take place over months or years. Throughout that period, there needs to be an adequate level of communication between the participants and, due to their distributed nature, this is hard to sustain amongst individuals who have many demands on their time *and* who may be separated by significant distances.

Research with such communities indicates that a significant proportion of the necessary communication can be provided by the use of quite modest telecommunication channels. To facilitate this process, however, different functions and characteristics of media have to be researched and their potential made clear in order that they may be used in the most efficient way*.

4. LEARNING

The use of communication technology provides opportunities for universities to enhance their educational offer. For example, they may take steps to:

- use the campus network to allow traditional students better access to resources (including tutors);
- widen the accessibility of existing courses to off-campus students (including those in other countries);

As has been suggested earlier, in thinking about learning, it is necessary to identify the form of knowledge which is to be 'learnt'. In the classical case, universities have been engaged in offering opportunities for the learning of formalised ('scientific') knowledge; the learners have come to universities with the *intention* of learning some fairly well prescribed formal knowledge.

The two steps suggested above address the classical diffusion of knowledge but, as illustrated earlier, there is another equally important form of knowledge, that which is grounded in practice and professional activity. It is often informal, tacit and is developing continually in all working communities through the experience and the exchange of information among professionals. University staff have no exclusive or even particular insight into such knowledge but they are under pressure to facilitate the *process* of the exchange of this knowledge as well as more formalised knowledge. To this end information technology may be a communication medium which could help. There are a number of ways in which such mechanisms could work:

- by the creation of *discussion networks* between academic and professional tutors or workers in industry (linked perhaps to collaborative research or practicum programmes) which existing students could observe as a way to become, as Lave and Wenger (1991) would suggest, 'legitimate peripheral' participants;
- to provide a context for those seeking continuing learning to set the agenda for 'learning' in such a way that learning becomes predominantly a *process of*

---

*The Virtual Mobility and Distributed Laboratories project, supported by DGXII of the European Commission, examined such issues (Heeren & Lewis, 1997). The final report may be found at: http://www.lancs.ac.uk/users/ktru/vmdl.htm

knowledge exchange with peers (tutors providing process rather than content contributions);
- to create *explicit 'courses'* which engage students in action-research projects with industrial partners which might facilitate initial contacts with enterprises making the shift from academic to work cultures smoother.

Some tentative trials with the latter mechanism have taken place and others are planned. These will now be discussed.

5. LEARNING THROUGH ACTION-RESEARCH

Information and communication technology may have a crucial role in integrating perspectives on knowledge and the issues facing universities and enterprises in the current socio-economic climate which have been outlined above. Is it possible with the aid of ICT for universities to address both their research and teaching roles by combining these two key functions?

One model for exploring this possibility has been tried on a small scale at the University of Twente in a course module for final year undergraduate students.

5.1 Nieuwe Media en Media Management

The course description included the following perspective:

> "In a society which, it is claimed, is increasingly dependent on information, cognitive processes which transform information into knowledge must become a major concern. This course explores, reviews and compares the ways that communication technology can be used to support distributed groups of workers and learners in the transition from information to knowledge. It blurs the distinction between 'work' and learning' by drawing on mainly professional communities in which the distinction hardly exists. It considers the individual and organisational dimensions of work in communities in which interaction between members is wholly or partly dependent on a range of electronic communication media. It looks at ways in which professional knowledge, often tacit and informal, may be elicited and shared during the process of which action organisational memory is significantly enhanced."

The key element of the course was an action-research project in which groups of four students visited a local company and negotiated with that company to define a research question which related to communication patterns in the company; they then devised a semi-structured interview schedule or questionnaire to use with members of the organisation and wrote a report which identified particular problematic communication mechanisms. There were four face-to-face seminars during the course which lasted three months (part-time) and during the other times the students interacted electronically with local tutors and another (the course leader) who was in another university. The advantages seen in such an approach were:

- the students experienced setting up and undertaking an action-research project as a team;
- they also experienced support from a remote tutor communicating electronically with them;
- the company benefited from an outside analysis of its ways of working;
- there was reinforcement of the collaboration between the university and the enterprises with the potential for future partnerships;
- the outcomes contributed additional, much needed, naturalistic case study data about ways in which knowledge is shared in organisations.

Student reactions

Following the course, the students were asked to provide feedback on a number of issues related to the way the course ran and if and how how they saw benefits in the approach taken. Some of the questions and the feedback illustrate a number of the issues that require further attention.

- *were the face-to-face seminars of the right form? too many new concepts?*

Feedback from the students generally indicates that they can cope with a wide array of new concepts as long as the seminars are highly structured and allow them to track their own progress in the work they are doing:

> ". . . What I missed was the structure. Some 'syllabus' with an overview of the course (why is what subject taken into account..) and the most important articles neatly organised would have been really good. Sometimes I missed a real thread. It is nice to know what subjects are treated when and why."

Some students also demanded more active participation:

> "The course could have benefited from more interactivity during classes. If there would have been some challenging statements, more discussion would have taken place. In that way it could have become clearer what the goals of the course were, and maybe an interesting goal could have been negotiated."

- *was the on-line support adequate? could it have been more helpful?*

It was generally felt to be adequate.

> "It was adequate. Better not to write very often and give useful information, than writing for instance every day while there is nothing to say."

There was a suggestion to make all email interaction 'public'; a possibility which, however, was rejected by the group when offered at the beginning of the course:

> ". . . My suggestion: organise a mailinglist for the course and see to it all the online communication is done through this mailinglist. Since most TO-ISM students read their email you 'force' them to read the mailinglist communication. . . . "

- *should the local tutors have done more; if 'yes' is that role (time allocation/ availability) one that the remote tutor should have taken on more? how?*

Naturally, there was a view that tutors could always do more but an important point related to a clearly defined role.

> ". . . I don't know what their role should be exactly, but I think that their role has to be clear and mutually distinct. . . . . Like the students had a monitor in

their group, the professors could have the roles 'lecturer, organisational manager and technical manager' or something like that."

- *did all the students read the group email? how could you be better motivated?*

The technical aspects of using email were not a problem and students used it habitually. However, it is necessary to define the purposes of the exchange quite explicitly for the students (even though this seemed clear to the tutors).

"... I think the only way to get students communicating on-line is through email. They read it anyway. WWW is less frequently visited - messages do not get to their address. . . ."

"I checked email every day, but we didn't use it very much within our group. Sometimes to make appointments. But we saw each other regularly and then we discussed every thing face-to-face."

"I usually read my email two or three times a day, during the course maybe a little more. Roughly stated short-term goals could have made the interaction . . . more frequent and clearer."

- *how did you find the experience of working on a project in a team?*

The students had previous experience of groupwork and expressed their frustration as some members did not take an active role. On the positive side, they felt it was useful to share ideas but at times it was difficult to keep everyone informed of how personal tasks were progressing .

"... one of the frustrations in groupwork among students, is that every member is equal and in many cases no one has or takes responsibility. Group members should therefore been assigned to a specific role with specific responsibilities. Assigning monitoring tasks to one of the group members is a good start, though."

- *should the research question be defined by the tutors or is this a part of the research design which needs to be negotiated with members of the company;*

The students generally thought it was a significant part of their work but would have appreciated more clear information on the overall goals as well as better information given to the organisations in the way of what could be expected of them.

"It took quite a long time to specify the question. But it wouldn't have been useful to have it specified. It took a long time, because we needed certain information about the company that was difficult to get and we also had to change our research question a couple of times after having talked to the company manager and having received new information."

- *should more pressure (formality) have been used during the course?*

They generally appreciated the opportunity of self-guidance but also thought some more structure at the beginning would have been useful.

"... You don't have to give 'ready-made' instructions as what to do. A little 'self-guidance' can be expected from students I guess. A more clear statement of goals and a clear 'framework' of the course would have been very welcome though."

And yet:

"It was quite clear from the beginning. It would have been helpful if we had received more suggestions along the way."

- *do we need more or fewer face-to-face sessions?*

Although some felt that more face-to-face sessions would have been useful, they were able to get all the help they needed:

"No. More and better on-line communication!"

"Officially there should have been more I think. But we had in between a few times a meeting with our local tutor and also some informal talks where we posed some questions."

Some other suggestions were offered, one of which related to experience on another course which used the Web:

"Even in this well-designed and frequently updated environment it was sometimes hard to keep track of the goals and plans for the course. But the web-site was the central 'face' of the course, it gave some handhold in the virtual community. During the MMMT course there were a lot of misconceptions and misunderstandings on planning and delivering of products. When this information would have been available on a web-site, it could still be flexible, but also be available clearly stated on the screen."

Overall, difficulties with the kind of open work which was required were also expressed. These issues could perhaps be dealt with in other versions of the course but some may have to do with a dramatic change in the nature of the tasks which are required as students face open, naturalistic problems and may thus need significant changes in their perspective of the processes of learning, always a difficult goal.

"I don't think any of the groups had a well defined idea of what they were doing exactly. This was partly due to the assignment being so broad. I sensed that the groups really had problems narrowing the assignment down to one problem in the company that could be dealt with within the confines of this course. Too much time was spent on getting to know the company and trying to find out whether they really DID have a problem. For instance with TSM we had the impression that everything was going as good as it could be in these times of rapid changes."

Tutor observations

Some of these difficulties were foreseen by the tutors before the start of the course. Their reflection on students' feedback is that it highlighted a number of key issues, some of which could apply to a more traditional group project run with regular face-to-face sessions. However, the remote tutoring aspect meant that these issues became more pronounced. The main tension which existed lay in the desire, on the one hand, to 'force' the students to be autonomous in their actions whilst, on the other hand, providing adequate guidance. There also seems to be a tension between the complexities and ambiguities of the functioning of the enter-prise "in the real world", the ingrained habits of working on the part of students and the time limit of the course. However, clarity of purpose, the establishment of a shared understanding of the goals of the activity, and, closely linked to that, explicit expectations and role of both tutors and students could have helped. Both these dimensions require particular attention in the distance tutoring context. As one tutor said:

> " . . . I think that a little more structure in the course and a clearer goal orientation, as well as a better role division between us, would have been appreciated".

It was also felt these demands could have been 'forced' or more strongly demanded by the students during the course. However:

> ". . . anyway, all by all it was a good experience. It is clear that all of us (including the students) have still to learn a lot about how to deal effectively and efficiently with the opportunities of new pedagogical approaches . . ."

One important perspective, that of the organisations studied was missing from this preliminary study. If this mechanism is to be used to promote university-enterprise collaboration, future work must ensure that these views are elicited.

5.2 Universidad Autonoma de Madrid

A second experiment with a similar philosophy, which will build upon the insights gained in Twente, will take place at Universidad Autonoma de Madrid (UAM) in a course for doctoral students.

Course structure

The course will be part-time over three months and there will be four course elements plus the main action-research project itself. The course elements have been selected to be directly related to the carrying out of the specific form of action-research envisaged.

- *Introduction to communications technology*

It will involve aspects of the design and practical use of computer conferencing, email, Internet. intranet systems, www etc. This will be essentially practical and the tools used will be used later in the course for interaction within the teams and in interaction of members with tutors.

- *Research methods*

The focus will again be practical and relate directly to the needs of the action-research case study which will be undertaken. This means it will cover issues related to elicitation of knowledge and perceptions of people working in organisations. Elements will be: the formulation of the research question; forms of data elicitation - semi-structured interview schedules; questionnaires; data analysis and reporting.

- *Structures, communication and knowledge exchange in organisations*

Patterns of communication, legitimacy of information, accessibility, decision making processes, power, control, management structure, collaboration, competition, capitalising on knowledge, learning organisations.

- *Social and cognitive processes of learning*

Cooperation and collaboration, communication as a key learning process, communication channels, knowledge creation, sharing knowledge in groups, working and learning, activity theory, social structures and processes.

Methodology
The basic structure of each module will be a half-day seminar/workshop run by one or more of the tutors followed by tele-tutoring support. Each module will be assessed by a team report on an assignment. The assignment will be written to ensure that the team draws on the 'introductory' seminar/workshop and on a supplied list of associated reports, papers, books etc. The teams will be set up and the assignments designed so that the work of writing the report can be divided up - for example one member focuses on a specific part of the literature and they work together to create the final collective document. Tutors will interact with the students by tele-conference during this work - commenting on drafts, suggesting lines of thinking, etc. All this work has the aim of preparing the students for their case study investigation during which tutors will provide tele-tutoring support by commenting on drafts (e.g. of the research question; of the data elicitation methodology; of the elements of the final report; etc.)

General goals
The activity is aimed at providing a significant experience of team working for the students whilst at the same time involving them in research related to working in teams and associated issues in a real-world context. Their research should enable them to uncover the explicit and implicit communication channels and structures in organisations. From this they may ask such questions as whether those channels and structures support the sharing of professional and operational knowledge in the organisation and pose the question as to whether alternative channels (using electronic communications for example) and an alternative management structure could impact positively on the effectiveness, efficiency, culture, morale and competitivity of the organisation.

Following an effective analysis and report, the students (in partnership with the organisation) could plan, implement and evaluate an innovation in the organisation. This could become a follow-up 'course' as part of a doctoral thesis or a further diploma. This would require a fully developed evaluation and framework for the management of change to support such extension work.

6. CONCLUSIONS

The aim of this paper has been to explore alternative approaches to the ways in which universities can fulfil their role in research as well as in teaching and learning, and to suggest ways of collaboration between universities and enterprises. It is suggested that the distinction between learning and research is one which can impose artificial boundaries to activities especially when the emphasis is on tacit, craft knowledge rather than on formal 'scientific' knowledge. The work is on-going and aims to assess the conditions under which ICT can provide support for the sharing of professional and craft knowledge, that is continual apprenticeship, both in working and learning contexts. It also stimulates an analysis of the cognitive processes involved in learning and working and the extent to which research activities are similar to learning and need to be grounded in a social and cultural context.

Experiences of the action-research approach to learning so far seem to open new and interesting perspectives. However, it is also important to note that major difficulties appear: students may ask for more structure than is possible under these naturalistic conditions and this way of learning may be fraught with uncertainties, mistakes and ambiguities. There are also serious difficulties in convincing enterprises of the benefits of this collaboration. In summary, it can be concluded that more experience in the design of courses of this kind is needed.

But, to end positively, communications technologies do seem to open up exciting opportunities to bridge the gap between academic and professional knowledge, something which is currently highly valued.

7. REFERENCES

Bannon, L.J. & Kuutti, K, (1996) Shifting Perspectives on Organisational Memory: from storage to active remembering, in *Proceedings IEEE HICSS'96* Hawaii.

Conklin, E.J. (1992) Capturing organizational memory, in *Groupware '92* (ed. D. Colman), Morgan Kaufman, San Mateo CA.

Heeren, E. & Lewis, R. (1997) Communication media for distributed communities. *Journal of Computer Assisted Learning*, **13**, 2, 85-98.

HMSO (1986) *Exploitable Areas of Science*. Her Majesty's Stationery Office, London.

IFIP (1970) *The IFIP Guide to Concepts and Terms in Data Processing* (ed. I.H. Gould). North Holland, Amsterdam.

Lave, J. & Wenger, E. (1991) *Situated learning*. Cambridge University Press, Cambridge.

Lewis, R. (1992) Strategies for Research - integrating outcomes into practice. Keynote Paper in *Information Processing 92 - Education and Society* (ed. R. Aiken), Elsevier Science Publishers, Amsterdam.

Nardi, B.A. (1996) Studying Context: a comparison of Activity Theory, Situated Action Models and Distributed Cognition, in *Context and Consciousness* (ed. B.A. Nardi), MIT Press, Cambridge, MA.

Newby, H. (1992) *Social Sciences in the 1990's*. Economic and Social Research Council, Swindon.

Sigurdson, J. & Tallving, M. (eds.) (1977) *Universities in the Cross-Streams of Globalisation and Information Technology*. The European Institute for Japanese Studies, Stockholm School of Economics, Stockholm.

8. BIOGRAPHIES

Robert Lewis has been engaged in research into the uses of information and communication technologies to support learning and knowledge exchange more generally. Recent research, some of it supported by the European Commission, has focused on the sharing of tacit, informal knowledge in communities of professional practice. He has been the Editor of the *Journal of Computer Assisted Learning* since its foundation in 1984 and has edited many IFIP proceedings.

Carmen Vizcarro is Profesora Titular at the Faculty of Psychology, Universidad Autonoma of Madrid and Director of the Service of Staff Development (SADU) at this University. She recently co-edited a book on the use of computers in education ("Nuevas Tenologias para el Aprendizaje". Madrid: Ed. Piramide, 1997).

Cultural contextualisation of learning with the World Wide Web

M. Wild
School of Management Information Systems, Edith Cowan University, Pearson Street, Churchlands, Western Australia 6018.
e-mail: m.wild@cowan.edu.au

L. Henderson
School of Education, James Cook University, Townsville, Australia 4811.
e-mail: lynette.henderson@jcu.edu.au

Abstract

There is a developing urgency about how Australian universities should make use of the World Wide Web to best meet the needs of culturally diverse students, especially those of Asian origin. This urgency is the result of both global and internal pressures, some political, (consider the imminence of the 'Hanson movement' against a multicultural Australia[1]) some technical, some social. To miss the current opportunity to exploit Web technologies to design, implement and market effective instructional courses will be to hand over a potentially billion dollar market to overseas competitors, especially those of the United Kingdom and the United States. One of the most pressing problems in this context is how to provide instructional materials in a model of teaching and learning that is cost effective, makes extensive use of Web technologies to provide for flexibility in learning, and that is culturally appropriate. This paper outlines an approach and model for investigating and developing culturally appropriate instructional materials.

---

[1] P. Kelly (1997). The challenge of Pauline Hanson. *Focus: The Weekend Australian, 26-27 April, 1997,* pp 21-22. In this article, Paul Kelly outlines the urgent need for all Australians, to address the 'racial isolationism' and anti–multicultural sentiments propagated in Hanson's One Nation Party, and in its manifesto: *Pauline Hanson: The Truth* .

The Virtual Campus F. Verdejo & G. Davies (Eds.)

The following hypotheses are central to our work:

- Existing cultural influences in instructional materials designed and delivered on the World Wide Web by (Australian) universities, and intended for use by culturally diverse students, are minimal and ineffective.
- The efficacy of learning based in the use of the World Wide Web for instructional purposes can be improved by the adoption of a culturally appropriate model of instructional design.
- Culture is a significant factor in determining the effectiveness of learning materials created in the World Wide Web and intended for use by culturally diverse students.

In testing these hypotheses, we intend to provide the empirical research to help determine the most appropriate ways of using the Web to stimulate effective learning at tertiary level for all learners, whatever their cultural heritage or perspectives.

Keywords

Distributed learning systems, WWW, Multi-cultural tertiary education, Multimedia instructional design, Flexible learning

1. INTRODUCTION

'In the age of cyberspace education, interactive learning and globalisation of the learning process ... universities webbed together by electronics and learning systems based upon new academic paradigms will not be easily denied in the twenty–first century.' (Pelton, 1996 20)

Here Pelton gives an insight into the imperatives presented by widespread usage of new communication technologies. Tertiary education will necessarily assume a new shape in a communications rich world, and be driven by developing customers' demands for greater sophistication, flexibility and cultural appropriateness in learning systems. In particular, universities are increasingly targeting culturally diverse students and will need to develop culturally contextualised applications of these new technologies.

The Internet and especially the World Wide Web is increasingly being used as a vehicle for flexible learning, where learning is seen to be free from geographical, time and participation restraints (Nguyen, Tan, and Kezunovic, 1996; Rossman, 1992). Numerous tertiary institutions are rapidly investing considerable resources and faith in the Web as a means of conveying both the administrative and the pedagogical materials for student learning. Australia figures prominently amongst the nations of the world which use distributed information systems, such as the Web, to deliver education (Paulsen, 1992; Rudra, 1994). Too often however, paper based information resources are simply being converted into 'electronic page-turning' materials for accessing via the Web. There is little regard for appropriate pedagogic design models and strategies for exploiting the Web as an instructional medium (Alexander, 1995; Reeves, 1996; Wild, 1996b), particularly for students originating and studying with different cultural perspectives.

Distributed learning systems on the Web have the potential and often the intention of reaching greater numbers of culturally diverse students. The key to success in the use of the Web across cultural boundaries lies in the appropriate pedagogic design of on line educational environments (Harasim, 1995; Henderson, 1996). Our own recent research (Henderson, Patching, and Putt, 1996; Oliver, 1996; Oliver, Herrington, and Omari, 1996; Wild, 1996a; Wild, 1996b; Wild and Omari, 1996) has demonstrated that the Web is almost always chosen as a delivery medium for instruction primarily for its ubiquity and insignificant costs. However, it is not chosen for its instructional effectiveness. Nor is it chosen as a medium particularly suited to carrying a range of information types for culturally diverse learners. In this context, creating systems for teaching and learning with the Web may well work to limit efficacy in learning, despite the Web's ever developing technical capacities to carry multimedia materials and information, and its growing provision for various levels of complexity in learner material interactions. While many learners might possess the basic information and navigational skills to contend with information access on the Web, instructional designers are yet to consider those aspects of this medium that determine its effectiveness for all learners, whatever their cultural characteristics.

Henderson has determined, as late as 1996, 'the relationship between cultural context and instructional design has received little attention in the educational technology and instructional design literature' (Henderson, 1996 85). It seems apparent that the lack of research to target cultural issues in instructional design for distributed and interactive learning systems, such as those being placed on the Web by Australian and overseas universities in ever increasing numbers, is even more noticeable and is likely to have serious consequences, particularly for students as well as for universities. Indeed, a recently published government funded report in the area of Internet use by Australian universities, makes a clear recommendation that 'the university sector should be proactive in profiling and accommodating characteristics of user need that will require compatible network technologies' (Bruce, 1996 xi).

This paper rationalises a methodology for research into the use of Web sites as pedagogic vehicles for flexible learning, especially for students of diverse cultural backgrounds. It describes an original conceptual framework for conducting such research-one that is presently guiding our own work in this area.

2. FLEXIBLE LEARNING AND THE USE OF THE WEB

The concept of flexible learning has evolved alongside developments in new technologies in four main phases. The initial phases are considered by Nguyen, et al (1996), Peacock (1995), and others, to have focused on, (i) correspondence and radio broadcasts (directed at isolated learners in farming and mining communities); (ii) video and television broadcasts, which allowed greater approximation of the traditional classroom experience; and, (iii) computer conferencing, electronic mail and voice mail, which supported greater levels of synchronous and asynchronous communication across distance and time. A fourth phase is set to emerge in the later 1990's and will be focused on direct student access to computer based remote databases, hypermedia and multimedia information and dial up access to video materials. In this fourth phase, students will be in control of the time, place and pace of study (Peacock, 1995), and will have direct access to an expanding and dynamic knowledge base and extensive communicative facilities. The Web is an emerging technology but already possesses the functionalities described in this fourth phase: the Web is placed to be the technology most likely to carry flexible learning into a new phase of development.

Of course, the move towards flexible learning for all students, on campus and distance, is being driven not only by technological imperatives but also by economic and pedagogical ones. There is a declining ratio of academic staff to students; and students are increasingly being encouraged to invest greater independence in, and control over, their learning. Indeed, over the last 20 years or so there have been significant changes in policies, organisation, staffing, funding and management of universities in Australia, usually as a result of government directives and policies (Chalmers and Fuller, 1996). One consequence of these changes is that students are now a much more diverse group, particularly in cultural characteristics, and are more likely to study in mixed modes that are suited to flexible learning.

3. EDUCATIONAL POTENTIAL OF THE WEB

The nature of the World Wide Web has attracted a great deal of rhetoric in favour of its potential to provide for a student centred model of learning, where the learner is both intrinsically motivated and active in the learning environment (Becker and Dwyer, 1994). At first glance there is much in the Web that appeals to educators, for example, the hypermedia information structures in the Web allow for the chunking of information, a feature that, in light of information processing theories of working memory, might be seen to support the cognitive processing of knowledge (Biggs and Moore, 1993). There have also been suggestions that in providing for browsing and thematic exploration, the Web facilitates higher order cognitive processes, such as transfer and knowledge application (Jacobson and Spiro, 1995; Oliver, Herrington, and Omari, 1996); whilst at a more conceptual level, there has always been a case made for hypertext mirroring the ways in which much of human thinking occurs, by association rather than linearly or procedurally (Burton, Moore, and Holmes, 1995; Bush, 1945; Minsky, 1975). Furthermore the Web, in terms of being a dynamic, extensive and extensible information base, provides for the ultimate in resource rich learning.

It is important to remember that the Web, as hypermedia or hypertext, is itself only a medium for conveying information data. Hypermedia does not possess a single or normative information structure, hypermedia documents are created to conform or fit to a structure, imposed by their instructional designers. At one extreme this structure might be highly ordered, supported by a constrained and sequential set of links. At another extreme, the hypermedia may be nonsequential and supported only by referential links. In many cases, a coherent hypermedia document, such as a Web site, might comprise a mix of these structures. It is, then, the nature and application of these structures that determines the effectiveness of engagement with the data carried in the Web in order for generative learning to occur. Furthermore, to maximise engagement, the information needs to conform to a structure that best fits or suits both the type of knowledge being conveyed as well as the learning preferences and requirements of diverse groups of learners.

However, there is no guidance, and virtually no empirical research, to help determine the most appropriate ways of using the Web to stimulate effective learning at tertiary level for all learners that are so targeted. It is apparent that instructional design for Web based learning systems cannot, and does not, exist outside a consideration of cultural influences-both the cultural influences operating on the authors and instructional designers of Web based learning materials, and similarly, those influences that impact on the interpretation of such materials by learners.

4. THE INFLUENCE OF CULTURE

Defining culture is a difficult proposition. Many different classifications exist in relation to national culture (Kluckhohn and Strondbeck, 1961; Roackeach, 1973; Hall, 1959, 1990; Hofstede, 1984; Hofstede and Bond, 1988). Supporters of the convergence theory claim that, due to influences such as technology and trends towards globalisation of information, societies will become more and more alike (Child, 1981; Negandhi, 1985); others who support the divergence theory believe that national differences are not divisible by such influences, and that such differences will operate to limit or negate the value of distributed information and learning systems aimed at multiple cultures (Hofstede 1984, Cheung and Burn, 1994; Nelson and Clark, 1994; Lewis, 1996). Perhaps the most pervasive view is that culture is a manifestation of ways in which an identifiable group adapts to its changing environment; that people belong to more than a single cultural group, embodying a subset rather than a totality of a culture's identifiable characteristics; and that they do not remain totally allegiant to their birth culture (Henderson, 1996; Scheel and Branch, 1993).

Whatever the theory, there appears to be consensus that culture has a definite and very strong influence on the design and use of information, communication and learning systems, as well as on their management, despite the lack of identifiable research in these areas. In all areas of human activity, the behaviour of people is affected by the values and attitudes that they hold and the societal norms which surround them. When values are widely shared by a group of people, they are provided with a common mechanism by which they can share understandings and interpretations of their world, and establish what is important and clarify priorities.

As nations develop and organisations become more technologically advanced and globally oriented, their culture changes and this, in turn, has an effect on individuals' attitudes and values (Adler, 1991). Culture, however, is more than just an abstraction. It also consists of a distinctive symbol system together with artefacts, that capture and codify the important and common experiences of a group. Distinctive significant symbolic meanings and values develop around information, its use and structuring in any cultural group. Also, at a practical level, when the act of instructional design translates this information into products or artefacts of learning, that artefact embodies cultural influences, such as the instructional designer's world view, their values, ideologies, culture, class and gender, and, their commitment to a particular design paradigm (Henderson, 1996).

These interacting cultural factors have a particular importance for the diffusion and efficacy in use, of distributed learning systems, such as the Web, and the products and materials of learning provided in those systems.

5. A MODEL FOR INVESTIGATION

We presently have a situation where cultural influences in distributed information, communication and learning systems, especially those centred in the Web, are present and are identifiable, but are largely created unknowingly. As a result, such systems probably work to the detriment of large groups of culturally diverse learners who cannot identify with the instructional designs in Web–based systems of teaching and learning, originating as they do, in single cultural identities. Given the instructional agendas currently being set by universities for the present and future use of the Web, it is reasonable to suggest that there will be a mismatch between instructional intention and learning outcome. This mismatch will become more noticeable as Web based flexible learning systems are increasingly put into place in the later 1990s and into the new millennium.

Henderson describes three existing instructional design paradigms in static instructional multimedia: (i) culturally unidimensional or exclusionary; (ii) inclusive; and, (iii) inverted (Henderson, 1996). In the first paradigm, cultural minority groups go unrepresented. Scheel and Branch (1993) have attempted to describe the reasons for this, and in doing so explain various manifestations of what Rattansi (1992) has termed, *deracialisation*.. Deracialisation occurs when there is an unintentional or intentional exclusion or avoidance of, or insulation from, issues of appropriate cultural contextualisation in the production of multimedia learning materials. In the second paradigm, Henderson (1996) acknowledges the adoption of an inclusive or perspectives instructional design approach, where the instructional designer includes the social, cultural, economic and/or historical perspectives and/or contributions of minority groups. 'In this paradigm, instructional design is driven by social justice and equity issues, while instructional design solutions range from soft to hard multiculturalism' (Henderson, 1996 91), or what Scheel and Branch (1993) term 'mild to strong interventions' (p. 9). In a third paradigm, the instructional designer will attempt to approach the design task from the perspective of one or more minority cultures, that is, from an inverted curriculum or critical theory-postmodernist paradigm (Henderson, 1996 93).

Each of these instructional design paradigms has been determined by Henderson (1996), to be unsatisfactory in terms of providing culturally appropriate instruction in static (ie. CD–ROM) multimedia products. It is reasonable to hypothesise that these are the very paradigms that currently also dominate in distributed information, communication and learning systems, presently being provided on the Web by universities for teaching and learning for culturally diverse students.

6. A RESEARCH METHODOLOGY

The following research programme is promulgated to enable a triangulation of qualitative and quantitative data in order to assess the cultural contextualisation of learning with the Web as a distributed learning environment. It is envisaged that this research programme will commence in Australia in 1998.

In selecting a research methodology, we have been guided by both Howe and Eisenhart (1990) and Reeves (1993), who argue that any methodology employed should be judged in terms of its success in investigating educational problems deemed important. Moreover, Salomon (1991) describes the contrast between analytic research that is focused on isolating effective instructional treatments and systemic research focused on understanding how instructional treatments work in practice. This suggests that analytic and systemic approaches are complementary: 'the analytic approach capitalises on precision while the systemic approach capitalises on authenticity' (Salomon, 1991 16). Both analytic and systemic methods are being used in this research programme. Also, the nature of learning based on the Web, with its high degree of individualisation, 'meshes precisely with the naturalistic assumption of individual constructions of reality' (Neuman, 1989 48). Indeed, specific strategies based on case study methods are highlighted in our research program so we can elicit these individual constructions.

At all stages of the research programme, it is crucial that a mixture of strategies be used to collect and analyse data within methodologies that are based in narrative, case study, and survey approaches (Patton, 1990).

The aim of this three year research project is to identify the nature and improve the efficacy of models of flexible, open and distance learning created in the World Wide Web by universities. The following hypotheses will be tested:

- Existing cultural influences in instructional materials designed and delivered on the World Wide Web by Australian universities, and intended for use by culturally diverse students, are minimal and ineffective.
- The efficacy of learning based in the use of the World Wide Web for instructional purposes can be improved by the adoption of a culturally appropriate model of instructional design.

- Culture is a significant factor in determining the effectiveness of learning materials created in the World Wide Web and intended for use by culturally diverse students.

In testing these hypotheses we intend to provide empirical research to help determine the most appropriate ways of using the Web to stimulate effective learning at tertiary level for all learners, whatever their cultural heritage or perspectives.

There are three phases in the research, corresponding to three temporal stages.

Phase one-year one

The major focus for this phase is to identify the existing instructional design paradigms that exist in distributed information, communication and learning systems provided by Australian universities for culturally diverse groups of learners, both internal and external to Australia. This will be accomplished in five stages:

1. Administering brief written survey questionnaires to Australian universities via email and/or post, with the intention of identifying those that provide for open, distance and/or flexible learning in courses that are studied in part or in whole, on the Web, using distributed communication, information and/or multimedia technologies.
2. From this database, randomly select Web course sites: (a) at undergraduate level, (b) with large to small enrolments, (c) across a number of disciplines, (d) from various large urban to small country universities, and (d) ranged across the Australian States and Territories.
3. Create data collection instruments to enable identification of instructional design paradigms used in the distributed learning systems on the Web sites selected in (2). Identification will be based upon how well the Web sites conform to critical identifiers of the three existing instructional design paradigms identified by Henderson (1996) that are hypothesised to exist in Web based systems created for flexible learning.

   Currently, we are hypothesising that the instruments will involve checklists that include the following sorts of relevant instructional design elements seen to belong to the three cultural paradigms: (a) the underlying pedagogic philosophy of each Web course site; (b) the Web course site's epistemology; (c) each site's instructional sequencing (for instance, is there a holist (horizontal hypertext) or partist (linear hypertext) layout to the interface design of what is usually seen as the content menu page/s?); (d) the degree of inbuilt individual versus collaborative strategies; (e) hypermedia navigation pathways that cater for individual learning styles (Carver, Howard and Levelle 1996) as well as novice, expert, and the progression from novice to expert, Web users; (f) the ratio of American, Canadian, British, Australian and New Zealand active internet links to non Anglo Western active internet links included within each Web course site; (g) word count of key concepts and examples of, for instance, a single 'truth' or multiple theoretical perspectives; (h) semantic chunking of text versus traditional paragraph structure; and (i) appropriate/inappropriate culturally contextualised graphics, animation, video clips, sound, and colours.

4. Undertake collection of data from the instruments devised in (iii) above. This will involve the following strategies to promote reliability amongst the researchers of their coding of the data. One Web course site will be selected; each researcher will use the data collection instrument/s to codify the site; their respective codification will be comparatively noted. Each researcher's codification will be tabulated and put through a reliability check devised by Marland, Patching and Putt (1992) and subsequently ratified by Henderson, et al. (in press). This reliability check will be administered randomly throughout the codification of all selected Web course sites. We would be expecting above an 80% agreement for validity. Where discrepancies occur in the codification, the researchers will negotiate an unanimous decision.
5. Report the findings of the first phase. These findings should stand alone as a significant contribution to the literature on the pedagogic design of Web distributed learning materials. As well, they will highlight the cultural contextualisation of such teaching learning materials. Additionally, the findings provide the conceptual entry point to the second major phase of the research program.

Phase two-year two

The major aim of this phase is to (a) create and implement a number of Web sites based on a fourth instructional design paradigm centred in a view of multiple cultures (Henderson, 1966) and (b) implement a pilot study to test the paradigm's effectiveness.

The primary endeavour of the multiple cultural model is to design a learning environment that promotes equity of outcomes for all learners. A major weakness in the multicultural, inclusive and inverted paradigms is avoidance of the cognitive, epistemological, and philosophical aspects of inter related cultural educational contexts. A multiple cultural model that has been used and researched since 1990 is offered as an alternative way to conceptualise the cultural contextualisation of instructional design in distributed learning environments (for a synthesis of some of the research corpus, see Henderson, Patching and Putt, 1996). The multiple cultural model strives for a coherent interplay between various implicit and explicit cultural logics: those of the academic, 'mainstream' and 'minority' cultures. First, instructional design in a multiple cultural model needs to overtly recognise the specific requirements of the 'mainstream' tertiary culture. These are expressed through the content to be taught, types of assessment, the written and oral genres, research methodologies, and culturally–specific ways of promoting cognitive development within an academic environment. Second, as academic culture is embedded in each society's dominant culture, aspects of the macro culture, particularly systemic factors, need to be included in the overall instructional design of any distributed learning environment. Third, it is also necessary that instructional design incorporate the cultures of the other identifiable groups of learners, that is, their knowledge and preferred ways of thinking and doing in a manner that goes beyond tokenism.

Thus, the multiple cultural model does not assume one instructional pedagogy as immutable but provides an epistemological and pedagogic pluralism in which multiple ways of constructing knowledge and understanding are valued, and it prompts learners to interrogate those pedagogies in the construction of their own knowledge. In this way cultural contextualisation is visible in the instructional design of the Web learning materials.

There are six stages in this second phase of the research plan.

1. Select a number of existing foundation units offered in the School of Management Information Systems at Edith Cowan University and in the School of Education at James Cook University. The criteria for selection are that students enrolled in these units will have culturally diverse backgrounds and be internally and externally enrolled.
2. Instructionally design a series of Web sites using these foundation units in accordance with the multiple cultures paradigm, and focussed on providing student learning for students of diverse cultural backgrounds. Because the multiple cultures paradigm is centred within Vygotsky's socio-cultural historical theory of learning, scaffolding strategies within the student's zone of proximal development are incorporated in the instructional design of the Web sites. Such scaffolding will target the various strategies of modelling, coaching, cognitive apprenticeship, etc., as propounded in the theory of situated cognition (Choi and Hannafin, 1995). The strategies will necessarily be aimed at canvassing a range of cognitive and metacognitive thinking skills.
3. Program the series of Web sites, utilising the expertise of computer science postgraduate students. Programming will also incorporate tracking of student movement within the Web site. The tracking has dual purposes. Firstly, it will provide students with self determined and program determined access to appropriate scaffolding support that provides cognitive and navigational guidance from a 'more capable other' (which, in this case, is the scaffolding strategies instructionally designed within the Web sites). Secondly, the tracking will be utilised as research data to ascertain the where, how and when of students' intranet and, hopefully, internet movements within and outside the Web sites.
4. Undertake a pilot study of these Web sites at the Perth Institute of Business and Technology to test the veracity and appropriateness of (a) the instructional design in the Web sites and (b) the data collection instruments. This Institute and its foundation units typically attract students of diverse cultural and national groups, enrolled internally and externally, and who are representative of students studying these same or similar foundation units at Edith Cowan and James Cook University. Some students from diverse cultural groups will be invited to be involved in the trailing evaluation of the Web sites. Checklists, student diaries, observations, open ended questionnaires, data from the programmed tracking, interviews, and stimulated recall interviews will be used.

The main function of the first four instruments is to obtain data about the multiple cultural contextualisation of the content and the instructional design features of the Web sites. Tracking data will provide evidence of its efficiency in actually doing what is intended, that is, providing cognitive scaffolding and navigational support to the learners and obtaining their 'what, where and when' navigational movements. Interviews based on the analysis of the tracking data should provide us with an understanding of why students took certain paths, options, and actions while studying with the Web materials. Interviews will also provide data about the students' perceptions of whether these strategies promoted their learning and were related to culturally identified ways of thinking and doing.

The last methodology, stimulated recall audiotaped interviews focussed on a replay of a split screen videotaped session of the students as they studied with the Web materials, is based in the mediating process paradigm (Shulman, 1986). The paradigm directs attention to student thought processes that mediate or come between instructional stimuli and learning outcomes. Analysis of the coded data allows the researchers to elicit the thinking and attitudinal processes actually engaged in whilst the students studied with the Web materials. The mediating process paradigm has been successfully tested in previous research with culturally diverse groups (Henderson and Patching, 1995; Henderson, Patching and Putt, 1996; Putt, Patching and Henderson, 1996).

5. Edit the Web sites based on analysis of the data collected in (4).
6. Commence initial visits to universities in Australia and other countries (based on previous enrolments of students studying externally to Edith Cowan and James Cook universities, it is predicted that these countries will include Malaysia, Taiwan, Thailand and Hong Kong), to identify likely subjects and organise qualitative and quantitative collection strategies, as preparation for Phase Three as described below.

Phase three-year three

This phase aims to investigate the degree of success in student learning that students of different cultural groups have as a result of using the Web based materials designed in the paradigm of multiple cultures. The students (n>1500) chosen for investigation will include students enrolled both at Edith Cowan and James Cook Universities, students who are enrolled internally and externally to these universities, and who are therefore studying within and outside Australia. They will also include students who can be, collectively, identified with a range of representative cultural groups. The study will incorporate quantitative and qualitative data collection instruments, such as:

1. pre, post, and post delay content questionnaires;
2. pre and post attitudinal, anxiety, and usage questionnaires (King, Henderson and Putt, 1996), to be incorporated within the Web site pages;
3. a five category Likert questionnaire focussed upon the interface design features of the Web sites, to be incorporated within the Web site pages;

4. case study of 12 ethnically diverse students; two from each Web unit site;
5. diary kept by each of these, and a random sample of other, students;
6. stimulated recall audiotaped interviews with these 12 students;
7. observations of the students identified in (4) and (5) at the various Australian and overseas study sites;
8. other evaluative open ended questionnaire interviews of the students identified in (4) and (5);
9. tracking data.

7. CONCLUSION

It is anticipated that various outcomes will be achieved which will add to the body of knowledge on flexible learning, instructional design, cultural influences in learning and teaching, and pedagogically effective culturally contextualised World Wide Web instructional materials. Such outcomes include an empirically researched evaluation of (a) the impact of teaching and learning based on the Web for culturally diverse tertiary students; (b) an instructional design model which can be applied to develop culturally appropriate teaching and learning on the Web; and (c) flexible learning materials provided by Australian universities on the Web in terms of their cultural sensitivities.

8. REFERENCES

Adler, N. J. (1991) *International dimensions of organisational behaviour* (Second ed.). PWS-Kent, Boston.

Alexander, S. (1995) Teaching and learning on the World Wide Web. Paper presented at *AusWeb95: The First Australian World Wide Web Conference*, Southern Cross University, New South Wales, 30 April-2 May, 1995.

Becker, D., and Dwyer, M. (1994) Using hypermedia to provide learner control. *Journal of Educational Multimedia and Hypermedia*, **3**(2), 155-172.

Biggs, J. B., and Moore, P. J. (1993) *The process of learning* (Third ed.). Prentice Hall, Sydney.

Bruce, H. W. (1996) *Internet, AARNet and academic work: A longitudinal study*, Department of Employment, Education, Training and Youth Affairs (DEETYA), Canberra. November, 1996.

Burton, J. K., Moore, M., and Holmes, G. A. (1995) Hypermedia concepts and research: An overview. *Computers in Human Behaviour*, **11**(3-4), 345-369.

Bush, V. (1945) As we may think. *The Atlantic Monthly*, **176**(1), 101-108.

Carver, C., Howard, R., and Levelle, E. (1996) Enhancing student learning by incorporating learning styles into adaptive hypermedia, in *Interactive multimedia and hypermedia* (eds. P. Carlson and F. Makedon) (pp. 118-123). Association for the Advancement of Computers in Education, Charlottesville, VA.

Chalmers, D., and Fuller, R. (1996) *Teaching for learning at university* . Kogan Page, London.

Cheung, H. K., and Burn, J. M. (1994) Distributing global information systems resources in multinational companies: A contingency model. *Journal of Global Information Management*, **2**(3), 14-27.

Child, J. (1981) Culture, contingency and capitalism in the cross-national study of organizations, in *Research in organizational behavior* (eds. L. L. Cummings and B. M. Staw),(pp. 303-356). JAI Press, Greenwich, CT.

Choi, J., and Hannafin, M. (1995) Situated cognition and learning environments: Roles, structures and implications for design. *Educational Technology Research and Development*, **43**(2), 53-69.

Harasim, L. (1995). The virtual university: New approaches to higher education in the 21st century. Paper presented at *ASCILITE95. The 12th Annual Conference of the Australian Society for Computers in Learning in Tertiary Education*, Melbourne, 3-7 December, 1995.

Henderson, L. (1996) Instructional design of interactive multimedia: A cultural critique. *Educational Technology Research and Development*, **44**(4), 86-104.

Henderson, M., and Patching, W. (1995). Multimedia interactivity: Relating cognitive processing and click and drag activities. *Educational Multimedia and Hypermedia, 1995*, Association for the Advancement of Computing in Education, Charlottesville, VA. 318-323.

Henderson, L., Patching, W., and Putt, I. (1996) Off-campus preservice teacher education via interactive multimedia technology: An indigenous cohort case study, in *Interactive multimedia and hypermedia* (eds. P. Carlson and F. Makedon), (pp. 300-305), Association for the Advancement of Computers in Education, Charlottesville, VA.

Henderson, L., Patching, W., and Putt, I. (in press) Non-indigenous students thinking: Studying with interactive multimedia courseware designed for indigenous students.

Henderson, L., Putt, I., Ainge, D., and Coombs, G. (in press) Comparison of students' thinking processes when studying with WWW, IMM, and text-based materials.

Hofstede, G. (1984) *Culture's consequences* . Sage, Beverly Hills, CA.

Howe, K., and Eisenhart, M. (1990) Standards for qualitative (and quantitative) research: A prolegomenon. *Educational Researcher,* **19**(4), 2-9.

Jacobson, M., and Spiro, R. (1995) Hypertext learning environments, cognitive flexibility and the transfer of complex knowledge. *Journal of Educational Computing Research*, **12**(4), 301-333.

Kluckhohn, F., and Strodtbeck, F. (1961) *Variations in value orientations* . Row Peterson, Evanston, IL.

Lewis, R. D. (1996). *When cultures collide: Managing successfully across cultures* . Nicholas Brealey Publishing Ltd.

Marland, P.W., Patching W.G. and Putt, I. J. (1992) *Learning from Text: Glimpses inside the minds of distance learners*. James Cook University, Townsville.

Minsky, M. (1975) A framework for representing knowledge, in *The psychology of computer vision* (ed. P. H. Winston), McGraw Hill, New York.

Nelson, K. G., and Clark, T. D. (1994) Cross-cultural issues in Information Systems research: A research program. *Journal of Global Information Management*, **2**(4), 19-29.

Neuman, D. (1989) Naturalistic inquiry and computer-based instruction: Rationale, procedures and potential. *Educational Technology Research and Development*, **37**(3), 39-51.

Nguyen, A. T. A., Tan, W., & Kezunovic, L. (1996). Interactive multimedia on the World Wide Web: Implementation and implications for the tertiary education sector. In R. Debreceny & A. Ellis (Eds.), *Proceedings of AusWeb96: The Second Australian World Wide Web Conference. (Also available at, http://www.scu.edu.au/ausweb96/)*, (pp. 551-557). Gold Coast, Australia: Southern Cross University.

Oliver, R. (1996) Interactions in multimedia learning materials: The things that matter in *Proceedings of Third Interactive Multimedia Symposium, The learning superhighway: New world, new worries?* (eds. C. McBeath and R. Atkinson), (pp. 303-308), Promaco Conventions Ltd, Perth, Western Australia.

Oliver, R., Herrington, J., & Omari, A. (1996). Creating effective instructional materials for the World Wide Web. In R. Debreceny & A. Ellis (Eds.), *Proceedings of AusWeb96: The Second Australian World Wide Web Conference. Also available at, http://www.scu.edu.au/ausweb96/*, (pp. 485-491). Gold Coast, Australia: Southern Cross University.

Paulsen, M. F. (1992) Computer mediated communications and distance education around the world. *From Bulletin Boards to Electronic Universities*, **7**, 31-37.

Peacock, K. A. (1995) *Distance education in a univesrity setting: connecting to the global classroom*. Available, http://www.utirc.utoronto.ca/Distance_Ed/disted-report.html [on-line]. University of Toronto, Canada, October, 1995.

Pelton, J. N. (1996) Cyberlearning versus the university. *The Futurist, November–December, 1996*, 17-20.

Putt, I., Patching, W., and Henderson, L. (1996) Teachers' Thinking Elicited from Interactive Multimedia Professional Development Courseware. *Educational Technology Research and Development* **44**(4), 7-22.

Rattansi, A. (1992) Changing the subject? Racism, culture and education in *Race, culture and difference* (eds. J. Donald and A. Rattansi),(pp. 11-48). Sage, London.

Reeves, T. (1993) Pseudoscience in computer based instruction: the case of learner control research. *Journal of Computer Based Instruction*, **20**(2), 39-46.

Reeves, T. (1996) A model of the effective dimensions of interactive learning on the world wide web, in *Interactive multimedia and hypermedia* (eds. P. Carlson and F. Makedon), AACE Charlottesville, VA.

Rokeach, M. (1973) *The nature of human values* . Free Press, New York.

Rossman, P. (1992) *The emerging worldwide electronic university: Information age global higher education* . Greenwood Press, Westport.

Rudra, A. (1994) AARNet and ERNET: An era for fostering international academic research, in *Proceedings of International networking: Education, training and change* (ed. N. F. Ellerton), (pp. 104-109), Edith Cowan University, Perth, Western Australia.

Salomon, G. (1991) Transcending the qualitative–quantitative debate: The analytic and systemic approaches to educational research. *Educational Researcher*, **20**(6), 10-18.

Scheel, N., and Branch, R. (1993) The role of conversation and culture in the systematic design of instruction. *Educational Technology*, **3**(3), 5-14.

Shulman, L. S. (1986) Paradigms and research programs in the study of teaching: A contemporary perspective, in *Handbook of research on teaching* (ed. M. C. Wittrock), (pp. 3-36), Macmillan, New York.

Wild, M. (1996a) Designing appropriate learning environments in instructional multimedia: The role of theory. Paper presented at *Higher Education Research and Development Society of Australasia (HERDSA) Annual Conference: Different approaches-Theory and practice in Higher Education*, Perth, Western Australia, 8-12 July 1996.

Wild, M. (1996b) *Invited Presentation: The future of flexible learning and the use of technologies in tertiary education*. Open Learning Seminar, University of Technology, Sydney. 15 July, 1996.

Wild, M., and Omari, A. (1996) Developing educational content for the Web: Issues and ideas, in *Proceedings of AusWeb96: The second Australian World Wide Web Conference. (Also available at, http://www.scu.edu.au/ausweb96/)*, (eds. R. Debreceny and A. Ellis), (pp. 353-355), Southern Cross University Gold Coast, Australia.

9. BIOGRAPHIES

Martyn Wild teaches in the School of Management Information Systems, Edith Cowan University, Western Australia. He has published in diverse fields of information technology research, including, IT use in teacher education; interactive multimedia and learning; instructional design in on-line and multimedia environments; interface design; and human–computer interaction. He is currently developing performance support systems for teaching and learning.

Lyn Henderson is senior lecturer at James Cook University, in North Queensland, Australia. Her fields of research interests concern the cultural contextualisation of instructional design in multimedia and the World Wide Web, mental models, thinking processes and teaching–learning strategies used by teachers and learners when interacting with electronic databases, interactive multimedia and the World Wide Web.

13

Questions and Discussion

J. Wibe

The Norwegian University of Science and Technology, Trondheim Norway

The general discussion was very animated and many important issues were raised and discused. Ten minutes were allowed for discussion after each presentation and about half an hour at the end. There was a lively exchange of comments. Many questions were asked and few answers were given. This may be because most of the contributions were about «learning» and as said by one participant: We know very little about how learning takes place. How does learning take place and how is the technology used in the learning process?

- *Staff Development:*

A question was raised concerning the need for staff development in the use of CIT in order for it to be properly implemented in an institution. An approach of encouragement rather than obligation was suggested. A basic knowledge of using CIT was seen as necessary not just for supporting student learning but also to be more effective in collaboration and in research.

- *Instructional Design and cultural differences:*

Is it possible to find one solution for Instructional Design taking into account cultural differences? For example by setting up a list of cultural differences and a benchmark for a particular environment.

There are microdesign questions like icons and colour. These may not be solvable as the solutions are very small grained and therefore not applicable on a larger scale. It may be possible to develop some generic tools. It was also argued that we need local adaptation.

There are also macro design questions like frameworks and strategies. Openness is important. Currently we have the culture of the designer and the cultural attitudes of the teacher, not the learners.

- *Learning:*

Most of the discussion was about learning.

The Virtual Campus F. Verdejo & G. Davies (Eds.)

It was argued that our aim is to enrich the learning experience, we need to evaluate how that occurs using different media, producing not a direct comparison of media but an exploration of the unique nature of each medium.

Evaluation methodology: "How do we know certain levels of learning takes place?"

Is it better to have one code (culture) shared by everyone or enable people to master different codes and exist and learn in different contexts? A comment to this question was: Don't think we can force one code!

We must aim to support insecure learners who are facing open/natural contexts where the truth is not known.

The learning process and the research process are the same. For example using skills of browsing, collaboration and constructing ideas. "Research" may be said to be the development of knowledge for "humanity" and "learning" as the development of knowledge for the "individual".

The promotion of learning as constructivist and the emphasis on discovery learning and learning by doing brings the process of learning quite close to that of research. In an exchange between Lewis and Paquette, it was agreed that the cognitive processes of learning and research are more or less the same, the only difference being that in learning it is usual for someone to 'know the solution to a problem' and this is not the case in research. However, the fact that someone may know the 'answer' does not affect the individual engaged in a problem solving activity.

The Rapporteurs general impression of the session is that it contained excellent papers, very good presentations and the discussion was lively, with contributions and argument from many people from different countries and different backgrounds.

BIOGRAPHY

Jan Wibe is Chairman of IFIP Working Group 3.6. He is involved in several projects related to Distance Learning through Telematics in the *Centre for Continuing Education* of *the Norwegian University of Science and Technology*. He is engaged in the organization of a number of international conferences on the use of ICT for Distance Learning.

PART FOUR

Collaborative Learning and Group Activities

New Approaches for Collaborative Learning and Group Activities

A. Paiva
INESC and IST,
Rua Alves Redol, 9, 1000 Lisboa, Portugal
e-mail: Ana.Paiva@inesc.pt

Abstract

One of the most promising topics of study and exploration for the last decade in computer based learning has been collaborative learning. However, it is only recently that the approaches explored are being tested and effectively used. This brief summary focuses on the problems and new approaches of collaborative learning, as highlighted by the discussions held during the collaborative learning session at the IFIP 3.3 & 3.6 Joint Conference.

Keywords

Computer supported collaborative learning, Collaborative learning, Active support, Joint space, Interaction, Coordination

The Virtual Campus F. Verdejo & G. Davies (Eds.)

1. INTRODUCTION

The last decade has seen not only the impressive development of computer based collaborative learning, but also the exponential emergence of Web based tools. So, it is not surprising that the new approaches in this area are centred on the use of Web based technology. Indeed, the emphasis has shifted on learning as a constructive process where the learners are emerged in a social environment for task execution. Furthermore, this process has crossed the borders of the small classes to embrace a world wide scenario where collaboration at a distance is now a reality. One can predict that in the "Virtual Campuses" of the next decade, now starting to be built, collaborative learning and Web based distance learning will play important roles.
However, although the telecommunications infrastructure supporting the collaboration at a distance has had an almost explosive development, it is also true that these technological facilities do not replace the need for contextual and task oriented support. This kind of rich support was a common theme in all the presentations and discussions held in the session of "Collaborative Learning" of the IFIP 3.3 and 3.6 Joint Working Conference. This paper summarises their finding with a focus on distance learning systems which "support collaborative critical discussions at a distance" with the goal to promote learning. The present document is structured as follows: first a small overview of tools for collaborative learning is made. Then, some of the aspects found and reported in the Conference are highlighted, and the intriguing results obtained are discussed. Finally, some questions that were raised at the discussion are presented, leaving them open as new problems to be addressed.

2. SUPPORTING COLLABORATIVE DISCOURSE AT A DISTANCE

According to the socio-constructivist (see (Dillenbourg et al. 1997)) approach to learning, it is through the interaction with peers, and by comparing one's views with those of the others, that learners start to understand new approaches to reality (see (Doise, 1990)). The presence of learning companions with whom the students can interact, change information and share task execution, gives to the learning process a more real social context, and thus provides more effective environments for learning.
During the last decade, several environments have been proposed in order to support these collaborative situations. Results were obtained in classes of students exchanging email as well as in using collaborative virtual environments. In fact, the tools that support collaborative learning have changed considerably during the last few years, and at present, they range from the general purpose environments (that support email, talk, chat, etc.) to the more specific ones, tied to one task in

hand. In general, they intend to support some of the mechanisms that are observed in collaborative learning scenarios such as (see (Dillenbourg, 1995)): (1) conflict (socio-cognitive conflict), (2) mutual and auto-explanation, (3) internalisation, (4) appropriation of the knowledge and tasks of the peers, (5) mutual regulation, and (6) social grounding.

However, from the present state of research, it is not clear which approach should be adopted for building a collaborative learning tool, nor which type of support should be given in order to support some of these mechanisms. Such support can range from a very basic one with only communication infrastructure mechanisms to highly task oriented ones. In general, one can divide the support given by collaborative learning tools in three main types: social support, task support and cognitive support.

Social support: A tool must promote the emergence of social activities, including conflicts between peers, helping learners to achieve a shared understanding. This type of support includes support for information and knowledge share.

Task support: A tool must promote task level execution and its coordination. This includes the support of a shared working space, in which the students can construct in their activities.

Cognitive Support: the tool must promote cognitive and meta-cognitive episodes, such as reading, understanding, planning and analysing. They can support the construction of mutual explanations between students, or promote individual internalisation.

Taking a different perspective, one can also divide the support given to collaborating students into two main classes: active support and passive support.

Passive support is given by a tool in the form of implicit imposed restrictions on the ways learners interact, collaborate, solve problems and think. For example, both the work by (Barros, et al. 1998) and (Hietala et al. 1998) describe tools which include passive support by embedding in the interface a set of pre-defined collaborative interactions.

Active support is provided by an external element that helps the learners to overcome difficulties in the collaboration process. This active role of support can be played by a teacher or even by the tool itself (for example, in the Quorum project (Canas et al. 1995) the real teacher plays a role of a mediator).

2.1 Collaborative Tasks

The nature of the task (e.g. whether it is shareable or not) influences the results of the collaboration (see (Dillenbourg 1997) for a discussion) as well as the whole process. This influence is well illustrated by the papers (Barros et al. 1998) and (Hietala et al. 1998).

The intriguing findings obtained by (Hietala et al. 1998) demonstrate that even using the same collaborative learning environment, different results can be obtained for different tasks. Since the tasks can be set up by the teacher, several topics were explored and better results were achieved if the task at hand depends significantly on achieving a common objective. Similarly, the task to be executed by the learners described in (Barros et al. 97) was writing a summary, which clearly establishes an objective to be achieved. This required mastering two types of skills. First, a content based one, where the students had to relate aspects of a certain subject and create a summary of that subject, and second, students had to learn how to work in a cooperative manner, which included skills such as being able to propose or explain ideas. In both of these studies there is a clear need for supporting the process of collaboration towards achieving a common objective.

2.2 Joint Problem Space

Participation in a joint problem solving process is a way to foster the understanding of the problem, where each partner, in the collaboration process, changes his views by giving meaning to the others actions according to his or her own conceptual framework. Indeed, one essential property of collaborative problem solving is that it enables the construction of a shared conceptual structure that is called Joint Problem Space (introduced by (Teasley & Rochelle 1993)). The Joint Problem Space is intended to support the collaborative activities by integrating semantic interpretations of the goals, features, operators ad methods.
Both the work by (Barros et al. 1998) and (Hietala et al. 1998) illustrate the creation of a joint problem space.

2.3 Types of Interactions

The achievements of the collaboration not only depend on the task but also on the types of interactions. The interactions required in the collaboration process may prompt learners to express beliefs in ways that serve to organise what they know and identify gaps in their understanding. However, some interactions have a more positive influence in the learning results than others. So, which kind of interactions can be identified as collaborative? And how do systems trigger such interactions?
For example, the Collaboratory Notebook (see (Edelson et al. 1996)) provides shared hypermedia databases that the learners construct based on specific scientific inquiry forms of interactions. The information exchanged and stored by the students through *questions, conjectures, evidence for and against conjectures, plans, steps in plans, information and commentary.* In the shared workspace the students make links from each one of these components of the inquiry model.
Indeed, as mentioned in (Hietala et al. 1998) an important stage of learning (called dialogue) shapes and re-organises the material learned through discussions, mutual questioning and reflection in a social environment. However, the main problem lies in the fact that students need appropriate support in order to be assisted in the dialogue phase.
One solution to this problem is offered by (Barros et al. 1998) and (Edelson et al. 1996) through the use of a restricted set of pre-defined interaction types allowed between the learners. In the passive support introduced by (Barros et al. 1998) the interactions are task oriented and structured by the use of *proposals*, *contra-*

proposals, *questions* and *comments*. These collaborative dialogue acts, support the students in following a pattern of communication such that they are forced to justify their actions.
Field studies results with such systems indicate that supporting collaboration through structured and restricted dialogue acts lead to better results, both at University level (in the case of (Barros et al. 1998) and (Hietala 1998)) and school children (see (Baker & Lund 1996)).

2.4 Coordination Spaces

Finally, in order to support the concurrent execution of activities by the learners, some of these tools provide a coordination space. This coordination varies from tool to tool, which in general rely on "versions" and "voting" principles. The final result may pass through different versions demarcating different stages of the work (e.g. from the stage of "proposed" into the "final" stage (Barros et al. 1997)).

3. SOME RESULTS AND DISCUSSION

It is interesting to observe the convergence of the results presented by (Barros et al. 1998) and (Hietala 1998) with those found previously by (Baker & Lund 1996). A common theme is the provision of passive support to collaborative learning through the use of "structured" collaborative interactions. This is usually embedded in the interface in a way that forces the learners to follow a pattern of collaboration. However, the findings also suggest that such structuring is not enough to captivate the students that are unable to play active roles in collaborative tasks. Students may even avoid using these very structured tools, and prefer a more free style of interaction. Since the motivation factor is indeed important to obtain good results is there a need for the students to introduce their own "communication acts"? This question remains to be explored in the future.
On the other hand, (Hietala 1998) showed that the more positive results were achieved when the students where "obliged" to use the system. So, how can these tools motivate students that do not participate? In trying to find answers to such question it was suggested that the motivation factor can come from an "elected student", a "teacher", or some "computer based mediator". However, such a solution raises other questions such as what is the impact on the role of the teacher resulting from the use of computer based collaborative learning tools.

4. REFERENCES

Baker, M. & Lund. K. (1996) Flexibly structuring the interaction in a CSCL environment, in *European Conference on Artificial Intelligence in Education* (eds. P. Brna, A. Paiva & J. Self), Edicoes Colibri, ISBN 972-8288-37-9.

Barros, B., Rodriguez-Artacho, A. & Verdejo, F. (1998) Towards a Model of Collaborative Support for Distance Learners to Perform Joint Tasks, in *The Virtual Campus: Trends for Higher Education and Training*, (eds. F. Verdejo & G. Davies) Chapman & Hall (in this volume).

Canas, A., Ford, K., Hayes, P., Brennan J. & Reichherzer T.(1995) Knowledge Construction and Sharing in Quorum, in *Proceedings of the AIED'95*, (ed. J. Greer), AACE..

Dillenbourg, P., Baker, M., Blaye, A. & O'Malley, C. (1997) The evolution of research on collaborative learning, in *Collaborative Learning*, (ed. C. O'Malley) Springer Verlag, 1997.

Doyse, W. (1990) The development of individual competencies through social interaction, in Children helping children (eds. H.Foot, M.Morgan & R. Shute) J.Wiley & sons..

Edelson, D., Pea, R. & Gomez, L. (1996) The Collaboratory Notebook, *Communications of ACM* 39(4), April.

Hietala, P., Niemirepo, T. & Ovaska, S. (1998) Using the World Wide Web to promote educational discussion on university level courses, in *The Virtual Campus: Trends for Higher Education and Training*, (eds. F. Verdejo & G. Davies) Chapman & Hall (in this volume).

S.Teasley, S. & Rochelle, J. (1993) Constructing a Joint Problem Space: The Computer as a Tool for Sharing Knowledge, in *Computers as Cognitive Tools*, (ed. S. Lajoie & S. Derry), Lawrence Erlbaum Associates.

BIOGRAPHY

Ana Paiva is a Professor of Computer Science at IST, Technical University of Lisbon and a Research Fellow at INESC. She completed her PhD in 1996 in the University of Lancaster, UK, in the area of Learner Modelling for Interactive Learning Environments. Since then she has been working on Learner Modelling, Pedagogical Agents and Collaborative Learning. She participated in many international conferences and was one of the co-chairs of the 1996 European Conference on Artificial Intelligence in Education held in Lisbon.

Currently, she is co-ordinating several Computer Based Learning projects in collaboration with Universities, industry and schools. She also lectures on Computer Science undergraduate courses and is responsible for MSc courses on Computer Based Learning and Intelligent Agents.

Towards a model of Collaborative Support for Distance Learners to Perform Joint Tasks

B.Barros, M.Rodriguez-Artacho and F.Verdejo
UNED - Dep de Ingeniería Eléctrica, Electrónica y Control
Ciudad Universitaria s/n 28040 Madrid Spain
e-mail: bbarros, martacho, felisa {@ieec.uned.es}

Abstract

This paper describes the design and implementation of a prototype to support collaborative learning. It is part of a larger effort dealing with the study of mechanisms of cooperation and collaboration between distance learners while performing joint tasks involving complex interactions. The final goal of the project is to produce a conceptual model and a tailorable system for describing a variety of collaborative distance learning scenarios providing active group support. A first web-based prototype integrating private and shared workspaces has been implemented, and a testbed carried out with graduate students. The learning scenario and the collaborative facilities offered by the system are presented.

Keywords

Computer supported collaborative learning, Distance learning, Cooperative tools, Higher education, Coordination

The Virtual Campus F. Verdejo & G. Davies (Eds.)

1. INTRODUCTION

The shift from individual to collaborative learning is an emerging approach in recent learning research and experiments. Distance learning is one setting in particular that deserves more and more attention due to the spread of web-based facilities. The scenario may include: a) a group of students performing different kinds of cooperative learning activities such as discussion or problem-solving, using conventional or multimedia-based material; b) a group of teachers, organising, facilitating and supervising the cooperative learning; c) a group of authors creating courseware and sources of information; and d) a telecomputer environment supporting all these activities.

Collaborative learning is based on the idea that learning occurs when students have to explain, develop or justify their ideas to attain a shared goal. The variation on the underlying model of learning is from a classical information-processing and transmission oriented model to a more social-process orientation centered on promoting learning through constructive activities (doing) and interactions (communicating) in a meaningful context.

Distance collaborative learning can be shaped in different ways (Verdejo, Cerri 1994), a joint project is appealing for a range of scientific and engineering subjects. Proposals for computational group support differ in the type of structure and the degree of genericity they offer to users, ranging from general purpose tools for communication and shareworking to fully typified spaces with specific primitives and communication protocols related to the task at hand. To mention just a few of the current educational projects exploring this area, Edelson et al. (Edelson et al, 1996) offer a shared Notebook with a set of page types corresponding to a task model of scientific inquiry to be used for collaborative science learning. The page types include questions, conjectures, evidence for and against, information, commentary as wells as plans and their steps. Students can create instances of these pages and link them as their work progresses. A learner interface built upon their scientific inquiry model, suggest the next steps for a student to pursue. Wan et al. (Wan, Johnson 1994) report on CLARE, an environment supporting the task of learning to understand scientific literature. They define an explicit process model: summary, evaluation, comparison, argument and integration and provide specific representations and structure for each of these individual and group activities.

Our aim is to explore collaboration at a distance for a range of tasks involving complex interactions, and to study in which ways an active computer-based support could benefit the learning process. Although we do not exclude interaction in real time, we focus on asynchronous interactions because this is the preferred mode for real distance learning students. They usually have tight time constraints making it difficult to establish common real time slots for groupworking.

2. THE PROJECT AIM AND BACKGROUND

This paper describes the design and experimentation of a prototype to support collaborative learning. It is part of a larger effort[1] dealing with the study of mechanisms of cooperation and collaboration between distance learners while performing a joint task. The final goal of the project is to produce a conceptual model for describing a variety of collaborative distance learning scenarios based on active support. A tailorable system built on this model, will provide functionality to generate an adapted computational environment to perform personal and shared activities for specific learning purposes. The project methodology includes iterative steps of prototype design, user experimentation and evaluation. Our approach benefits from a diversity of sources, mainly linked to three research streams (1) learning as a process of social knowledge construction (Scardamalia, Bereiter 1993), where students could work cooperatively in a context and with problems relevant to real practice (Schank, Kass 1996) (2) activity and conversational models from CSCW, proposed and implemented for teamwork in professional environments (De Cindio et al 1988) (Winograd, Flores 1986) (Ellis et al 1991) (Manole, Fry 1992) (Collis, 1994) and (3) distributed cognition theories (Coelho 1996) to model expertise and behaviour of a group of interacting autonomous agents to execute a task.

In this paper we will describe a first prototype and a preliminary testbed set up in our University. The next section defines the type of learning situations we have considered. In section four, the main features of the current prototype are outlined. We will conclude with a summary of current and planned experimental work.

3. THE LEARNING SITUATION

We will characterize the situation as a set of small (2 to 4) groups of graduate students, geographically distributed, carrying out together a learning task in a period of time. A computer environment providing a variety of resources and tools, some of them shared, offers to each group of students support to carry out the learning activities in collaboration. Teachers are also available though their intervention is primarily to give response to explicit learner's requests and to detect deadlocks in groups. At the moment their main role is to prepare the learning tasks and to observe and analyze the whole process, in order to give feedback to designers for further development and experimentation.

We distinguish two learning tasks, one content-oriented, related to a knowledge domain, the other one related to the ability to work cooperatively, including skills such as being able to propose, explain and discuss ideas with co-workers through

---

[1]The project includes a Spanish-Portuguese collaboration. Participants in the project are : B.Barros, A. Garcia Serrano, M. Rodriguez, and F. Verdejo from Spain. H. Coelho and A. Paiva from Portugal. Users are graduate and Ph.D students belonging to two Portuguese Universities and two Spanish Universities.

electronic tools, to negotiate and manage a plan to achieve a task, to establish and follow a common schedule to reach a goal in due time.

The learning situation involves personal and joint work; for the first experiment, students have to read and understand a collection of papers and elaborate a synthesis of the main ideas. It is recommended to students that they should organize their work into two main phases, a first phase centred on reading and understanding the material individually, a second one to elaborate a paper in collaboration with their peers. In further experiments a third phase would be added: comparing and evaluating their results with others' group work.

For the first phase, defined mainly as personal work, communication is also encouraged. Questions, doubts, clarification, further information can be interchanged within the student group to facilitate to each other a better understanding of the material.

In the second phase students have to use their understanding to elaborate a synthesis of the papers. Their final product, a document in this case, has to be written according to the topic contents and structure specified by the teacher. They can create the essay in an incremental way, section by section. For each section they can open a period of discussion, interchanging and refining proposals, and once they arrive at an agreement about a written version for that section, the text is automatically integrated into the document.

The prototype offers to each student a private workspace and an agenda and, to each group two interlinked but separated shared spaces: the working space and the communication space. Each space provides different functions.

The main events of the learners' interactions are recorded by the system. In this way tutors can analyze not only the final results obtained by the students but also the processes carried out by the group. For the experimentation phase this information is crucial, a main goal of the project is to determine, describe and evaluate how the cooperation works and in which way it can be facilitated or improved. What to gather and the level of abstraction required representing events and their links in order to perform learning task analysis is still an open matter. Too much fine grained information can cause an overflow of data, difficult to handle without automatic filtering techniques. At this point we have decided to include in the prototype three types of facilities:

> (1) The explicit notification (performed automatically by the system on each personal agenda) of new contributions happening within each group. This warning is not only useful for learners, to be aware of the activity going on within its group, but also helps teachers to have a quick overview of the task evolution

A shared summary of the group activity to accomplish their work in form of:

> (2) an automatically structured index of the set of contributions, labelled with author' s names

(3) an automatically updated index of the semi-structured set of messages interchanged by the members of the group while performing the learning task.

4. THE SYSTEM PROTOTYPE

We have implemented a first web-based prototype to support distance learning students to elaborate a synthesis paper through a structured coedition process. The system supports two kind of users/roles: students to perform joint activities related to a learning task and teachers to prepare the task and to follow and analyze the students' activities and results. In this paper we will present the prototype services for the students.

The prototype has been designed taking into account four claims (1) collaboration takes the form of a structured discussion between peers, without explicit moderator role. A set of conversational primitives allows the group to organize their joint work process. However (2) coordination between students (and teachers) should be done using flexible but explicit mechanisms to clearly state responsibilities and commitments. (3) The task for each student group is to produce a common document sharing a common workspace. (4) All the information generated in the process should be accessible, extractable and visualized from a variety of viewpoints, such as group related, time related, student related, task related.

Our aim is to offer a system supporting the exchange of information, helping to co-ordinate the discussion and letting the group work at its ownpace, to generate a common essay. To achieve these objectives, we have two separate but interlinked shared spaces: the coedition space and the coordination space. Nevertheless the prototype offers also in an integrated way a private, individual workspace, to each student.

4.1. Individual Workspaces

Two options of the bar menu provide access to private areas: "individual work" offers to users a kind of personal notebook while "agenda" allows the representation and management of information about activities and commitments.

Figure 1 shows the screen when the option individual work has been selected by one of the students participating in the testbed.

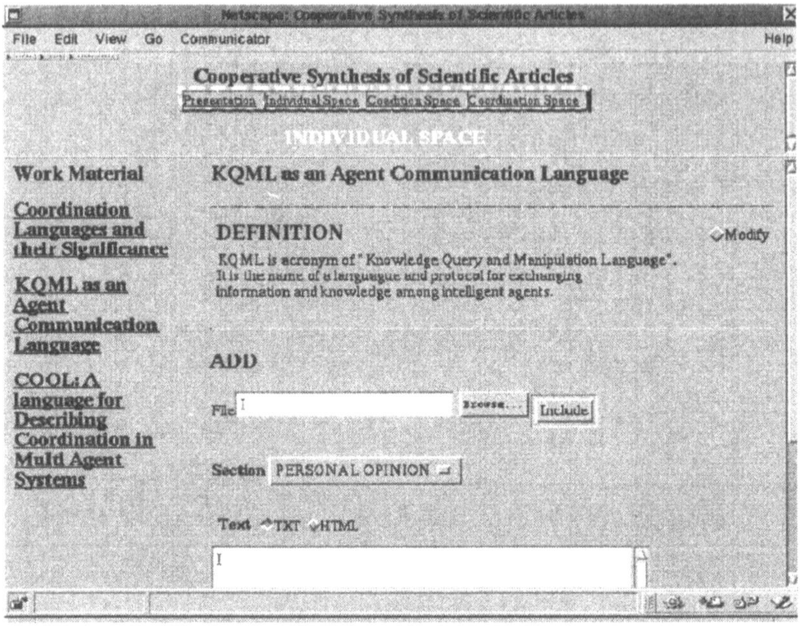

Figure 1 Individual Workspace

On the left part appears the list of papers assigned to its group. During the personal phase, he has to read them and in this case to write for each paper a brief summary, following some key points provided by the teacher. The list of titles works as an index. Clicking on one of the titles the pages of the notebook corresponding to the paper summary become available on the upper right part of the screen. The pages are empty at the beginning of the task and can be created by the student in an incremental way using a standard set of editing operations. Pages of the notebook can either be forms (predefined by the teacher) or have free format.

4.2. Shared Workspaces

Collaboration is required for carrying out a joint task, the prototype provides two options of the bar menu for such purpose: collaborative synthesis and coordination. Both include shared spaces belonging to each working group, we call them working space and coordination space respectively. The last one includes a Bulletin Board service, allowing the posting of messages for the group.

The working space consists of three related subspaces: a coedition space for the draft version been currently discussed by the group, a final version space for storing portions of the synthesis document considered as finished parts by common agreement, and a history space to store other previous draft versions, although discarded at some time, they are nevertheless available for an eventual reconsideration.

4.2.1. WorkSpaces components

The production of an essay can follow a variety of approaches, ranging from a well established plan of work to a completely unstructured process. An example of the former could be to organize the task in form of subtasks like: global brain storming to fix key ideas, writing a schema, develop the content for each section, revision and refinement of the text, etc. When this same task has to be done collaboratively, the process become more complex because not only the approach and the task management have to be agreed and successfully accomplished by the members of the group, but also each substask can be matter of argument and negotiation.

Let us assume that the learning task starts from a given schema, provided by the teacher in this case, and students should focus on the writing of the content of each section. We can consider this phase as a coediting task, where the students should participate in writing their own proposals, discussing the peer proposals, commenting, mutually asking questions and giving answers until this process converges to a written text satisfactory to the group.

A way of providing some structure to organize automatically the contributions and arguments generated during the writing discussion is to type each student contribution, so as to link and thread a set of related interchanges in the Coedition Space. We propose coedition as a structured discussion process where group members interact with each other to create a content section by means of the following types of *contributions*:

- Proposal: the first contribution
- Contraproposal: alternative text for an existing proposal. It is another original proposal or made by extending an existing proposal
- Question: someone asks for something related to an annotation.
- Comment: text for commenting an existing annotation.
- Clarification: text for answering a question or for extending the information on an existing annotation
- Agreement: annotation where the user declares his agreement with another annotation

4.2.2. The structure of the co-edition space

As stated before the Coedition process has two phases for every section, namely construction and agreement. During the former, the group members propose ideas or comments, they write, refine and polish a text. The first annotation becomes a proposal. This proposal can be made by any member of the group. Once a proposal is there, students can make contributions, contraproposals, questions, comment or clarifications. New contributions can be linked to these, and so, a tree named *coedition process scheme* is automatically generated. This scheme is a representation of the group dynamic.

In figure 2, we can see a snapshot of the Coedition Space during the discussion phase.

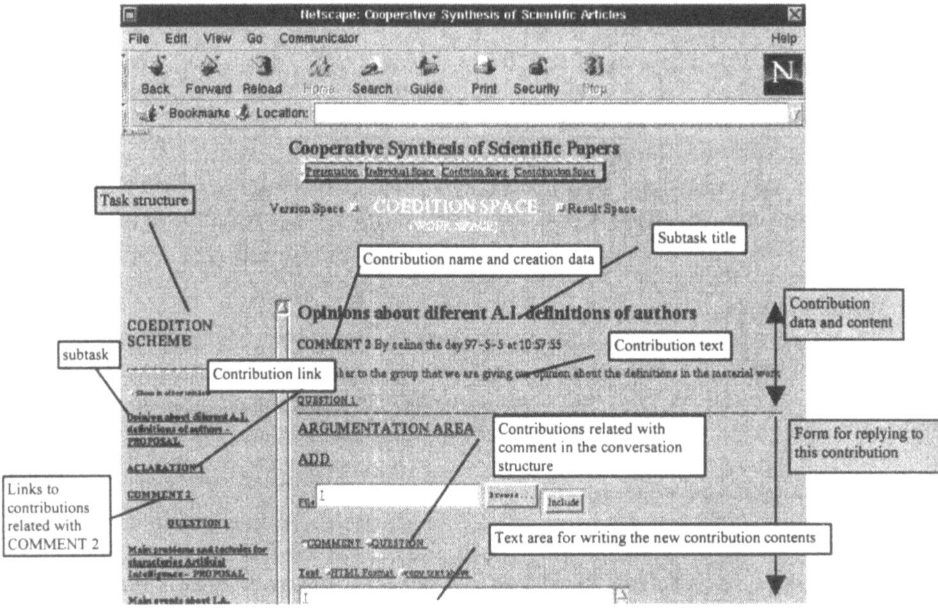

Figure 2 Coedition Space

On the left part the coedition process scheme is shown. It contains part of the content, and on the right part, - after clicking on one of the contribution names - the whole content for this contribution. At the top of the right part there is the annotation information, below the names of contributions related to it, and below, a form where the student can write a new contribution if he wishes.

While working on the coedition process, an image of the current state of the Coedition Space can be saved in the Version Space. Figure 3, shows the Version Space interface appearing when this option is clicked on the bar menu.

On the left, the available operations in this workspace and the list of existing versions appear. The user can see a complete old version contents by clicking on its name.

The following Version Space operations allow for the interchange of information between both spaces:

- STORE: primitive that stores the current state of the Coedition Space as a new version in the Version Space. The result is a new version
- BACK primitives for restoring a version in Version Space to the Coedition Space

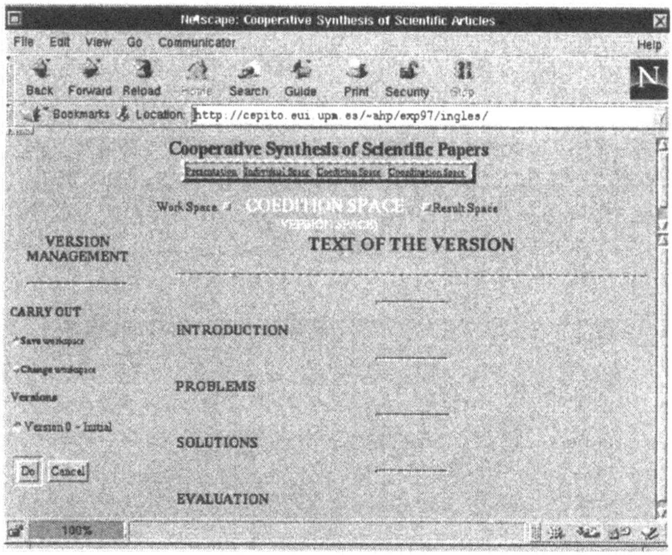

Figure 3 Version Space

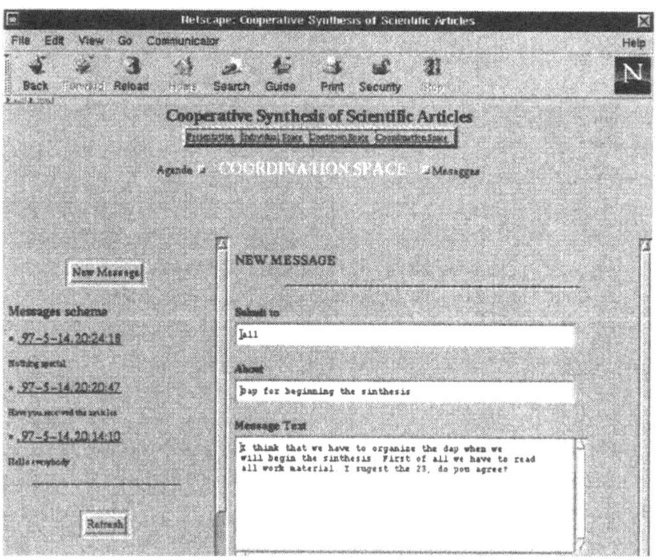

Figure 4 Notice Board Space

4.2.3 The Coordination Space

The coordination space includes a Notice Board Space and an agenda.

- The Notice-Board Space

Here the group members can post messages about their plans, comments about the work, as well as general management affairs. Figure 4 shows the Notice-Board Space. On the left, there is a list of messages ordered by data. If the user clicks on one message title, the whole message contents will be displayed on the right side: title, content, author, and sending data.

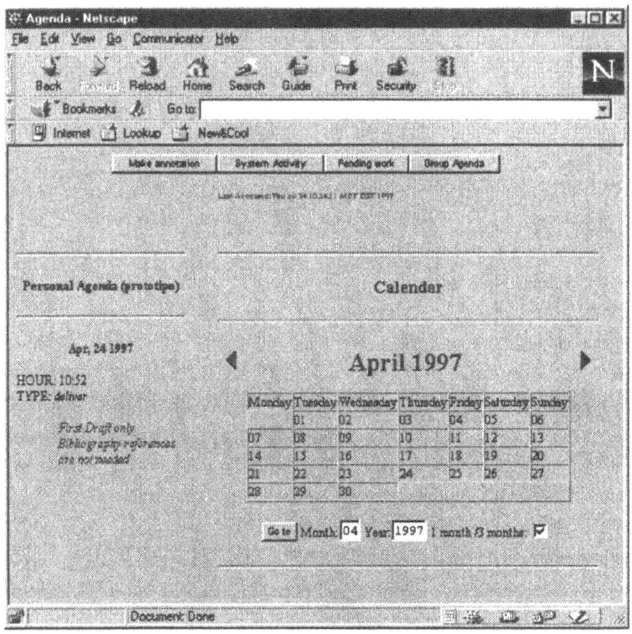

Figure 5 Student Agenda

- Agenda

The Agenda is a tool integrated within the Coordination Workspace. As mentioned in previous sections, the agenda organizes and updates information relative to the development of the joint task.

During this process of development, the user has to plan his individual and group activities, annotate some information, arrange deadlines with others members of the group, etc. Additionally, when a user logs onto the system, it is useful to know what have been the last activities performed by the other members of the group and which are the new contributions to the task at hand.

Thus, it becomes necessary to offer a way to plan both individual and group work by means of a tool allowing the user to (a) schedule the activities involved in performing a given task, whether they are part of a personal scheduling, or cooperative activities, and (b) trace the development of the task and the activity of the members of the group in order not only to inform students but also to facilitate the subsequent analysis of the process by the teacher.

Figure 5 shows a snapshot of a student agenda, obtained by clicking the option *agenda* in the coordination space window. The upper part contains a menu bar, with four options: make annotation, system activity, pending mark and group agenda. The bottom right part visualizes the calendar by months. Clicking on a day, the appointments of the personal agenda for the selected day are shown on the left side.

Both personal and group annotations in the agenda are typed in order to classify and distinguish the different kind of information that a user may need to manage for scheduling his personal and group work. Selecting the *make annotation* option of the menu bar opens a window allowing the creation of a personal annotation as shown in figure 6.

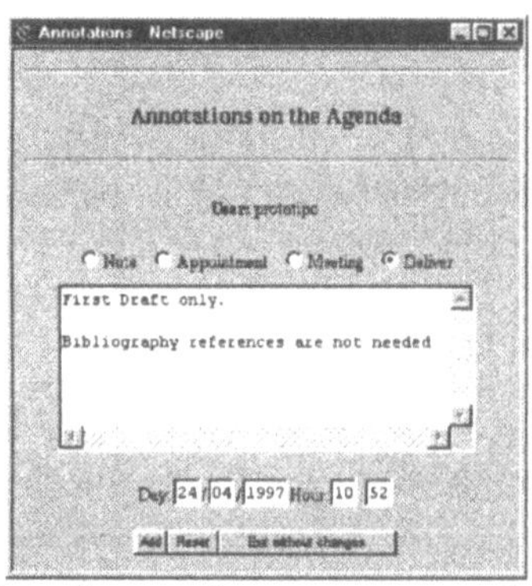

Figure 6. Window for creating a new annotation in the agenda

The prototype considers four types of agenda annotations :

- NOTE : Information to remember. Acts as a "post-it" note.
- APPOINTMENT: Two or more members decide that the group or some of its members have to perform a synchronous activity
- MEETING: There is a synchronous meeting to discuss the development of the task
- DELIVER: There is deadline to deliver a given work.

The agenda is updated in two manners, by the user whenever he makes annotations in his personal agenda, and by the system, that, in addition, makes annotations automatically inherited from the group agenda.

The types of contributions can be enriched according to the nature of the joint task. The choice of these four types is however a first step in distinguishing different types of information that a user may need to annotate, but at the same time, this set can be modified as the analysis of the system activity reflects that a more or less extensive set of types is needed. Furthermore, it becomes important to notice that very structured and enriched information involves also more complexity to the interface and this can lead to laziness in the use of the system as the user can get tired of clicking and popping too many buttons or menus.

As mentioned before, the system also offers to the user a list of the new contributions made by the other partners since his last login (system activity option on the bar menu in figure 5). This additional feature of the agenda is useful for the student as it allows him to know the progress of the joint task, and also for the supervisor as it constitutes interesting information about the behaviour of the group members.

In short, the agenda offers a high perspective of the performed task, much better than a simple scheduler of the user work. This constitutes a first step in the organization of a structured scheduling of the development of a joint task. Much more work has to be done in this aspect in order to anticipate some behaviour patterns allowing the system to offer active support to dynamize the group.

5. FUTURE WORK

First sets of experiences have been organized in April-May 97. Three groups of PhD students have been working together to prepare an essay on A.I. topics. Each group (two to three students located in different towns) used the system for three weeks. The aim of this first pre-test was to check the accessibility and reliability of the prototype, as well as the acceptability from the students. This pre-test has been successful and next term a wider set of experiences will be carried out. The experiences will involve PhD students and tutors in a similar scenario but in three different universities. We expect more diversity in this trial, both from students and tutors. After this second technical pre-test the experimental phase will consist of a series of evaluation experiences, focusing on the analysis of the collaboration process. The results of the educational investigation will be discussed and their interpretation will help to enhance the design of the final version of the software. Our plan is to have the system operative for general use at the UNED server.

6. ACKNOWLEDGEMENTS

This work has been partially funded by the *Ministerio de Educación y Cultura* through *Acción Integrada* HP97-0050 and by CICYT (*Comisión Interministerial de Ciencia y Tecnología*), Spain, project number TEL97-0328-C02-01.

7. REFERENCES

Coelho, H. (1996) Distributed coginition. Panel on Proceedings of EUROAIED.

Collis B. (1994) Collaborative learning and CSCW: research perspectives for interworked educational environments, in *Lessons from learning*. (ed. R.Lewis and P.Mendelsohsn), North-Holland. 1994.

De Cindio, F., Simone C. Vassallo and R. Zanaboni, A. (1998) CHAOS: a knowledge based system for conversing inside office, in *IFIP tc8/WG 8.4 Int Workshop on Office Knowledge: representation, management and utilization*. (ed. W. lamersdorf), North-Holland 1988.

Edelson,D.C., Pea R.D. and Gomez L.M. (1996) The collaboratory Notebook. *Communications of the ACM*, **39**, No 4, 32-33.

Ellis, C.A., Gibbs, S.J.and Rein, G.L. (1991) Groupware: some issues and experiences. *Communications of the ACM*, **34**, No. 1, 38-58.

Malone, T.W. and Fry,C. (1992) Experiments with OVAL: a radically tailorable tool for cooperative work, in *CSCW 92 Proceedings*. (ed. M.Mantei, R.Baeker), 289-297.

Scardamalia M., Bereiter C. (1993) Technologies for knowledge-Building discourse. *Communications ACM*, **36**, No. 5, 37-41 .

Schank R.C. and Kass, A.(1996) A goal-based Scenario for High School Students. *Communications of the ACM*, **39**, No 4, 28-29.

Verdejo, M.F. (1996) Interaction and collaboration in Distance Learning through computer mediated technologies. In *Advanced Educational Technology: Research Issues and Future Potential*. (ed. T.Liao). Computer and System Sciences, **145**, Springer-Verlag , 77-88.

Winograd, T. (1986) Flores F. *Understanding computers and cognition: a new foundation for design*. Norwood Ablex.

Wan D. and Johnson P. (1994) Experiences with CLARE: a computer-supported collaborative learning environment. *Int. J. Human-Computer Studies*, **41**, No. 6, 851-879.

8. BIOGRAPHIES

Beatriz Barros received her Computer Science degree in 1994 at Technical University of Madrid, and now she is working for her Ph.D. in Artificial Intelligence. She is Assistant Professor at UNED since 1996. Her research interest areas are computer supported cooperative systems, collaborative learning and distance education.

Miguel Rodríguez-Artacho is Assistant Professor at the Universidad Nacional de Educaci6n a Distancia. He received his Computer Science Engineer Degree from the Technical University of Madrid in 1994.Now he is working in his Master of Science Degree on Telecommunication and Network Systems and also in his Ph. D. about architectures for distance learning environments.

M.Felisa Verdejo is Professor of Computer Science at the Universidad Nacional de Educacion a Distancia, UNED, since 1991. She received a 3rd-cycle Thesis in Computing Science from the University Pierre et Marie Curie (Paris, Francia) in 1976, and a Ph.D in Sciences at the Universidad Complutense (Madrid, Spain) in 1981. She was formely professor at the Universities of El Pais Vasco (San Sebastian, Spain) and Politécnica de Cataluña (Barcelona, Spain). Her main research interests are in the areas of Natural Language Processing, and Interactive Systems to support human learning. Major national and international projects she has been involved related to the last topic are: CAPRA an intelligent tutoring system for novice programming , EPOS, developing european learning through technological advance, TOSKA, tools and methods for knowledge based authoring ESCAD, a computer environment to support cooperative work for distance learning activities, and STEED, telematics support for learning at a distance. She is co-editor of the book *Collaborative dialogue technologies in distance learning.* (Vol 133, Nato ASI Series, Springer-Verlag 1994) and has published several papers on these subjects.

Using the World Wide Web to promote educational discussion on university level courses

P. Hietala, T. Niemirepo and S. Ovaska
University of Tampere, Department of Computer Science
P.O. Box 607, FIN-33101 Tampere, FINLAND
e-mail: {ph, tkn, ov}@cs.uta.fi

Abstract

In this paper we describe our efforts in promoting educational discussion and collaborative work on university level courses. This research has been carried out in a research project entitled "Conferencing on the Web for Group Learning" (CoWoGLe project). The goal of the project is to augment the participation in and quality of educational discussion by using Web-based computer conferencing. We also aim at producing systems easily tailorable for use in various course settings, to suit different learning and teaching approaches. In this paper we report on our first efforts in this direction, by outlining the theoretical background of our work and the two prototype systems designed and implemented in the project. We provide empirical data describing the use of our systems on four courses with more than 200 students. We also indicate how our systems have evolved during the field experiments and end with a few suggestions for further work.

Keywords

Distributed learning system, Tools for distance education, Web-based conferencing systems

The Virtual Campus F. Verdejo & G. Davies (Eds.)

1. INTRODUCTION

The problems in university level higher education are well known. First, the ratio of students per teacher is growing, for both on-campus students and those studying at distance while working. Secondly, traditional methods of teaching (such as lectures) have been heavily criticized as old-fashioned and non-efficient from the point of view of modern educational theory. The larger number of students makes it difficult to abandon the traditional approaches, though. Evidently, the opportunities for fruitful discussion between the teacher and the student are diminishing (Mayes & Neilson, 1995). Yet, as Laurillard (1993) has pointed out, dialogue lies at the heart of the educational experience, and has been an essential part of higher education in the past.

Dialogue, not only with teachers, but also with peer learners, is very important in learning, thus collaborative learning should have a prominent role in higher education. Any university should prepare its students for teamwork situations common in the workplaces of today, by providing team and project work opportunities. Typically, these opportunities are associated with lab work (as in computer science), but even lectures could be alternatively organized as collaborative learning events (Yerion & Rinehart, 1995). Still, the demand for more discussion, collaboration and group work in higher education may cause problems for those students who do not fit the 8 to 4 university day, e.g., extension or graduate students, or students working outside the university.

The use of telecommunications seems one promising solution to the problems outlined above. In fact, textual Computer Mediated Communication (CMC) and computer conferences have already been used as means of organising group discussions and distance education (Turoff, 1991). There are many commercial systems available today, but many of these systems are too expensive for schools or universities and some are also somewhat difficult to learn to use (Klemm & Snell, 1994).

Recently, the World Wide Web has been marketed as the panacea for most of the problems in education, also for those in higher education. Most uses of the Web so far, however, concentrate on how to organize and present information content on the Web pages or how to find the latest material created by others. For our purposes, we would like to explore more the use of the Web to support educational discussion. Some researchers (Reeves, 1997) even suggest that Web-based tools for groupwork and collaboration are potentially the most powerful factors of the Web in promoting learning. Already tens of Web-based discussion forums have been developed (Woolley, 1997). However, not many are in use in higher education on a regular basis and even fewer have been analyzed or evaluated.

In order to study these issues we have implemented experimental discussion forums with varying support for structured discussion, and introduced them in several courses in our department (four courses with more than 200 students). In this paper we focus on the field experiments we have conducted so far, and report mainly on qualitative findings concerning the discussion forum used in each case. We also indicate how these systems have evolved during the experimentation period and end with a few suggestions for further work.

2. RELATED WORK AND BACKGROUND

Mayes and Neilson (1995) describe learning as a cycle of stages leading to the growth of understanding. In this model learning starts with conceptualisation where the exposition of material to be learned is important. Most educational programmes (*primary courseware*) are concentrating on this aspect. Although there is a shift from this kind of instructivist learning, in the direction of providing exploratory and constructivist environments, programmes of the latter kind (*secondary courseware*) are not very common. Finally, the third stage of learning (called dialogue) shapes and re-organizes the material learned through discussion, mutual questioning and reflection in a social environment (the learner together with peers and the teacher). In this paper our goal is to consider especially those educational environments assisting the dialogue stage of learning (*tertiary courseware*). Furthermore, how to assist more than one of these three stages in one learning environment emerges as an important research question.

For there are many possibilities the assisting the dialogue as defined above. On the one hand, the more expensive groupware systems (e.g., Lotus Learning Space™) integrate all the three stages presented above but may not offer much scaffolding for the third stage. At the other end, standard network tools, such as e-mail, bulletin boards, and news groups are useful in enhancing discourse. However, there are also problems (Klemm & Snell, 1996): for example, in many mailing systems sequencing and structuring is non-existent, all messages are intermingled, switching between private and public is not easy, and lacks the media of graphics and photos. Bulletin boards (news groups) are more user friendly than e-mail and have some organization of content but there are problems with poor graphics, linking to older messages, and other means of supporting dialogue.

One problem with standard network tools is that their support typically concerns only the social aspects of communication. We believe that both cognitive and social perspectives should be scaffolded in the educational use of computer mediated communication. By the cognitive aspects we mean that the systems should provide some structure that scaffolds or guides the discussants. Structured discussion can be established, e.g. by requesting that the students indicate the type of their messages, or the source from where they have obtained their arguments. The support for cognitive processes can be domain dependent or independent. One source that can build the basis for the design of domain independent support are the theories of problem solving and critical thinking (Newman et al., 1995; Mason, 1991). After all, the abilities of critical thinking, evidently, are an integral part of the "pedagogical residue" that our students should carry with them when leaving the university.

Of the similar approaches to support argument and group work we can mention e.g. systems like CSILE (Scardamalia & Bereiter, 1993), or The Collaborative Notebook in the CoVis project (O'Neill et al., 1995), but many of them are for pre-university levels and some basically LAN solutions. As for the university level solutions, we can mention e.g. WebCamile (Turns et al., 1995), FORUM (Klemm & Snell, 1996) and the work of Verdejo et al. (1996). Most of these are more oriented towards supporting collaborative design and problem-solving than just conferencing. However, not much empirical evidence has yet been published on the use of these systems.

An interesting idea is to save the discussion as a knowledge base for later student inspection (e.g. to alleviate next year's students familiarization with systems and topics of the course). The Axis system (Chaplin, 1996) has this kind of knowledge base incorporated. A related project is AnswerWeb (Mayes & Neilson, 1995), an attempt to accumulate a knowledge base of question-answer pairs connected to simulations of engineering phenomena. In this kind of approach locating relevant information is of utmost importance (even if questions with no earlier answers are routed to lecturers). It would be very interesting to have empirical evaluation studies of this approach.

3. THE COWOGLE PROJECT AT THE UNIVERSITY OF TAMPERE

The CoWoGLe (Conferencing on the Web for Group Learning) project has set out to study existing (Web-based) computer-conferencing systems, build lightweight conferencing systems that can be used with ordinary Web browsers, and experiment on the conferencing systems as part of course work. Our main motivation is pragmatic: we want to collect experience on different ways of integrating a computer-conferencing forum as part of course work, and learn about the user requirements of students and teachers using the software. As we already have interest in both CSCL and CSCW at our department this seemed a fruitful starting position for a project (of the need of research synergy for these two research communities see Collis (1994)).

In our experiments we have varied several aspects of the use: course goals and assignments, the properties of our conferencing systems and means of adding structure to the discussion. As the settings vary a lot from course to course, we do not aim at providing any conclusions or generalizable results at this point. Instead, we hope to elaborate on our ideas and eventually develop good strategies for integration of the conferencing software meaningfully into course arrangements for the benefit of both learners and teachers.

Course assignments

In some courses the use of the computer-conferencing software has been mandatory to a certain extent (number of messages sent), while in other courses the usage has been voluntary. We have experimented with the length of the time period devoted to commenting so that in some cases the students have had two weeks of time to work out their comments in the system, in some cases only a couple of days. The assignments have been different in all courses ranging from broad discussion topics to more group work oriented problem solving exercises. Also voting tasks have been used. In some courses we have restricted the length of the individual postings and the student's possibilities to create new discussion topics. The conferencing has so far been only one part of the courses, we have not yet tried to build a course based entirely on the Web.

Adding structure to discussions
As we wish to promote meaningful and structured discussion, we have also varied several aspects of the conferencing systems. One way of adding structure to the discussion is to give a set of annotation types for the user to select from before (or after) writing his/her annotation. The discussion topics have been specified together with a set of annotation types. Thus the number and nature of annotation types may vary even between topics in the same discussion forum. Another way of adding structure is to ask the user to specify the source of the annotation, for instance, lectures, other literature, or a personal opinion.

Versions of the conferencing systems
The CoWoGLe project has so far developed two versions of a computer-conferencing system: 3Wcomments and Dyn3W. The prototypes differ mainly in their user interface: 3Wcomments does not use frames while Dyn3W does, and Dyn3W uses folders to encapsulate branches of the annotation tree while in 3Wcomments the leaves are shown all the time. Both systems keep track of the poster's and reader's identity. Also, both systems allow anonymous annotations where the poster's identity is not revealed to other readers but only to the teacher. We have also built tools for the teacher to analyse and keep track of the activity of the students.

The development of the systems is ongoing, and sometimes even in the middle of a course we have switched to a new version or to the other conferencing system. This enables us to learn about user reactions to analyse the usability of the system. The system versions are always tailored to suit the course at hand.

Next we outline briefly the two systems implemented at the University of Tampere. Both prototype systems are implemented using CGI programming in standard Web browsers.

3.1 3Wcomments

The 3Wcomments system has a standard Web interface where new pages are retrieved after clicking hotwords or buttons on a page. Each topic in 3Wcomments (see Figure 1) has a title, a short description with perhaps a link to an interesting web-page, and information about the author of the topic and date. In this paper we will use the word "annotation" for all user contributions (sometimes in the literature also called comments, notes, or messages). A button for adding an annotation to the topic is located under the topic, and the annotation is written into a form. The type of the annotation is chosen after the annotation text has been written, and it may also be left empty. Each individual annotation in the annotation tree may be commented in the same way: clicking on the title of the annotation shows the text of it, and associated is a button for adding an annotation. The underlined author names are mailto-links for individual feedback.

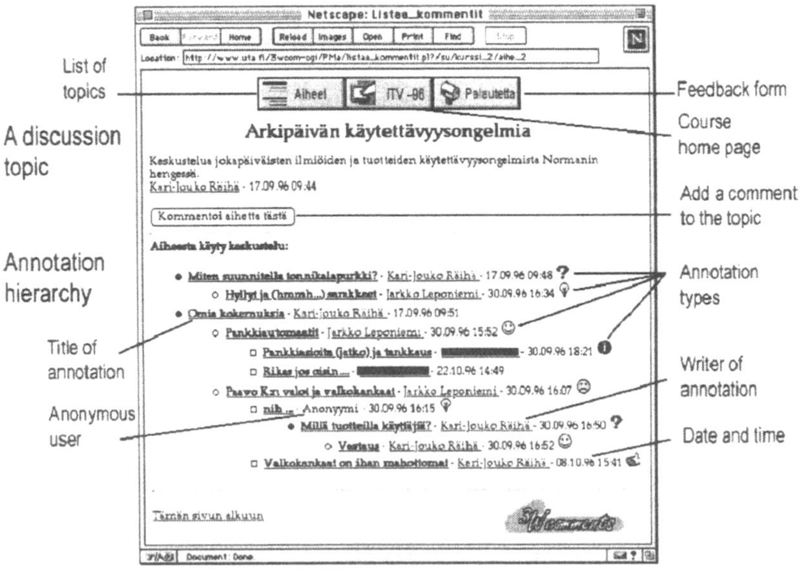

Figure 1. A discussion tree in 3Wcomments.

3.2 Dyn3W

The Dyn3W system utilizes frames to divide the interface into different parts in such a way that is supposed to help the user to better perceive and participate in the discussion. The frames make it possible to show the annotation hierarchy in one frame while the selected annotation can be read in another frame (see Figure 2). When adding an annotation, the frame on the right side is split into two parts. The frame for writing the annotation is located at the bottom of the right side. The top right hand side frame can be used for reading the other annotations as well as previewing one's own annotation before saving it.

Dyn3W tries to help the user to clarify his/her argumentation by forcing him/her to select the type of the annotation before he/she can write it. For the same reason, the user has in some Dyn3W versions to determine the source for his/her argument before the annotation is saved. When adding a topic one must define the title, the text, the annotation and source types and optionally an http-link to some essential source. The topic can be defined to be open to everyone or for the named participants only. For the annotation one must define the type of the annotation and the source of the argument the title, the text and optionally an http-link. Before the annotation is saved the system checks the compulsory parts and gives an error message if something is missing. Only after the annotation is in order it is saved. The annotation can not be changed afterwards but the user may cancel it before it is saved.

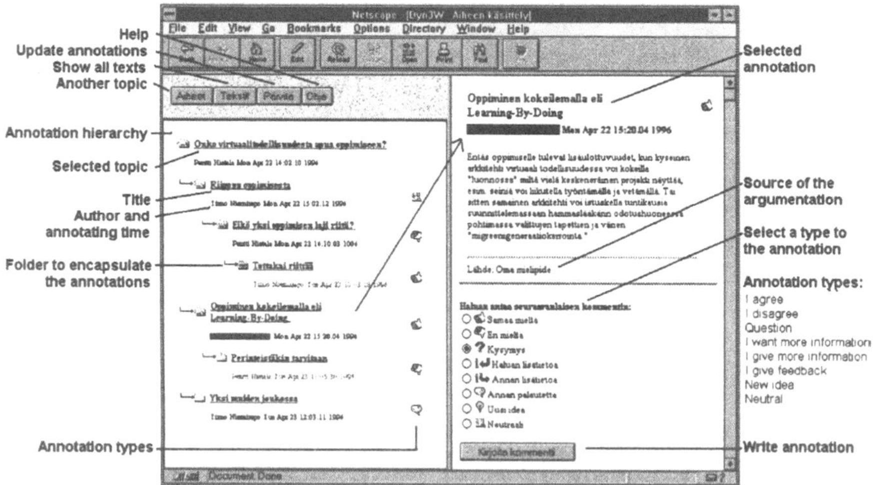

Figure 2. Working with a selected topic in Dyn3W.

4. FIELD EXPERIMENTS WITH THE SYSTEMS

In the academic year 1996-97, the systems described in the previous chapter were in use at our department on four courses (and a seminar, which is not reported here). The goals for the system use varied from course to course. Two courses (see Table 1) utilized the discussion forum to support free discussion, while the other two had more obligatory assignments to be worked on with the system.

Because the courses were given by the Department of Computer Science, most of the students were majoring in computer science or mathematics. However, many of the students participating were non-science undergraduates, e.g., from education, psychology, literature or information science. None of the courses is mandatory to the participating students, except the Computer Aided Instruction course for those mathematics students majoring to become teachers in mathematics.

Course	*Course topic*	*Main goal for conferencing system use*	*How conferencing systems were used*	*Students*
HCI Fall 96	Human Computer Interaction	Free discussion, mainly on interface issues	voluntary	2nd year, mainly Comp. Sci.
Groupware Spring 97	Groupware and CSCW Systems	Exploration of various groupware systems	voluntary for credits	3rd or 4th year, mainly Comp. Sci.
CAI Fall 96	Computer-Aided Instruction	Discussion on CAI topics	obligatory (5 comments)	extension students
CAI Spring 97	Computer-Aided Instruction	Structured work in small groups, after which public discussion on results of small group work	obligatory (1 own suggestion) plus credit from extra use	1st or 2nd year, mainly Comp. Sci. Also various non-science students

Table 1 Courses in a nutshell

Table 2 presents an overview of the systems used in each course. In the following chapters these courses are elaborated on together with our preliminary findings. The analysis of the four courses varies because the corpus of data collected varied from course to course. In this paper we report mainly on issues concerning the usability of the systems and on the support for argumentation and annotation. A more thorough analysis of the collaboration, including content analysis of the annotations, will follow in a later paper.

Course, semester	*Systems used*	*Number of students*	*Styles of conferencing*	*Possibility to create own topics*	*Private/ public discussion space*
HCI Fall 96	3Wcomments Dyn3W	83	- annotating - voting	Yes	- public
Groupware Spring 97	Dyn3W	40	- annotating - voting	yes	- public
CAI Fall 96	Dyn3W	21	- annotating	no	- public
CAI Spring 97	Dyn3W	76	- annotating - working in small groups - voting	restricted	- private - public

Table 2 Systems in use on the four courses

4.1 HCI Fall 1996 with 3Wcomments and Dyn3W

Background and goals
Our hypothesis was that the discussion forum could be useful in promoting discussion on topics introduced in the lectures. The discussion forum could also be used for questions and guidance about the large Web-based development assignment the course included. The assignment was rarely discussed during the lectures. The students (83) were introduced to both of our prototype conferencing systems in order to provoke discussion on the interface issues.

Usability
The first system in use was 3Wcomments, and in November (after seven weeks of use) the contents of the still valid discussion topics were moved to Dyn3W. The new forum increased the number of comments written about the system features.

The frames received most negative feedback. Three frames on a small screen made scrolling a necessity, and especially the space reserved for writing one's own annotations was considered too small. Opinions concerning positive aspects were given too: the frames enabled staying on the same screen while reading the annotations, since only one frame was updated at a time.

Folders in Dyn3W were liked by most students, since they allow some branches of the annotation tree to be encapsulated and thus make the tree smaller. The issue of obligatory selection of an annotation type in Dyn3W was brought up only in one negatively toned comment.

Scaffolding argumentation and annotation
Our expectations about promoting discussion in 3Wcomments and Dyn3W were not met. The discussion topics were set by the lecturer about issues related to the lectures, but they did not receive more than a couple of student annotations. The students raised five topics themselves, and these topics dealt with different aspects of the assignment. We tried several means of promoting the use of the discussion forum, for instance by setting up a topic of extra exercise groups with enrolment as annotations in the discussion forum. Also a poll was organised at the end of the course using Dyn3W. The students were asked to vote on the best Web service developed in the course. To our surprise, at this late stage still some students logged on the conferencing system for the first time. Apparently the poll task was motivating for the students, and we received about 20 votes; but many more students read the voting task options in Dyn3W.

A minority (39 students, 47 %) of the 83 students attending the course were somehow active (by voting, enrolling, etc.) in the new forum. If we exclude the discussion promoting tasks, an annotation was written by 14 students, six of which contributed only anonymously. Anonymity was felt to be an important feature of the system also by the six students who filled in a questionnaire presented them in Dyn3W.

The experiences we had on the HCI course brought clearly forward the need to motivate students to participate in a public discussion. The objectives of the shared discussion forum were not presented to the students in a manner promoting shared benefit; instead, the forum was mainly used for public administrative announcements and detailed questions about the difficulties in the assignment. Total freedom in taking part in the discussion meant that the more urgent affairs were given precedence. The gains for the students of devoting their time to the discussion forum were not high. A clearer coupling between the lecture material and the discussion forum would be needed to enable discussion on each individual issue in the material, and when new annotations or topics appear in the system, the users' attention should be triggered, for instance, by e-mailing them, to start using the system.

4.2 Groupware Spring 1997 with Dyn3W

Background and goals

Dyn3W was only one of the groupware systems (like BSCW and TeamWave, among others) tried out during the course. One goal was to provide the students (40) with both theoretical knowledge and hands-on experience on the major design and evaluation issues of groupware systems. As in the HCI course, all participation was voluntary but active participation was credited. The students were able to write new discussion topics, and comment on the earlier ones. Also votes were collected on several issues.

Usability

The user interface of Dyn3W was criticized by some students: "*Discussion with the system is rigid. It is annoying to read the messages. Since they are short, you end up clicking fast when following the links. It is difficult to comprehend the annotation space.*" As one possible solution, another arrangement of the three frames was presented and adopted during the course. In this version all the three frames were placed under each other, the annotation hierarchy above the frame for showing the annotation text. The placement received only two comments, the first stating the user should be able to select the orientation of the frames, and the other complaining about unnecessarily showing the annotation hierarchy even while writing the annotation.

Scaffolding argumentation and annotation

A spontaneous discussion emerged in Dyn3W about the benefits and drawbacks of anonymity. The students took opposite stands about the value of knowing who is the writer of an annotation. Two opposing annotations:

- "*... I do not have the energy to read anonymously written comments...* " and, later: "*... There's nobody backing up an anonymous comment.*", and, "*...in the real world, it appears that a person has more weight than another.*"
- "*I do not evaluate an annotation regarding if it has been written anonymously or not. In a conferencing system, most people are anyhow totally unknown.*"

A poll was organized by one of the students who took part in the discussion. He posted the results of the poll: 1 student voted to abandon all anonymity, 2 students admitted they read also anonymous postings but do not give much value to them, 1 student said that all writings are equally valuable, and the majority of 5 students admitted reading and sometimes even thinking about the contents of anonymous annotations.

4.3 CAI Fall 1996 with Dyn3W

Background and goals

The course on Computer-Aided Instruction is typically taken by first or second year students. However, the Fall 96 course was organized at the Institute for the Extension Studies within our university. The students were adults from working life extending or continuing their earlier studies, and so the course was organized a little differently, e.g. the lectures took place in the evenings and during weekends.

Dyn3W was used for three weeks by 21 students. This was the first time Dyn3W was in real use and the goal was to find out how usable the system was and how the support for discussion was received. Three topics relating to the theme of the course were given. To pass the course a student had to write at least five annotations. After the fifth annotation the system presented a questionnaire. We report some data from the questionnaire concerning the usability of the system.

Usability

Dyn3W was found easy to use by 81% of the students and 76% felt that discussion with Dyn3W was pleasant. In free feedback they stated, e.g. that "*You don't have to be dependent on the time and place*" (subject 1) and "*In this way everyone has the opportunity to express his opinion*" (subject 17). The students liked that they were able to plan their contributions in peace and when they have an opinion they have a chance to expose it. The main obstacle seemed to be the fact that the frames left too little room for the contents, e.g. "*Quite small windows ... scrolling gets quite annoying sometimes*" (subject 14) and "*... it is difficult to write to the annotation window because of its small size*" (subject 17).

Scaffolding argumentation and annotation

The most used annotation type for the first three annotations was "*I agree*" (39.7 %) and the next two were "*I give feedback*" (22.2 %) and "*Neutral*" (12.7 %). For the three next annotations the most used annotation types were "*I agree*" and "*I give feedback*" (both 25.0 %) and then came "*Question*" (16.7 %). It is noticeable that the "*Question*" and "*I give feedback*" types increased their popularity. Perhaps we can draw such a conclusion that after the preliminary phase the system encouraged the participants to demand more information and to give their own contributions to the discussion.

At the beginning the most used source for the argumentation was "*My opinion*" (68.3 %) and the next were "*Conversation with other*" (9.5 %) and "*The Media*" (6.3 %). At the later stage "*My opinion*" is still the most used (54.2 %) but "*My idea*" (14.6 %) had taken the second place and "*Common fact*" and "*Conversation with other*" (both 10.4 %) took the third place. It seems that taking part in a public discussion where the annotations remain to be read by other participants creates a reluctance to give to the others the possibility to verify the argument with the help of some precise source. An own idea or opinion is always a safe source because they can be based on the prevailing feelings that can be changed later on.

The possibility of reading other annotations at the time of writing one's own annotation was found to be a helpful feature by 76% of the students. Note that in the Groupware Spring 1997 course this possibility was considered as unnecessary by one student.

This experiment made us suspect that an open discussion without any specified structure or goal would not be a fruitful arrangement to promote educational discussion. In the next experiment we used a well-defined assignment with a more strict time schedule.

4.4 CAI Spring 1997 with Dyn3W

Background and goals

The Computer Aided Instruction course in Spring 1997 was attended by 76 students, mainly from Computer Science and Mathematics. In this course we wanted to analyse the support for group work and learning, not only public discussion among all students. The goal for this experiment was to find out what effect does Dyn3W have on the development of the critical thinking of the students. A further analysis will be made by examining the changes in the contents of the annotations. However, in this paper we only report on the issues concerning the usability and support for annotation.

Assignment

The students were divided into ten groups each with the goal to produce one solution for a given task. Every group had its own private discussion space in Dyn3W, where each member of the group had to prepare his/her own suggestion for the solution and other members commented by giving "*A good feature*" or "*A weak feature*" annotations. After a one week annotating period every group voted for the best solution and the winning solution (polished by its author) was published so that the other groups could comment it. The work was structured by a strict schedule and by forcing the solutions to be given in a certain form. Furthermore, there were only two types of annotation that could be given, and the source of argument had to be defined. To pass the course a student had to give at least one solution and if he/she wanted to gain extra points he/she had to give at least five annotations to the solutions produced by the other groups.

Usability

The old Web-browsers could not handle the frames in the way Dyn3W required. The "server error" messages caused a lot of frustration especially to those students who participated from outside the university. Furthermore, the possibility of scrolling each frame of the page separately was not obvious to all students.

Scaffolding argumentation and annotation

Students gave more "*A good feature*" (277) annotations than "*A weak feature*" (167) ones. All in all 444 annotations were given by 76 students so each of them wrote on an average 5.84 annotations. In other words, the students typically gave one annotation more than was required for the extra points. The most used source for argument was "*Other source*" (95.5 pct). The other types for argument were based on the course material. As in the CAI Fall 1996 course (see 4.3), the same hesitation to use verifiable sources appeared. Perhaps this problem can be overcome with more support for the writing process of the annotation. One possibility to increase process support is that the system will reflect the choice of annotation type by giving the user a set of predefined questions that need to be answered for that kind of annotation type. This hypothesis will be tested in the next version of Dyn3W.

5. DISCUSSION AND FUTURE PLANS

Already a preliminary analysis of our experiences so far has given us confidence that systems like ours are useful in promoting discussion on university level courses, thus being an important part of the virtual campus of tomorrow. However, computer conferencing will not succeed without mindful planning. As we have shown in this paper, several intertwined dimensions of use must be carefully taken into account in planning and running a course. What follows is a partial list of issues we have learned that should be considered in arranging the next courses using the systems:

- Various modes of collaboration and utilization of the system should be supported. Both forum type public discussions and small group private work situations are needed. In our current courses there has typically been one discussion area dedicated to familiarization with the system, and on some courses we have also had an area for free discussion after the credit discussion period has ended. In addition, we see the need for private areas for one-to-one teacher-student discussion within the conferencing framework. This is an extension we intend to provide in the next courses.
- Our (see also Kurland & Barber, 1996) data on the use of conferencing systems has shown that annotating and discussion should be tightly coupled with other activities such as construction of reports or other artifacts.
- If the system is to be used to support small group activities, some kind of positive interdependence (Salomon, 1992) must be established within the groups, if good results are hoped for. Evidently, the teacher can have various other goals for using computer conferencing besides small group work. Moreover, there will always be "lurkers" (students not participating by adding annotations but only reading them) who will learn from following the discussion. However, based on our experiences reported in this paper, our overall recommendation is that our busy students will not find the time to use

these systems if interdependent group situations are not established (more of these techniques in the connection to computer conferencing, see e.g. Klemm (1995)).

From the technical side, the number of annotations seems to increase very easily to proportions that are not manageable for the student - some kind of assistance is needed also in this respect. We have plans for augmenting our systems with a search facility and some kind of visualizations of the annotation space, e.g. using 3D and color techniques.

Acknowledgements

The authors want to thank Päivi Majaranta and Jouni Salonen for fruitful discussions during the project. An early version of the 3Wcomments system was designed and implemented by Sami Lehtonen, Päivi Majaranta, and Ari Viljakainen, after which Päivi Majaranta extended the 3Wcomments system for the HCI course described in this paper. The Dyn3W system has been designed and implemented by Timo Niemirepo. We also want to thank Professor Kari-Jouko Räihä and Aulikki Hyrskykari for using our prototypes on their courses.

6. REFERENCES

Chaplin, D (1996) Creating web communities. *CMC Magazine*, May 1996. In electronic form: `http://www.december.com/cmc/mag/1996/may/chaplin.html`

Collis, B. (1994) Collaborative learning and CSCW: research perspectives for internetworked educational environments. In Lewis, R., Mendelsohn, P., (eds.), *Lessons from learning*. North-Holland, 81-104.

Klemm, W.R. (1995) Computer conferencing as a cooperative learning environment. *Cooperative learning & College Teaching* 5, 3, Spring 1995. In electronic form: `http://www.cvm.tamu.edu/~vaph/klemm/cl.html`

Klemm, W. R. & Snell, J. R. (1996) Enriching Computer-Mediated Group Learning by Coupling Constructivism with Collaborative Learning. *Journal of Instructional Science and Technology* 1, 2, March 1996. In electronic form: `http://www.usq.edu.au/electpub/e-jist/klemm.htm`

Klemm, W. R. & Snell, J. R. (1994) Teaching via networked computers: what's the best medium? T.H.E. Journal 22, 3, October 1994. In electronic form: `http://www.cvm.tamu.edu/~vaph/klemm/thej.html`

Kurland, T. & Barber, P. (1996) User requirements from a group perspective: the case of distance learning mediated by computer conferencing. In Thomas, P. (ed.), *CSCW Requirements and Evaluation*. Springer-Verlag, 57-74.

Laurillard, D. (1993) Rethinking university teaching: a framework for the effective use of educational technology. Routledge, London.

Mason, R. (1991) Methodologies for evaluating applications of computer conferencing. In Kaye, A.R. (ed.), *Collaborative learning through computer conferencing*. Springer Verlag.

Mayes, J.T. & Neilson, I. (1995) Learning from other people's dialogues: questions about computer-based answers. In Collis, B., Davies, G. (eds.), *Innovative adult learning with innovative technologies*. Elsevier, 31-47.

Newman, D. R., Webb, B. & Cochrane, C. (1995) A content analysis method to measure critical thinking in face-to-face and computer supported group learning. *IPCT-J*, 3(2), 56-77.

O'Neill, D. K., Edelson, D. C., Gomez, L. M., & D'Amico, L. (1995) Learning to weave collaborative hypermedia into classroom practice. In J.L. Schnase & Cunnius, E. L. (Eds.), Proceedings of CSCL '95: The First International Conference on Computer Support for Collaborative Learning, October 17-20, 1995, Bloomington, Indiana. Hillsdale, NJ: Erlbaum. In electronic form: `http://www.covis.nwu.edu/Papers/CSCL95/CSCL95_weaving.html`

Reeves, T.C. (1997) A model of the effective dimensions of interactive learning on the World Wide Web. In the Proceedings of *ITK-97: Interaktiivinen Teknologia Koulutuksessa* (Interactive Technology in Education) Aulanko, Hämeenlinna, Finland, April 1997.

Salomon, G. (1992) What does the design of effective CSCL require and how do we study its effects? Proc. CSCL'92, *ACM SIGCUE Outlook*, 21, 3 (Spring 1992), 62-68.

Scardamalia, M. & Bereiter, C. (1993) Technologies for knowledge-building discourse. *Communications of the ACM*, 36(5), 37-41.

Turns, J., Mistree, F., Rosen, D., Allen, J.K., Gudzial, M. & Carlson, D. (1995) A collaborative multimedia design environment. In Maurer, H. (ed.), ED-MEDIA 95 - Proceedings of World Conference on Educational Multimedia and Hypermedia, Graz, Austria, June 17-21, AACE, 654-659.

Turoff, M. (1991) Computer-Mediated Communication Requirements for Group Support. *Journal of Organizational Computing* 1,1, 85-113.

Verdejo, M.F., Abad, M.T. & Barros, B. (1996) Modelling groupware for computer-supported collaborative learning. Paper presented at IFIP TC 3.6 Working Conference on "Collaborative Learning and Work", Vienna, Austria, September 1996.

Woolley, D.R. (1997) Conferencing on the World Wide Web. In electronic form: `http://freenet.msp.mn.us/people/drwool/webconf.html`

Yerion, K.A. & Rinehart, J.A. (1995) Guidelines for collaborative learning in computer science. *SIGCSE Bulletin* 27, 4, December 1995, 29-34.

7. BIOGRAPHIES

Pentti Hietala and **Saila Ovaska** are Lecturers, and Timo Niemirepo is an Assistant at the Department of Computer Science, University of Tampere.

17

Distance Education and Distributed Virtual Environments

H. Trefftz, C. Correa, M. A. González, G. Imbeau, J. Restrepo, M. I. Vélez and C. Trefftz
Universidad EAFIT
A.A. 3300
Medellín
Colombia-SouthAmerica
e-mail: htrefftz@sigma.eafit.edu.co .
Funding for this project has been provided by EAFIT University and Colciencias-BID under grant number 150-97.

Abstract

The possible applications of Distributed Virtual Environments to support Distance Education are being explored. A first experience with IRC (Internet Relay Chat) is described.

Keywords

Distance education, Virtual reality

The Virtual Campus F. Verdejo & G. Davies (Eds.)

1. INTRODUCTION

Distributed Virtual Environments (Burdea 1994, Broll 1995, Benford 1995, Hagsand 1996, Wexelblat 1993) are benefiting from two trends in the computer and communication marketplace: The increase in speed of networks and microprocessors and the decrease in price of hardware. These trends open the door to a number of new applications, among others "Virtual Classrooms" (O'Malley 1995, Kelsel 1996, Pantelidis 1994).

The project described in this paper explores the possible applications of Distributed Virtual Environments in the area of distance education. Researchers working on the project include both educators and computer scientists. The project is planned to be developed in a number of stages. In the first stage, the concept of IRC (Internet Relay Chat) is being used as a basis for a first interface that will allow an instructor and a number of students to interact in "real" time. In a second phase of the project, 3D "immersive" environment will be incorporated in the interface.

In this paper the results of a first implementation of a modified version of IRC, called AVALON, the critique by the educators in the group of this first version and the resulting new version of AVALON are described. We also describe the long term direction of the project.

The rest of this paper is structured as follows. Section 2 describes the preliminary version of AVALON.

The critique to the first interface by the educators in our team is included in section 3. Section 4 contains the modifications performed on the first version of the software. Section 5 describes the experiments that will be performed next semester. Conclusions and future work can be found in section 6.

2. INITIAL VERSION OF AVALON

The structure of IRC is based upon 2 assumptions:

- All users are equal.
- Users are logged on to machines that are not necessarily in the same domain.

In the kind of environment being envisioned for this project, these assumptions do not hold.

The interaction among the participants will be directed by the instructor. A student who wishes to participate should ask the instructor before starting to communicate to the rest of the group. Therefore in AVALON, there are two different user interfaces available: One for the instructor, and one for students.

The instructor receives the requests for participation from the students and ``yields the floor" to a given student. In this first version of AVALON, a student wishing to speak signals the instructor by clicking on a particular icon which results in a square associated with the student flashing on the screen of the instructor and a message appearing in the common text area telling everybody that the given student wishes to talk.

It is also assumed that the students and the instructor will be connected through a dial-in service provided by an academic institution. Thus all users will be in the same segment. Therefore the implementation uses multicast services to improve the response time. As multicast services become more widely available through Internet, using multicast will be an alternative that will improve performance.

3. CRITIQUE OF AVALON'S FIRST VERSION

The members in our team with a formal background in education had the following critique about the first version of AVALON: Distance Education is based upon the assumption that the student does NOT have to be at a certain time in a given place. This system will require the student to have access to a personal computer with the appropriate connection. The concept of physical distance is kept but the participants have to be "present" at the same time.

The number of simultaneous participants cannot currently exceed three or four persons. Beyond four users, the interactions become so fast that it is hard to read what the other users are saying/writing. The fact that the system is appropriate for a small number of participants only eliminates a comparative advantage of distance education: It covers a large and sparse population that cannot attend, for reasons of time and space, a regular educational institution. Furthermore Distance Education is an affordable alternative for this population. Limiting the size of the groups has an effect in costs as it will require a larger number of facilities.

Virtual Environments would become an enabling technology: They will enable students to participate, to interact with an instructor and with other students. On the other hand it would diminish the opportunity of advancing at one's own self pace in one's available spare time.

This discussion has lead the team to refocus the goals of the project. The goal will not be to replace the classroom and to expect all students to be "present" in the virtual classroom at once. Rather, the tool will be a "virtual help-room" where the instructor will be present at certain times and the students can "come" when the instructor arranges a meeting. The traditional distance educational media will not be replaced by the virtual help-room. The virtual help-room will be an additional service available. It will enable students to interact with an instructor and with each other in ways that were not previously available in Distance Learning.

4. AN IMPROVED VERSION OF AVALON

The following changes were made to AVALON:

- To avoid a particular student annoying the instructor and the rest of the students with excessive requests for participation, a request for an opportunity to speak will now result on the change of an icon that represents the student but no text will appear on the common text area. Thus, the instructor will realize that a particular student wants to participate in the discussion by looking at the corresponding icon. Any further requests will not cause any additional effects.

- The observation that no more than 4 students should be active at once lead to a redesign of the interface for the instructor. Every active student in a session will have a small face icon associated. The shape of the face reflects the current status of the student. The possible states are:

1. Listening and understanding (happy face)
2. Listening and not understanding (sad face)
3. Requesting the chance to speak
4. Requesting the chance to send a private message to the instructor
5. Absent but will return soon
6. Absent and will not return

5. GENERAL OVERVIEW OF THE PROJECT

The project started this year. The project has two main stages. The first one will use a text based interface. In the second one, we will develop an immersive virtual environment including sound, 3D avatars and other media.

The experiment will be performed three times:

1. Once with the text-based version of the interface.
2. Once with the graphic interface with one-to-one interaction between the instructor ond one student.
3. Once with the graphic interface with many-to-many interaction between the instructor and a group of students.

5.1. The first experiment

The first experiment started in August of 1997 using the text-based version of the interface. An introductory course on Environmental Sciences is being taught to eight first-year college students. The group was divided into two subgroups: One is receiving the course using traditional Distance Education methods and the other one is using the text-based interface. A tutor was assigned to each group. The tutors are in charge of guiding the modules of the course being taught. A comparison will be performed between both groups. We present the results obtained in this first experience under two categories: Challenges and Strategies. The Challenges are the situations on which we must continue working to make the experience more effective and the Strategies are the tools or strengths that we relied on during this first experience.

Challenges

The instructor needs to acquire previous experience in using the interface and must be very familiar with the entire course, so he/she has an appropriate knowledge of the situations and problems that could arise during the use of the tool. The instructor and students must concentrate on the interaction; the interface should be as "transparent" as possible. It is also necessary to be more familiar with the procedures that the students are following when using the tool.

The tutor needs to have a plan for the class and he/she must be familiar with the key concepts in the modules.

Adequate pedagogical resources are necessary to make the tutorial sessions more dynamic. For instance: If a student has difficulties and is slowing down the pace of the group with a repetitive question, the tutor should ask him/her to find the answer to his/her question on the written material.

The students should study deeply the modules of the course and if possible they should prepare some questions before every session.

The tutor has to be able to maintain several conversations at once when using the tool.

Although, the tool offers the students the opportunity of telling the instructor how are they feeling in the session, the tutor misses the non-verbal clues that students provide in a regular classroom environment.

Strategies

Having a small number of students in every session (four).

The ability given to the tutor of yielding the floor to a student and being able to take the floor back has made the interaction much more orderly and more dynamic.

Both the students and the tutor have found the possibility given to the students to express their mood very useful. The tutor can react according to the feedback provided by the students.

We also want to emphasize several technical aspects of the future stages of the project:

Immersive Interface: In the immersive interface the participants will find themselves in a Virtual Classroom. Each student and the instructor will have a 3D simplified representation, called an Avatar.

The avatar will be the means of the participants to share non-verbal information with the other participants. Via the avatar, the user will be able to:

- Occupy a space
- Move inside the world
- See the location and movements of the other participants
- Ask for the right to speak

The interface will also handle voice. According to a certain protocol, the participants will be able to hear others and to speak to others. Based on the current experience with the text interface, we are planning to have only the instructor talking to the group by default. If a student wants to speak to the group, he/she will "raise their virtual hands" asking the teacher for the opportunity to speak.

Only the instructor can "yield" the ability to talk to the group to a student (and take it back) whenever he/she wants.

The individual workstations will have a digitizing pad. According to a similar protocol, the participants will have access to a White Board. When a participant writes on the white board, whatever he/she writes on the digitizing pad on his/her workstation, appears magnified on the virtual white board. This offers a means of sharing diagrams with the group.

Other media have been proposed, for instance a VCR and a cassette player, but this media takes a lot of bandwidth (communications speed). Experiments will be conducted to determine the viability of such media on different communication networks.

On the long run we are also considering importing Virtual Worlds (described with the VRML language Brol 1995) to our system. This would allow the group to take a "Virtual Field trip" to virtually anywhere.

5.2 Computer Networks

The system will be tried on two types of computer networks:
-On local area networks (LANs), with high bandwidth,
-On wide area networks (WANs), where the communication bandwidth is much lower.

There are some interesting challenges when using WANs. Some compromises will have to be made in order to maintain a reasonable response time. No part of a voice message, for instance, can be dropped, whereas the message describing the movement of an avatar inside the world can be delayed.

6. CONCLUSIONS AND FUTURE WORK

Our vision is having our system used as support for distance learning in our country. Our hypothesis is that the use of such a system would improve the quality of distance learning.

The presence of both educators and computer scientists in our group has resulted in discussions and improvements to the prototypes we are developing.

IRC was modified to provide a more orderly and richer in information environment for class interaction. Our preliminary tests seem to indicate that only a small number of users can interact effectively, from an educational point of view.

7. REFERENCES

Benford (1995),"User embodiment in Collaborative Environments ",S Benford and J Bowers and L Fahlen and C Greenhalgh and D Snowdown, Proceedings of CHI 95, Denver ,Colorado.

Broll (1995), "Adding Multi-User Support to VRML, W Broll and D England, Proceedings of the VRMUL 95 Symposium ACM,pp 87-94, Denver, Colorado,

Burdea (1994), "Virtual Reality Technology", Grigore Burdea, John Willey and Sons.

O'Malley (1995), "Computer Supported Collaborative Learning", C O'Malley, Springer Verlag.

Wexelblat (1993), "The Reality of Cooperation: Virtual Reality and CSCW" in "Virtual Reality: Applications and Explorations", A Wexelblat, Academic Publishers, Academic Publishers.

Hagsand (1996), "Interactive Multiuser VEs in the DIVE System", Olaf Hagsand,IEEE Multimedia, Spring.

Kelsel (1996), VR in Education, Sandra Helsel, VR News, July.

Pantelidis (1994), "Exploring Virtual Reality for Classroom Use", V Pantelidis and L Auld, Tech Trends, Jan/Feb.

IVU (1996), Virutal University's Home Page, http://www.vu.org/.

BIOGRAPHIES

Helmuth Trefftz. Currently studying a Ph.D. at Rutgers Unviersity. Interests: Distributed Multiuser Virtual Reality.

Carlos David Correa. Finishing undergraduate studies at EAFIT University. Interests: Computer Graphics for Virtual Reality.

Miguel Angel Gonzalez. Invited scholar at EAFIT University. Interests: Evaluation of Education processes.

Gilles Imbeau, Ph.D. Professor at Universite de Quebec au Chicoutimic. Interests: Computer Supported Learning.

Juliana Restrepo. Invited researcher at EAFIT University. Pre School Teacher at Gimnasio Los Pinares. Interests: Computer Supported Collaboravie Learning

Maria Isabel Velez. Gradute student in Paleontholgy, Scotland. Interests: Education and Earth Sciences.

Christian Trefftz, Ph.D. Professor at EAFIT University. Interests: Parallel computing, distributed systems, Distributed Virtual Reality.

Self Organised Group Activities Supported by Asynchronous Structured Conversations

C. Viéville and A. Derycke
Laboratoire TRIGONE
University of Sciences and Technologies of Lille
Cité scientifique
59655 Villeneuve d'ASCQ CEDEX
FRANCE
email: Claude.Vieville@univ-lille1.fr

Abstract

This paper describes a communication system accessible through a Web browser. The main advantage of this system is to encourage a collaborative way of learning using asynchronous communication channels. The conversation is strongly structured by the system itself which helps the users to co-ordinate their actions playing their respective roles within a task. A conversation always occurs in the context of a task where each user plays a particular role. The system is built around the notion of an active form which is the single way for the user to communicate with the system. This system can be used by the actors of the educative process to self organise their work in a Virtual Campus. The first implementation is now finished and a usability test has been undertaken; the system has been modified in consequence.

Keywords

Asynchronous communication, Coordination, Group activity, Roles, Tasks, Forms, Structured conversation

The Virtual Campus F. Verdejo & G. Davies (Eds.)

1. INTRODUCTION

This paper describes an asynchronous collaborative learning system which aims to support a distance education process on the Web. What attracts the Internet to an educational institute is a large communication network to exchange information in two ways, the on-line browser and the courseware package distribution. So the challenge we have to face is to change information exchanges into learning activities. For this reason, we are interested in second generation servers which respond better to educational needs: better interactivity between video-clip, text, images, and so on; enabling re-use of all the supports we have developed in a fully integrated manner; inclusion of graphics and formulae is compulsory for many curricula; embedded courseware corresponds with the multiplicity of training pathways for individualised training and the ease of navigation required. As a minimum requirement, the system needs communication facilities to enhance real collaboration between users and tutors. In the EONT project[1], in which we are participating, we are verifying these hypotheses. And in the DEMOS project[2] we are designing, developing the asynchronous communication system presented more precisely in this paper. To develop our system we distinguish three spaces in which the activities of learners take place: information space, action space and communication space. The communication space depends on the institute, and organises the interactivity between the different spaces to correspond to a pedagogical practice. After a short introduction of the application field, the paper presents the functional specification of the system we are currently testing. A participative approach with a user group has been organised and usability metrics of the system are also presented.

Finally in the MODEM project[3], we are using the potential of ACLS to offer a way to organise the work of the teachers and students in a Virtual Campus. The ACLS is used to determine the scheduling of pedagogical activities, to manage the work to do for the teacher point of view as well as the student point of view. In the framework of this project we conducted a trial which has given us much useful information feedback.

---

1 An experiment in Open Distance Learning using New Technologies - part of the Socrates programme of the European Commission

2 Distance Education and tutoring in heterogeneous teleMatics envirOnmentS - part of the Education and training programme of the European Commission

3 Multimedia Optimisation and Demonstration for Education in Microelectronics - part of the Education and training programme of the European Commission

2. THE EDUCATIONAL CONTEXT

CUEEP (Centre Universite-Economie d'Education Permanente) is an institute of the University of Sciences and Technologies of Lille in northern France which is concerned with several activities: further education for adults, research into educational engineering (open learning and new communication technologies), transfer within the context of new technologies in education.

Since the late 70's, we have introduced new learning technologies and important work has been done in designing and experimenting courseware in traditional situations or in distance education and also in research and development of new tools with the help of European programmes like DELTA where a system of co-operative learning (the Co-Learn project) has been designed and experimented.

Since the late 80's, we have set up an open and distance system mixing several modes of training (group, individualised, distance, self-training in resource). At the moment, people who are registered in distance education are principally those who take a specific examination for adults equivalent to the baccalaureate. They learn from multimedia course material (written paper, audio-tape, video-tape, courseware) and they are in contact with a tutor by phone, fax and Minitel.

Some experiments of the co-operative system Co-learn have been set up during these two last years. Now we are looking to integrate this communication system into our distance education organisation.

To continue our work of research into the use of communication tools in distance education we are conducting a project to deliver a course on the Web based on collaborative learning. This project is mainly supported by the European Commission through the Telematics for Education programme. In this framework, we are setting an Asynchronous Collaborative Learning System in the DEMOS project. This system relies on a second generation of Web server (HyperWave from University of Graz - Austria).

3. THE USER'S DOMAIN

In this section the user's domain is clarified and the role of each *actor* in this area is given as precisely as possible to avoid confusion. From the user's point of view, the prototype that is specified in this document is an asynchronous communication system which favours the co-operation among people belonging to a same "social organisation". More precisely, in this document the organisation is a training institution which proposes this communication system in the framework of its distance education services. We focus only on the delivery side of the training institute - the course material production as well as the administrative side are outside the scope of this study. Two roles have been defined to provide an interface with both these other activities. People of this organisation have different roles such as:

- *teacher*: a person who is responsible for all the courses of a given domain proposed by the organisation to the trainee. He/she is the interface with the course material production teams.
- *tutor*: someone who gives daily help to a well defined set of learners. He/she works under the direction of a teacher.
- *trainer*: a person who leads a course, also under the guidance of a teacher.
- *counsellor*: a counsellor builds individual or group learning paths in negotiation with the learners themselves or human resource managers of the customer companies.
- *course manager*: somebody who is responsible for providing the requirements of tutors, teachers and learners in order to support the training services. This person is an interface with the administrative side of the training organisation.
- *learner*: someone who is trained by the institution. A learner may work for another "client organisation", but when he/she uses the services provided by the training institute they belong to the same "social organisation".
- *human resource manager*: a person working for an external organisation who negotiate learning paths with a counsellor.

Figure 1 represents the conceptual graph defining relations between roles and several basic objects of a training organisation. The number of roles portrayed inside a training organisation has been selectively limited as we are only interested in the "delivery side" of the process. Roles such as editors, course material designers, researchers, administrative staff, and many others are not taken into account in the specification of this communication system.

The system needs to be flexible enough to support various pedagogical scenarios. That means that it has to support several communication modes and it also needs to be adaptable, both during the installation phase and even during the operational process. Flexibility of the communication modes between users is one of the major challenges for this kind of system.

This section has described the context in which the communication system will be used. The following gives a description of the services that the system will provide to its users.

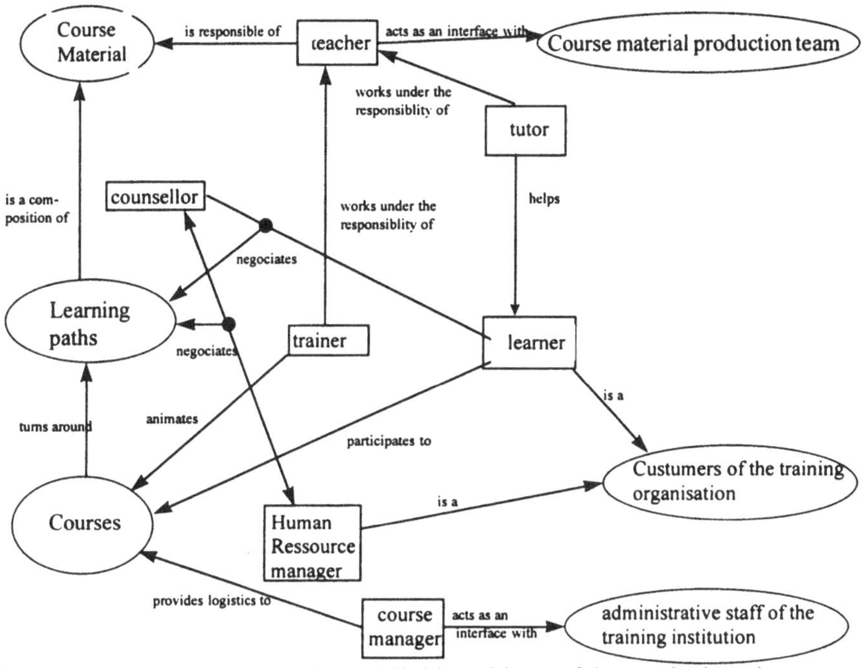

Figure 1. Conceptual graph linking objects of the user's domain

3.1 Overview of the services

This asynchronous communication system will provide a set of services from the same family as those already provided by electronic mail (email), electronic forums (forum), Bulletin Board Systems (BBS) and News. Its ambition is to give users real help with their tasks by avoiding several well-known drawbacks of current systems (Terry, 1991) and to propose a structuring of the conversation so that it is very efficient to communicate and collaborate via such a system (Viéville, 1995). The measurement of the efficiency of this system could be made upon :

- time-saved during the co-ordination phase of a collaborative process (Bussler, 1994),
- time-saved when reading each others contributions,
- enhancement of the quality of arguments produced during a debate (Desaranno, 1994),
- better involvement of users in the collaborative processes.

The Co-Learn project is an important input to the specification of such systems. In (Derycke, 1992), the interest of developing Collaborative Learning activities has been explained. It is outside the scope of this document to argue in favour of educational processes which are based on collaboration between learners and tutors.

In (Kaye, 1995) it is stated as result of the Co-Learn project, that "it might have been preferable to put emphasis on the Asynchronous Communication mode as the basic substrate for communication between learners and tutors. In this way the Asynchronous Communication Mode would provide the glue which would hold a course together, inter-linking the real-time sessions, and providing the forum for continuing discussion and collaboration after each of these sessions." The reader who is interested by this discussion will find pertinent papers on this subject in the reference section (Harasim,1993), (Henri, 1994), (Kirsche, 1994). Jonassen, in (Jonassen, 1996), gives an excellent overview of the possibilities of Computer Mediated Communication (CMC) in educational process.

3.2 Basic Services

The ACLS offers a set of basic services enhanced by a subset of complementary services which are needed to manage, adapt and integrate the system using existing communication tools to meet users' needs (Palme, 1992), (Palme, 1993), (Turoff, 1991).

Globally the basic services provided by this asynchronous communication system are:

- informal exchanges between people,
- question-answer exchanges between people,
- date negotiation between people (Woitass, 1990),
- pro-con argument production,
- action negotiation between people (Rogers, 1995),
- opinion collection.

Each of these services could involve people regardless of the context of a collaborative task, or be used in the framework of a task process involving the group. In this latter case the exchange is automatically classed as public, unless specifically defined as private. The task in which the communicators are involved is very fundamental as it will define the context in which the exchange has occurred (Ellis, 1994). In this ACLS electronic mail is not distinguished from electronic forums or news systems as a means of communicating between people. The ACLS provides an integrated view of exchanges whatever channel is used (i.e. email, forums, news, BBS etc.) (Benford, 1992).

This basic service will allow the members to select, fill in, edit, and submit a form which will complete an exchange. Exchanges are linked to each other by a temporal relation. The creation of a new exchange is a particular case of the creation of a contribution which becomes the root of the exchange.

3.3 Complementary services

The ACLS also proposes other complementary services to its basic services. To encourage co-operation ACLS will provide a service which gives information on its users. The communication needed by users during the task process will be supported inside a "group activity". The group activity is the context in which the "exchanges" of a communication occur. One and only one organisational group is attached to a group activity. The exchanges of a communication are structured sets of contributions. Each exchange is regulated by a set of global rules pre-defined at the installation of the ACLS. This set of rules depends on the way people of the organisation work together (Viéville, 1995). Obviously default rules are proposed during the installation phase. To participate in a group activity a user needs to be added; he then becomes a "member" of the group activity.

It is also possible task by task to create subgroups in which all the members play an identical role with regard to the aim of the task. For example, if a collaborative writing task is started, subgroups of "authors", "editors", "reviewers" are created by the initiator of the task. Belonging to a subgroup will give different rights to the objects in the ACLS.

A search service is available for all the users who want to find any objects in the ACLS. Users, group activities, sub-groups, forms, exchanges and tasks are searched and displayed to the user of the search service. To start a search operation, the user must fill in fields of a search form. The user has to define in the form which criteria the search should use. It is possible to search on the attributes and/or the contents of any kinds of objects of the ACLS.

Authorised users will use the administration service to create/modify attributes; delete/archive/open/close user and group activities. This administration is done by filling in an administrative form.

Users are added and removed from group activities by using the registration service. A subset of authorised users with appropriate rights will have access to this service. Registration is performed by filling out a registration form. Only when a group activity has appropriate parameters may a user register himself for that activity.

A service of notification allows members, who have subscribed, to be notified when something is appended to the group activity. Filling in a notification form is the proposed way to subscribe to the notification service. The notification service allows to the user to receive (or avoid reception of) the events generated inside the ACLS. The kinds of events are :

- "group activity" list has changed,
- list of users of the ACLS has changed,
- status of a group activity has changed,
- list of tasks for a particular group activity has changed,
- list of exchanges for particular tasks has changed,
- list of forms for a particular exchange has changed,
- a deadline relative to a task is going to arrive,
- a deadline relative to a task has been detected,
- a particular user activity has been detected,
- a particular group or subgroup activity has been detected.

The events are sent to the notification recipient which could be an electronic mail address, a news group, or another task of any other group activity.

4. SPECIFICATION OF THE USER INTERFACE

4.1 Basic principles

The principle of the user-system dialogue relies on the submission of active forms (Hammainen, 1991). This dialogue implements a schema of information interchange between the user and the system as already exists on the Web with the HTML form. This will remove constraints imposed by the selection of the user's workstation. This choice also allows complete mobility of the user and does not obviates the need to install specific client software on the user's workstation. Within these forms, there are three main objects manipulated by the user inside the ACLS. Another particular object is also manipulated - documents, however these are outside the scope of this study. The ACLS forms are too generic to be considered as an object; they are containers for the main objects presented in this section. The semantics which define articulation between these main objects are summarised in the figure 2.

Task : to perform a task the organisational group can decompose it into several sub-tasks. The aim of a task is achieved by performing actions external to the system. A task can be personal or collaborative. A task organiser manages the list of tasks by communicating with the mediation agent (mediator). Each group activity has its task organiser.

Exchanges and contribution forms : the contribution form (contribution for short) is the basic element by which users communicate, co-ordinate and work together. A contribution is a semi-structured message (Malone, 1987). It is a container for output and entry fields (list of items, dates, links etc.) and user actions (initiation and commitment of tasks, exchange, validation of forms. etc.). The exchange is the container which structures a set of contributions which appear as a tree-like structure. A mediator manages one and only one exchange; all contribution forms are communicated to the mediator. The mediation agent composes the contribution form according to its status and the role of the communication agent. A contribution is posted with a privacy level.

Documents : Documents are external to the ACLS, but can be attached to main objects of the ACLS. The following rules allows inheritance of attachment through interconnected objects of the ACLS :

- attached documents of a task are also accessible within children tasks
- attached documents of an exchange are also attached within children exchanges and in all the contributions of these exchanges
- attached documents of a group activity are attached to all the tasks and exchanges and contributions
- attached documents of a subgroup are attached to the relative tasks for which this subgroup has been created

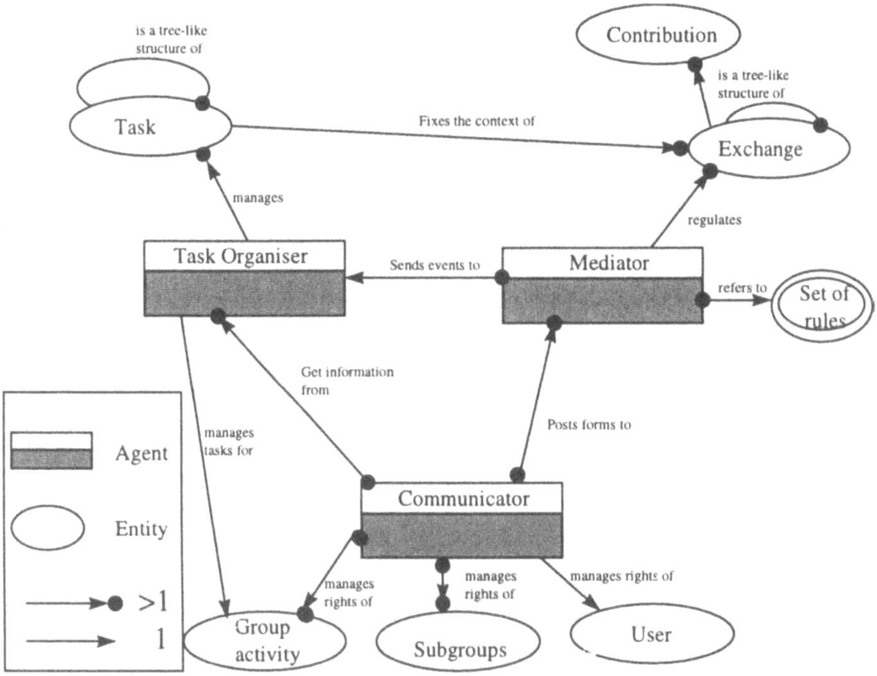

Figure 2. semantic network of basic objects of the ACLS

4.2 Agents of the ACLS

In addition to the main objects, there are also agents which "help" the users in their work.

The notification agent (notifier): this entity is responsible for distributing the events which occur in the ACLS to the subscribers who are users of the system. By default the notifier sends mail to signal each event. A notification agent is attached to a social organisation.

Communication agent: Is attached to one user. This agent knows the group activity, the sub-groups each user belongs to and using this knowledge is able to give rights on objects of the ACLS.

The mediation agent (mediator): Organises contributions and in conjunction with the communication agent proposes to the user a well chosen classes of forms to fill in. It also receives forms posted by the communication agent and sends back the form as it will be recorded by the ACLS if the user validates it.

Task organiser: The task organiser manages the users "to-do list". This to-do list is built from events sent by the mediation agent. The task organiser is associated with one and only one organisational group.

5. SEVERAL IMPLEMENTATION KEY POINTS

From the implementation point of view, the Virtual Campus relies on the architecture of an open system of CSCW called ODESCA which is built on the integration of an activity server using an object database for persistency with a WWW information server.

The access to the ACLS functions is realised by the way of the CGI mechanism of a web server. The CGI interface takes in charge the management of the transactions which is not supported by the web servers. This interface is also in charge of the management of the templates database of forms according the organisation and the users. Finally, it also communicates with ODESCA to obtain the conversation state, the list of types of templates allowed for a contribution and other functions less specific to asynchronous communication activities as the information on group members. This CGI application continuously updates a database where the interactions between users and ACLS are stored in order to give information to measure usability of the system.

The data forwarding from the user station and CGI application is done according the HTTP protocol. This protocol does not support a transaction by itself, so a mechanism has been designed to reject a non valid request which has already been submitted. For example, we must avoid a user submitting the same form several times when he uses the moving back functionality of a web browser.

A standard web browser of the Internet allows the user to get the list of the tasks in which he is involved in. Then, using the navigation functionality, he can get the list of the conversations of a selected task. Finally, he will get the list of the contribution of a particular conversation. A synthetic view of the state of the conversation remains always accessible as well as the set of the contents of all the contributions of a conversation (Figure 3).

Each time a user wishes to add a contribution at the heart of ACLS, the ODESCA server activates it self to propose him the list if the types of forms which are accessible. This list is computed by taking into account the state of the conversation in which the user wishes to converse, according to the role of the user and according to the kinds of the contributions he has already submitted. For example, in a conversation to define a date, the initiator of this conversation will receive from the ODESCA server a list of two forms: using the first one he will be able to meet the persons at a date selected by the members of the group; with the second one he will be able to announce the abort of the meeting for any reason. The submission of one or the other form will finish the current conversation. In this same conversation, all the other members of this group will receive from ODESCA a form in which he will indicate if the date is convenient for him.

ACLS makes a clear distinction between the presentation objects seen and manipulated by the user and the objects manipulated by it self. When a user creates a new object (i.e. new task, new conversation...) the system selects an appropriate list of templates and the user has then to select one of these. Then, he has to fill the fields of this template. The templates are HTML forms controlled by javascripts. Javascript controls the user input date for each field whose content is interpreted by the system. As the templates are semi-structured messages, some fields are not interpreted by the system but just stored and some other ones needs a strict control.

the system. As the templates are semi-structured messages, some fields are not interpreted by the system but just stored and some other ones needs a strict control. Before being submitted, a form which carries all the data of the template is locally controlled by a javascript. The designers of these templates encounter difficulties dued to the lack of standardisation of javascript among browsers. Netscape currently presents the most advance features as it is able to manipulate HTML objects such as select object.

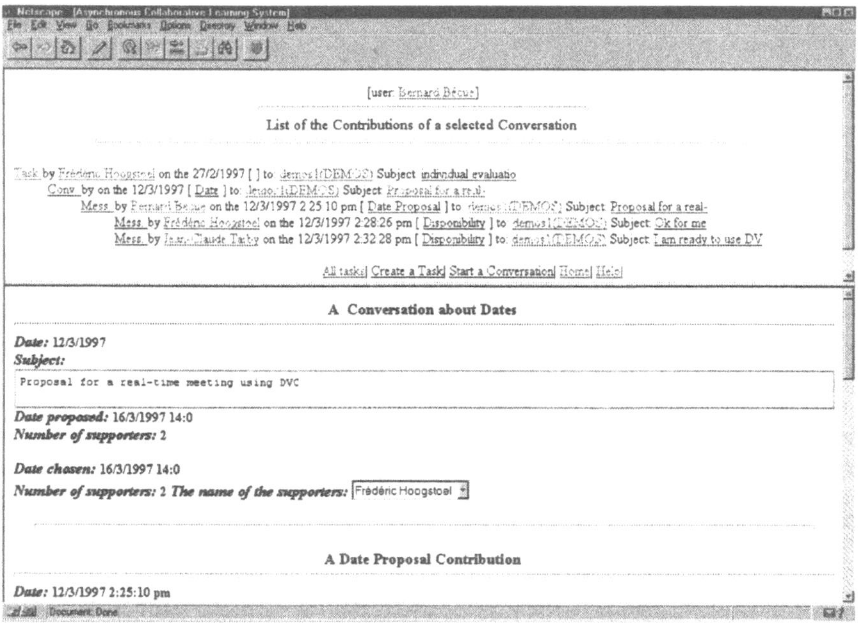

Figure 3. View of a Conversation to agree on a date

The current implementation takes in charge several parameters suitable for the organisations in which ACLS is used but also several other one suitable for the users.

An organisation can select from amongst an existing template database of forms but also edit its own database. The ACLS system uses HTML documents and proposes an extension which allows itself data on the flow according to the state of the conversation or the role of the user. The editing can be done by anybody knowing a HTML editor and the meaning of the variables of the ACLS system. By using a modification process, it is very easy to realise a new templates database in another language. This option is also proposed for use by the user. It can be used to reduce the complexity of a given set of information according to the skill of the users with the system.

As the models are stored in the HTML format, a classic web browser such as Netscape Navigator or Microsoft Internet explorer can be used to access the ACLS system. This choice allows a large usage of the ACLS.

browser and so more adapted to a specific context of work. The implementation can be done in any language as ACLS interface is just a definition of a protocol. JAVA seems to be a good candidate for this implementation.

The notification mechanism allows users to never consult the ACLS. They only have to let a email agent become active on their station. This agent will receive a notification message coming from ACLS telling them what is new in ACLS for them. A backward link helps them to consult directly the task and the conversation which includes the major events.

6. FIRST USABILITY TRIALS

A first usability campaign has been conducted during these last months. It involved ten learners whose work was to write a documentation about a camera. The analysis of the collected information shows a lack of efficiency in the browsing of the tasks, conversations and contributions. The interface designed as a three levels hierarchy needs to be changed. Moreover, we detected that all the users requested help about task objects. They have difficulties in deciding if they have to create a task before starting a new conversation. The result is that they never create a task. They always start conversation in the currently selected task. In consequence the task object never reflects a constextualisation of their work. The only utility of the task is to allow a selection of the appropriate group with which the user wants to discuss. Even if the task object is fundamental for the system to contextualise the conversations from the point of view of the designers, it seems to be an object the users have difficulties to manipulate.

Following this result, a second design of the HTML forms has been conducted. In this design, the system stores the conversation in a task by asking the user about the group and the objective of his work. If the objective does not exist, the system creates a task to support this new conversation without requesting more information from the user. In consequence, the users are no longer manipulating the « tasks forms ». The system appears simpler. Moreover, the number of levels of objects manipulation (tasks, conversations, contributions) has been decreased by one. This simplification without losing the main advantage of tasks (i.e. contextualisation of work) leads to a more efficient system. People responsible for the implementation of this system inside the organisation have to analyse the work of the users to set up a list of predefined tasks the users will have to conduct. This list can be manually or automatically extended during the live cycle of ACLS. If the user does not find a well suited task in the predefined list he can create a new one. The system administrator can decide to put it in the predefined list if this task seems to be frequently used by the users.

7. CONCLUSION

Particular attention has been paid to the methodology of design in order to work with the user group. Its usability has been measured to know how it reduces the co-ordination times during the self organisation of the asynchronous collaborative activities. This system has been designed incrementally; it means that, rapidly, with only a few functions it has been usable by the members of the user group who sent feedback to the designers. This participative approach has certainly given to this system a good level of usability.

8. REFERENCES

Benford S., Turroff M. and Palme J. (1992) An ISO standard to support asynchronous group communication. Elsevier Science Publishers B.V. (North-Holland)

Bussler C. and Joblonski S. (1994) Implementing Agent Coordination for Workflow Management Systems Using Active Database Systems. IEEE software

Danielsen T., Trine Folkow and Per Wiggo Richardson (1988) Relation and Inheritance in Group Communication. Message handling Systems. Elsevier Science Publishers B.V. (North-Holland)

Derycke A. and al (1992) Representation Models for Collaborative Educational Situations and Collaborative Learning activities. Deliverable 4 of Co-Learn D2005

Desaranno S. and Put F. (1994) Co-ordinating group communication. Computer networks and ISDN Systems, Elsevier Science B.V.

Ellis C. and Wainer J. (1994) Goal-based models of collaboration, in *Collaborative Computing* (Chapman & Hall)

Hammainen H. (1991) Form and Room: Metaphors for Groupware. COSC, ACM

Harasim L. (1993) Collaborating in Cyberspace: Using Computer Conferences as a Group Environment. Interactive Learning Environment Vol.3

Henri F. and Rigault C. (1994) Collaborative Distance Learning and Computer Conferencing. NATO ARW, ASI series, Springer Verlag

Hoogstoël F. (1995) Une approche organisationnelle du travail coopératif assisté par ordinateur. Application au projet Co-Learn, thése de Doctorat en Informatique à l'université des Sciences et Technologies de Lille

Jonassen D. (1996) Computers in the classroom; mindtools for critical thinking. Prentice Hall

Kaye A. (1995) Final Evaluation Report, Synthesis of Co-Learn Trials and Experimentation. Deliverable 33 of Co-Learn d2005

Kirsche T., Lenz R., Ruf T., Wedekind H. (1994) Co-operative Problem Solving using Database Conversations. IEEE software

Lindgaard G. (1994) Usability Testing and System Evaluation; a guide for designing useful computer systems. Chapman and Hall

Malone T. (1987) Semi-Structured messages are surprisingly useful for Computer-Supported Collaboration. ACM trans. On Office Information Systems Vol.5

Palme J. (1992) Computer Conferencing Functions and Standards *in Collaborative Learning through computer conferencing* (Kaye A.R.)

Palme J. (1993) Standards for asynchronous group communication. Computer communication V19 N9, 1993

Rogers (1995) The Use of an automatic "TO Do " list to Guide Structured Interaction. CHI 95

Smith C. (1994) Co-Learn Usability audit. Deliverable 29a of Co-Learn project D2005

Terry D. (1991) 7 steps to a better mail system. Message handling Systems. Elsevier Science Publishers B.V. (North-Holland)

Turoff M. (1991) Computer-Mediated Communication Requirements for Group Support. Journal of Organizational Computing

Vieville C. (1995) Structuring conversation in asynchronous communication systems to support collaborative learning at a distance. Telematics for Education and training, Held & Kugemann

Woitass M. (1990) Coordination of Intelligent Office Agents Applied to Meeting Scheduling. Multi-User Interfaces and Applications. Elsevier Science Publishers B.V. (North-Holland)

PART FIVE

Web Tools and Web Applications

Web tools and Web applications

E. Pastor
Dep. de Ingeniería de Sistemas Telemáticos - UPM
ETSI Telecomunicación, Ciudad Universitaria s/n
28040 Madrid, Spain
e-mail: encarna@dit.upm.es

Abstract

This paper is a summary on the issues raised during the Working Conference concerning Web based learning systems and tools. Its content responds to the full range of written and spoken contributions at the Conference.

Keywords

Evaluation, Implementation phase, Organizational aspects, Web applications

The Virtual Campus F. Verdejo & G. Davies (Eds.)

1 INTRODUCTION

The Word Wide Web is an emerging technology but already accounts for more Internet traffic than any other application, including email and simple file transfer. It increases the network capacities for information transfer and processing and it can support interactions between users over long distances.

Not surprisingly, the Web is increasingly being used as a platform to deliver education playing a central role in the development of new teaching and learning environments. Moreover, many institutions of higher education in the world are investing a large amount of resources in the Web as a vehicle to convey not only pedagogical material but also administrative information.

Confirming this trend, several papers presented at the Conference report on a range of Web based applications and tools, involving collaborative learning, individual learning, distribution of material and integration of facilities like, for example, simulators.

Web based applications relax some of the temporal and spatial constrains on communication while allowing for the presentation of multimedia information, collaborative work and provision for interaction. Although there is general agreement that Web applications have large potentials and benefits for education, there is no detailed view about how the Web should be used. Educators are still lacking appropriate didactical models to guide the realization of its potential. In this area, participants in the Conference pointed out several problems and some solutions.

Another important aspect raised by participants deals with the evaluation of Web based learning systems. It was noted that there is little regard for appropriate evaluation on the impact of new systems on the students' usual way of working as well as the effect on their already acquired study habits.

Finally, critical organizational issues to extend experiences to a real environment were mentioned like, for example, lack of infrastructure, some resistance of teachers to changes and rigid structures of current institutions.

All these issues will be summarized here as a result of discussions and written contributions.

2 USING THE WEB

The Web was originally designed as a mechanism for information access, not as an instrument to create systems for teaching and learning. In spite of the success of the Web, its technical capacity to carry multimedia materials and its facilities to build an extensible information base, it is not obvious how educational applications can take full advantage of the possibilities offered by the Web. Several solutions are possible and are evident in the systems presented at the Conference.

- *Organization of information*

Fernández-Manjón et al., in this volume, state that problems like lack of guidance in the access to information, disorientation as well as information overload affect seriously the usefulness of the Web as an educational tool. A new approach considers HTML as a tool that can help to organize and structure the content of documents according to pedagogical ideas. Using a richer and larger set of mark-up features it will be possible to apply pedagogical strategies in the presentation of the information.

- *Interactivity*

An important issue in distance teaching/learning is that of the evaluation, which could benefit the interactivity (self-learning assessment or automatic assessment (as addressed by Bedanokova and Teutsch in this volume) in the field of foreing-language learning). The incorporation of JAVA technology into Web browsers has emphasized the value of user interaction with a system. (Divjak; Tsironis and Neofotistos, both in this volume) suggests that the use of highly interactive systems based on JAVA enhances learning particularly in the field of science. JAVA is also the key for the development of virtual laboratories where students can directly interact with simulated artefacts (Llamas et al., in this volume) and be trained in virtual enviroments adapted to the particular target activity (Mc Daid et. al in this volume, which also elaborates on the production of training material addressing issues such as reusability or customisation).

- *Integration of tools*

Direct experimentation with learning materials like simulators or courseware is not sufficient (Adorni et al.; Llamas et al.; in this volume). Students need supervision by tutors as well as interactions with other students to discuss their own views and ideas. Some approaches consider that Web applications should integrate several resources to improve the effectiveness of learning such as hypertext material, simulated instruments for laboratory activities, tools for cooperative work, tools for self assessment and communication tools.

- *Software compatibility*

As a final technical remark, it is important to point out that the development of robust and stable Web based applications is sometimes limited by the rapid development of new software from different vendors using new technologies that are sometimes not compatible with previous environments. This fact represents a common problem to all Web based applications.

- *Resuability of corseware material*

Reusability could allow major benefits concerning the available learning material. Given the huge amount of such pieces of courseware a promising strategy could consist in organising the stuff coming from different sources into a large library of courseware (as proposed by M. Marolt and M. Privosnik in this volume).

3 EVALUATION

To assess the impact of Web based systems fully in the teaching/learning process a comprehensive evaluation of experiences is required. Usually the focus of the evaluation is on technical aspects of the system, usability or learning effectiveness.

However it is also important to know how the students integrate the system into their usual way of working.

(Adorni et al., in this volume) suggest that the way the students interact with the technology might interfere with their already acquired habits. The authors argue that it is therefore important to collect and evaluate subjective information in order to determine which facilities of the system fit in with the students needs and which ones have been overlooked.

Experiences with the on-line use of a course module and its related tutorials showed that to exploit the possibilities of the system the students should change their habits to include more independent study activity and less reliance on immediate feedback from the tutor as in face to face interaction.

4 IMPLEMENTATION PHASE: ORGANIZATIONAL ASPECTS

Educators introduce new forms of learning and working when using Internet technologies and Web applications as part of the educational process.

According to the change of educational concepts, organizational structures and processes have to be adapted to the new learning and teaching situations. For example, a lecture-oriented course where teacher and students meet in a classroom requires a different organization from a course where students work at home and interact with the teacher by means of asynchronous or synchronous communication tools.

There are many organizational aspects to consider related to the implementation phase of a new technology in a specific educational setting. However, bounds imposed by current organizational or pedagogical models are sometimes ignored.

Several basic aspects were mentioned in the Conference discussions like availability of technology, cost of the system for the student, accessible infrastructure and acceptance of technology/changes by teachers.

Too frequently such basic aspects are overlooked and thus, for example, the availability of the newest technologies is presupposed.

To overcome these weak points, a careful strategic plan for the implementation phase has to be designed. One of the aims would be to harmonize new requirements with current organizational structures and users' capabilities in a specific setting.

5 BIOGRAPHY

Encarna Pastor is Associate Professor at the *Departamento de Ingeniería de Sistemas Telemáticos* of the *Universidad Politécnica de Madrid.* She received the Ph.D. degree on Computer Science from the same University in 1988. For the last years she has been involved in R&D activities related to telematics applications, communication architectures and computer-supported cooperative work. Current interest research fields include distributed multimedia systems and collaborative learning.

How to distribute learning facilities by means of a network: some issues and a case study

G. Adorni[1], M. S. Barbieri[2], D. Bianchi[1], E. Calabrese[1] and A. M. Sugliano[3]

[1] *Dipartimento di Ingegneria dell'Informazione Università di Parma*
43100 Parma, Italy,
e-mail: adorni, bianchi, calabrese@ce.unipr.it
[2] *Dipartimento di Psicologia Università di Trieste*
Via Università 7, 34123 Trieste, Italy,
e-mail: barbieri@univ.trieste.it
[3] *Dipartimento di Scienze Antropologiche Università di Genova*
Vico S.Antonio 5/7 16126 Genova, Italy,
e-mail: sugliano@disa.unige.it

Abstract

In this paper we present a distributed client-server architecture which integrates hypertext tools with laboratory, evaluation, and communication tools, as a support for learning. A part of the architecture has been implemented and tested with undergraduate students. The preliminary results are encouraging and an extension of the system is planned with other communication tools such as bulletin board, blackboards, voice and images.

Keywords

Distance education, Web applications, Prolog, Evaluation

The Virtual Campus F. Verdejo & G. Davies (Eds.)

1. INTRODUCTION

According to a well-known theory in psychology, active learning produces better results than other forms of learning (Piaget, 1947; 1964). The possibility of acting on the learning material, observing the results of different actions and reasoning upon them, deepens the understanding of the learning material and consequently affects learning outcomes.

First hand experimentation with the learning material is however not sufficient. Students need supervision by the tutor as well as interactions with other students to discuss their own views and ideas and compare what they learned with their peers (Steffe and Gale, 1995). All these resources are usually provided in a traditional on-site learning environment where students sit in a classroom with a tutor and other students. This environment involves social comparison and interaction between the students as well as supervision by the tutor. It can also entail work in laboratory sessions which involves active experimenting with the educational materials.

By exploiting Internet facilities, computer and network technology have recently made all these resources easily available even to students who are not on-site. Access to the Internet allows distance students to sit at their personal computer and perform in a single place a number of different actions. For example, they have access to learning materials, contact with tutors and peers, do practical tasks and use the virtual laboratory. These are usually performed by on-site students by means of a number of different media (books, computers, telephone, face-to-face interaction), and sometimes in a number of different places (classroom, laboratory, cafeteria).

This new type of technology sometimes includes extra resources that may also improve the effectiveness of on-site learning such as hypertexts which can emphasise the conceptual links inherent in the learning material, or computer conferencing which can support topic-based asynchronous discussion among the students.

Though widespread acceptance of new learning technologies might require a long time (Cuban, 1986), it is worth trying out new resources to exploit their possibilities and assess their impact through different forms of evaluation.

The evaluation of these information technology resources is also a matter of extensive debate (Crook, 1997; McAteer et al. 1997). Usually, the focus is on the technical features of the system and their user-friendliness as well as on their learning effectiveness. However, the way the students interact with the new resource might clash with their already acquired study habits. It might be important therefore to know what the users actually did with it and why. Subjective data are important in order to know which features of the system the users felt met their learning needs and which ones were overlooked. As a consequence, a comprehensive evaluation of the resource requires putting together different pieces of information such as the students' activity patterns, their reason for proceeding the way they did, their acceptance of the resource, and lastly their learning outcome.

Further on in this paper, we discuss a distributed architecture for learning purposes which integrates different kinds of media. More precisely, section 2 is an introduction to the proposed architecture. Section 3 discusses a first implementation of part of the architecture used as a support for a course on "Logic Programming". Along with some concluding remarks, section 4 presents a preliminary evaluation of the implemented system performed during the present academic year for students enrolled in the first level degree called Diploma of Computer Engineering at the Engineering Department of the University of Parma.

2. PROPOSAL OF AN ARCHITECTURE

The Internet can be an important means for the diffusion of learning material and culture. In fact, a lot of news groups and Internet sites around the world offer learning material and information about educational topics. In this direction, the long-term goal of our project is to "break down the walls" of the classroom, which is the traditional learning environment, by means of a client-server distributed architecture through a network.

Each client supports a user-friendly man-machine interface integrating monitor, keyboard and mouse with a microphone and a CCD camera.

The server allows on-line presentation of a course module and its related tutorials. In the same environment, it integrates virtual instruments and tools to directly experiment with the learning material and to verify the "learning level of the student". Such an environment offers the possibility of asking questions to a tutor via e-mail facilities. Notes, comments and reflections related to the learning material can be posted on an on-line bulletin board and made accessible to all the students of the virtual classroom and to the tutor. The student can interact with the tutor (when he is on line) or with other students (if there are any) through the microphone. They can write text and draw sketches on a shared blackboard. By means of the camera they can even look "into the eyes" of the participants in the discussion.

The above facilities are available through the server by means of the network. More precisely, the server hosts the following: 1) teaching material organised as hypertext, integrating also animated text and parts of films; 2) software packages simulating instruments and tools for laboratory activities; 3) software packages for remote cooperative work which include management policies of the blackboard and management of voice communication as well as images; 4) tools for self assessment and final evaluation of the learning level (see Figure 1).

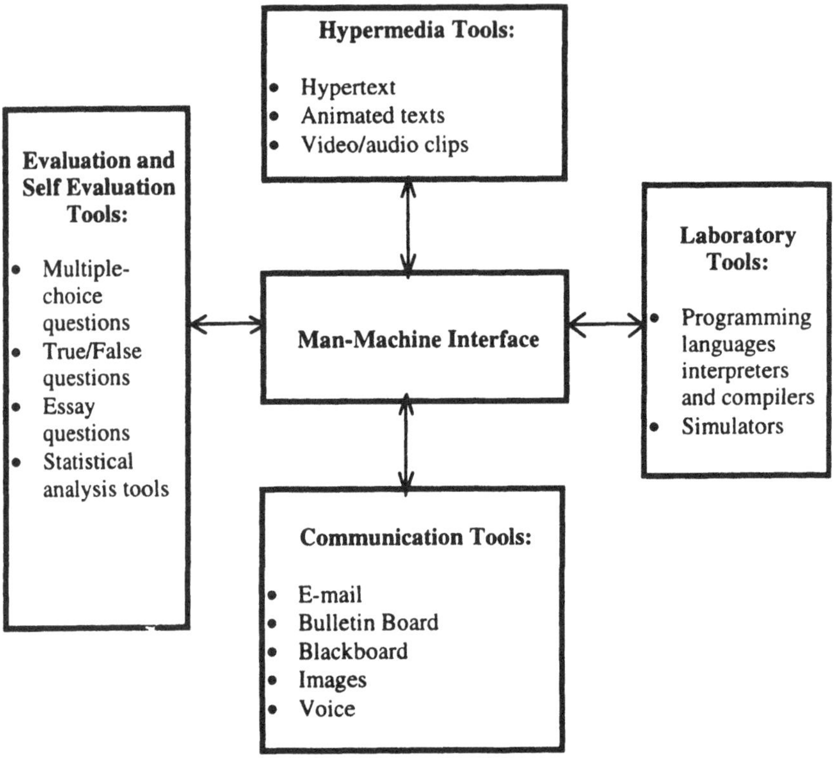

Figure 1. The proposed architecture.

3. A CASE STUDY

The architecture introduced in the previous section has been partially implemented as a system devised to allow the on-line use of a course module and its related tutorials. The subject matter of the module is "Mathematical Logic, Logic Programming and Prolog", which is used in courses for the diploma degree in Computer Engineering at the Engineering Department of the University of Parma. The client-server experimental setup is shown in Figure 2.

The theoretical part of the subject matter is presented through hypertext. Linked to the main topics of the key chapters there is a series of tutorials (guided training exercises), with questions and problems that the students are invited to solve.

Students can actually try out their answers and solutions by using within the browser an available Prolog interpreter on the server together with a number of files related to the examples presented in the tutorials. These sample files can be directly loaded and tried out in this environment which we called "PrologLab".

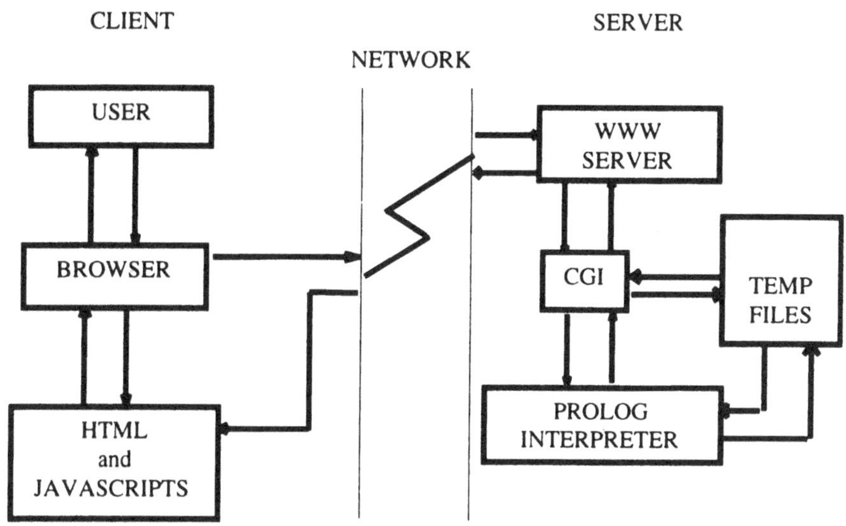

Figure 2. HyperProlog: experimental setup.

The students can easily switch from the hypertext (part of Hypermedia Tools) to the PrologLab (part of Laboratory Tools) or use both concurrently.

At the end of each tutorial there is a self-assessment test which the students can take and an e-mail facility where students can write their comments and send questions to the tutor.

The above implemented modules are integrated through a friendly Man-Machine Interface (see Figure 3).

The client-server architecture is based on a WWW browser and server. A platform independent user interface can be developed using HTML which was designed mainly as a markup language for creating hypertext. The use of CGI programs allows one to develop general user interfaces to almost any application. These interfaces can be further improved by using tools like Javascripts and Java applets. Anybody with a browser and an Internet access can use the system.

A Prolog interpreter is accessed as a part of a CGI (Common Gateway Interface) in order to process HTML forms. (Carpenter, 1996; Cabeza, 1996; Loke, 1996). A CGI program is started by the WWW server in response to the submission of an HTML form and stops when a response is generated for delivering to the client. This interaction procedure has two disadvantages. The first is that no state is preserved from one interaction to the next. States can be maintained by means of temporary files, Netscape "cookies", etc., but in some applications the state should be maintained by the application itself. An example would be if one wants to keep the contents of the Prolog database. The second problem is that starting and

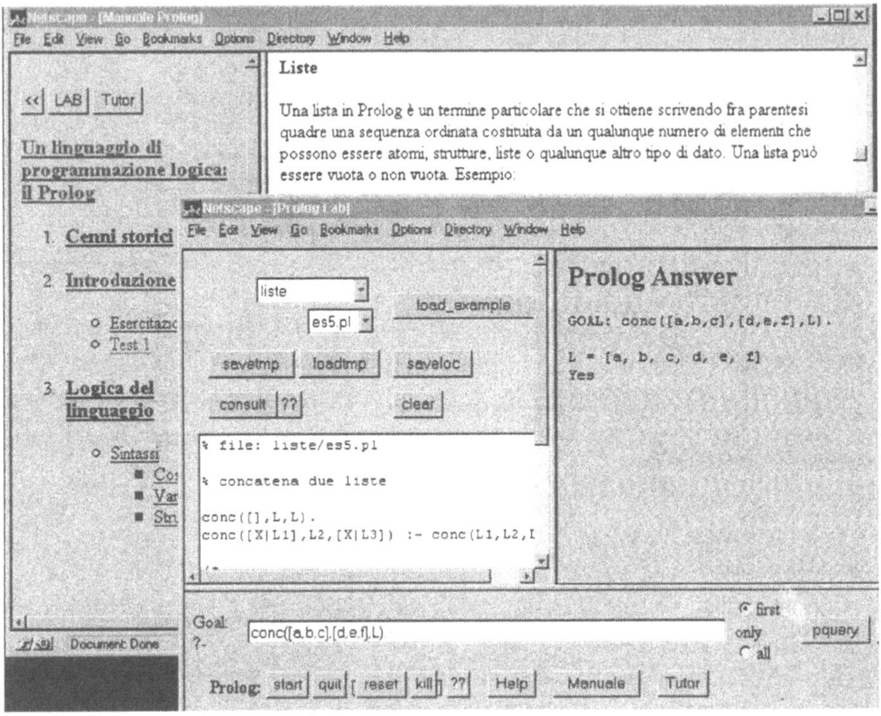

Figure 3. Man-Machine Interface.

stopping the application may be very inefficient. For example, it takes a long time to load the Prolog interpreter and to reload the previous state. A better approach is to have the application running continuously maintaining its status while the CGI program is only an interface between the WWW server and the application (the Prolog interpreter in our case).

In our architecture, the Prolog interpreter is the server, while the WWW browser, the client, is the user interface process. The CGI program or script converts the information coming from the browser to a Prolog query that is submitted to the interpreter. On the other side, the response of the Prolog interpreter is converted in an HTML format and is delivered to the client by the WWW server.

Many WWW-Prolog systems are designed to interface the client to a particular application such as a searching engine or an expert system, etc. The user input has the form of a query that Prolog has to satisfy.

Our purpose on the other hand is educational, so we have to allow the client to make basic actions with the interpreter. For example:

- consulting a user program in the Prolog database;
- executing a goal and showing the response to the user and the resulting binding of the variables.

It is also necessary to handle user errors like syntax errors in the program or in the query passed to the interpreter, or execution errors. These errors should be notified to the client.

Some debugging facility should also be provided. In our case, to avoid an overloading of the server only a trace facility is enabled.

The user can create and edit a temporary file containing his program. This temporary file, which resides on the server, is used for the consulting operation. For the sake of simplicity, the goals submitted to Prolog are also written to a file which makes it easy to check the goal's syntax. A log file managed by the Prolog interpreter is used to notify the occurrence of errors to the user.

Once started, the Prolog interpreter executes the following cycle:

```
while (communication is active) {
 wait for a command from the client (a Prolog goal);
 execute the goal;
send the output, in HTML format, back to the client;
}
```

An important issue is how to manage multiple HTML clients at the same time. In this case, it is necessary to keep track of each client's status. Many solutions were devised for this problem using some form of parallelism (Szeredi, 1996). We have preferred a solution in which each client has a different copy of the interpreter in execution. Each copy of the interpreter knows an identifier of the client, and a different set of copies of the temporary files is created for each client.

Going into more details, HyperProlog (which is how we called our integrated system) requires a browser that supports frames, forms, and Javascripts. It has been extensively tested with Netscape 3.0, but a few tests have also been done with Internet Explorer 3 with apparently no problems. The HTML files and the CGI's reside on an Apache server on a Pentium Pro computer running Linux.

The hypertext is composed of several HTML files. The browser window is split in two frames. The left frame contains the table of contents, while the text is in the right frame. By clicking on an item in the left frame, the corresponding paragraph is opened in the right frame and, if present, a more detailed table of contents is opened in the left frame. Navigating buttons are present in both frames. They allow one to move between chapters and to go back one level. All these buttons use Javascript functions.

Besides the usual hypertext links, the right frame contains buttons to go to the exercise section, to the test section, and to the PrologLab. In the latter case, the examples presented above the button are automatically copied to the edit area of PrologLab.

PrologLab starts as a new browser window and allows the user to interact with the Prolog interpreter on the server. The window is made up of three frames: the "edit" frame, the "query" frame, and the "answer" frame (see Figure 3).

The "edit" frame contains form elements to edit a Prolog program, to select one of the many examples which are part of or complement the hypertext, to insert the selected example in the edit area, to save, to retrieve, to clear the edit area, and to "consult" the Prolog program contained in the edit area. Context-sensitive help buttons are also available.

The "query" frame contains form elements to insert the Prolog goal and to submit the query. It also contains several buttons which allow one to start and quit Prolog, to kill the Prolog process in those cases in which the regular "quit" doesn't work, to jump to the hypertext window, to send an email message to the tutor. Context-sensitive help buttons are also available.

The "answer" frame is where the Prolog answers and information messages are displayed.

The PrologLab window and frames are generated and handled by CGI scripts written in Perl, which interact with the Prolog interpreter through some temporary files. One Prolog process is started and one set of temporary files is allocated for each user. The temporary files contain the user input, the Prolog output, the error log, the program to be consulted, etc.

Some buttons in the exercise section of the hypertext let students take a test. These buttons activate a CGI on the server which handles the whole test in a new browser window.

The information about the test and about the student taking it together with his/her answers is kept on a separate file for each student. This file is used throughout the test and its name is sent back and forth between client and server using a Netscape cookie, which allows keeping state information between separate browser requests.

The test window contains two frames. The right frame displays one question at a time, while the left frame contains buttons to jump to a particular question or to cycle through the questions. It also displays a "Finish" button. One can go back and forth between questions to check the answers given before clicking the "Finish" button.

When the student clicks "Finish", the CGI creates a summary table listing the answers given, the correct answers, and the ratio of the guessed, missing, and wrong answers. It displays the table together with all the questions in the test and the answers given by the student. At the same time, an e-mail is automatically sent to the tutor with all the information needed to evaluate the results of the test. While the multiple choice and the true or false questions are corrected automatically, the essay questions need to be graded by the instructor.

4. SYSTEM EVALUATION

The system was tried out by a group of 22 students attending the third and last year of a Computer Science program. They were all males and their age ranged from 21 to 23 years (mean 23). They worked with the system for about 30 hours.

A second group of 20 students of the fifth year of the Electronic Engineering program worked on the system for four hours in order to evaluate the system in terms of its robustness and the friendliness of the interface.

In the evaluation of this system we relied on three types of information:

1) Analysis of the students' patterns of activity by means of system logs. This analysis will give details about the students' use of the system; that is, which pages of the text they looked at most, which facilities they used the most (hypertext, tutorials, self tests, e-mail, PrologLab) or which ones they overlooked.

2) Effectiveness of the system in terms of the students' learning outcomes. This evaluation is based on the results of the final test.

3) Students' attitudes toward the resource. A questionnaire was administered to the students to assess how much they liked this resource in comparison with a traditional course. They were asked which part of the system they liked most and which ones least. They were also asked which parts they felt to be the most useful and why. The results of the questionnaires were integrated with the information gathered during group discussions on the topic.

Patterns of usage can be obtained by two sources. The first source is provided by the WWW server that automatically saves each transaction in a log file. In this file there is a record for each page accessed and for each form submitted. In the latter case, the associated query string is also registered.

By observing these data we can obtain statistics about page usage. For example, we can find out the topics the student read, or the operation that the user performed, such as loading a file in the edit area, consulting the file, submitting queries to the interpreter, etc.

Other data about the user activity can be directly recorded by the system. For example, when a form is submitted to the server and a CGI program is started, it can record information in a file. Every time that a student starts a session our system saves his user name, host name, date and time, etc. The data obtained from the system logs show that students did not access the general presentation of mathematical logic very frequently. The four related pages - propositional logic, introduction to mathematical logic, logic of first order predicates, logic for problem solving - register an average of 50 accesses each. On the contrary, the Prolog page registers almost 700 accesses.

Table 1. Number of accesses to tutorials, solution of exercises and to example files for laboratory use. (Tutorial contents: I - facts, rules and queries; II - syntax and structures; III - lists; IV - backtracking and cut; V - arithmetics).

	I	*II*	*III*	*IV*	*V*	*Tot*
tutorials	111	111	168	249	110	749
solutions	24	46	46	33	30	179
example files	184	65	312	255	74	928

The tutorials were also read a lot. Working on the tutorials includes checking the solutions of the exercises and loading the example files. Table 1 shows the number of accesses to the tutorials with the related files and demonstrates the interest shown by the students for practising what they learned in the Prolog presentation. We can see that tutorials 3 and 4 are the most accessed. This can be explained by the difficulty of their topics. Tutorial 5 is the very last and has not been accessed very much simply because of the lack of time. Self assessment tests were not meant for final grading, but were devised to give the students feedback about their understanding and mastery of the subject matter. There were five self assessment tests. Each one included a number of multiple-choice and true/false questions and one or two essay questions. These tests were automatically sent to the tutor for the correction of the essay questions and for general supervision. Multiple-choice and true/false questions were automatically graded. Immediately after having sent the test to the tutor, the students could see a screen showing the following information: how many answers to the multiple-choice and true/false questions were correct, how many were wrong and how many were missing. They could also reread the questions and since they knew now where they had made a mistake, they could then try to understand the reason for their error. Later on, the tutor would check the answers to the essay questions and send each student the necessary suggestions and advice by e-mail.

Self assessment tests were randomly generated from an available database. Therefore, each student received a different version of the test. This allowed the students to repeat the tests as many times as they felt it necessary. These tests were largely used by the students who appreciated the possibility of checking up on their progress. As it is shown in Table 2, many of them tried each test more than once. Some did it out of pure curiosity while others only wanted to be reassured about their performance.

Table 2. Median and mode of students' test usage. Each test refers to a tutorial (see Table 1).

Test #	*I*	*II*	*III*	*IV*	*V*	*Tot.*
Median	2	3	3	3.5	1.5	13
Mode	1	2	2	0	0	9
Total	45	77	75	78	52	327

It should be noticed however that the range of variation is quite large, especially for the last tests. Some students did not try them at all, while others tried them up to eleven times. This repeated trying however contributed to their learning.

Table 3 shows an increase in the mean percent of correct answers from the first to the last trial of each test. The increase is particularly evident and statistically significant for the last three tests. Students tried self assessment tests both during the course and in preparation for the final test.

At the end of the course, students were graded by means of a test also given through the Web. This test was the same for all the students. It included 10 questions and covered all the topics of the course. Although two of the students did not take the final test, those who did performed very well. The median of correct answers is 87 (range 60 to 100) and the mode 94. The students were motivated to do a good job, but these very high results also show that our environment was indeed very effective.

Table 3. Mean percentage of correct answers to the first and last trial of each test and overall mean percentage of correct answers to the same tests.

Test #	*I*	*II*	*III*	*IV*	*V*	*Tot.*
First	96.8	89.3	77.5	65.6	77.4	81.8
Last	97.9	91.7	86.0	85.6	90.5	90.4
Overall	95.6	85.9	84.2	85.1	86.2	86.7

Lastly, we collected some subjective data by means of questionnaires and interviews. The questionnaire included twelve questions. Students were asked whether they were familiar with the hypertext format and how much they liked it. Then, they were asked whether they had ever used an integrated tool such as HyperProlog. They were asked whether or not they liked it better than using a traditional book plus a separated Prolog interpreter and why. They were asked whether they had had any difficulty with HyperProlog and, if so, of what type. Lastly, they were asked what parts of HyperProlog they used most and least and to give their reasons.

Only a few of the students had ever had a course supported by hypertext material (18%) and none of them had ever followed a course with an integrated didactic tool such as HyperProlog. Nevertheless, they appreciated and enjoyed the experience. The majority of them (60%) said that in case they had to repeat the course they would rather choose an integrated tool instead of a traditional book and an interpreter. In a 7 point scale ranging from 1 (preferred the traditional book plus an interpreter) to 7 (preferred the integrated tool), with 4 as the indifference point, the median value was 5 and the mode was 6. This is a clear indication that they gave a positive evaluation to the use of this tool. Those who preferred the integrated tool justified their choice saying that it allowed them to try practical activities related to the theory they had just learned and that this made learning faster. Those who said that they would have preferred the traditional book plus a Prolog interpreter expressed their desire for face to face interaction with the teacher and also mentioned fatigue induced by reading the screen. They also said that they liked the PrologLab, but would have liked to have a personal copy of the material and felt limited by the fact that they did not have access to Internet from their homes.

The parts of the system that they said they had used the most were self tests (71%), tutorials (67%), and PrologLab (43%). These were also the parts they felt were the most useful: tutorials (67%), self tests (57%), PrologLab (52%). They felt that these three parts helped them to clarify their thoughts and doubts. They appreciated the richness of the examples and the possibility of practising. In the self test they liked the immediate feedback available in the computer corrected questions. They would have preferred not to have the questions sent to the tutor for correction though, because they thought that this had limited their possibility to try the self tests several times.

The parts that they used the least were the theoretical presentation (81%) and e-mail. In their opinion, the theoretical presentation was unclear and difficult. They do not justify their overlooking the e-mail facility but it should be remembered that the experience was on a campus where tutors were available. They preferred direct interaction as demonstrated by their active participation during face to face lectures.

In conclusion, it seems quite evident that this integrated environment has been appreciated by the students who liked the possibility of activity included in the tutorials by means of the PrologLab and used these resources effectively for their learning. In order to fully exploit the possibilities of this system the following will be necessary: a larger diffusion of technological resources such as individual access to Internet; changes in the students' study habits with more independent study activity and less reliance on immediate feedback from the tutor as in a face to face interaction; changes in the features offered by the system such as the availability of more different types of activity; a better automatic feedback in the correction of students' assignments and their evaluation; a wider range of different communication tools.

In this paper we presented a distributed client-server architecture as a support for learning. A part of the architecture has been implemented and experimented with undergraduate students. The preliminary results are encouraging and a more extensive use of the system is planned. The integration of hypertext with the virtual laboratory and the on-line evaluation which was presently integrated only with an e-mail facility for communication exchanges will be extended to the other mentioned communication tools such as bulletin boards, virtual blackboards, voices and images

5. REFERENCES

Cabeza, D., Hermenegildo, M., and Varmaa, S. (1996) The PiLLoW/CIAO Library for INTERNET/WWW Programming Using Computational Logic Systems, in *Proceedings of the 1st Workshop on Logic Programming - Tools for Internet Applications*, Bonn, Germany, September 2-6,1996.

Carpenter, B., (1996) A Prolog-based CGI handler. *http://macduff.andrew.cmu.edu/cgparser/prolog_cgi.html.*

Crook, C. (1997) Making hypertext material more interactive: some undergraduate reactions. In press *Journal of Computer Assisted Learning*, **13**.

Cuban, L. (1986) Teachers and Machines. New York, Teachers College.

Loke, S.W., and Davison, A. (1996) Logic programming with the Word-Wide Web, *The 7th ACM conference on Hypertext*, ACM Press. Available from *http://www.cs.unc.edu/~barman/HT96/P14/lpwww.html.*

McAteer, E., Tolmie, A., Duffy, C. and Corbett, J. (1997) The evaluation of Computer Mediated Communication as a learning resource in Higher Education. In press *Journal of Computer Assisted Learning*, **13**.

Piaget, J., (1947) La psychologie de l'intelligence. Alcan, Paris.

Piaget, J., (1964) Development and Learning, in *Piaget Rediscovered* (eds. R.E. Ripple and V.N. Rockcastle), Cornell University Press, Ithaca, NY.

Steffe, L.S. and Gale, J. (1995) Constructivism in Education. Erlbaum, Hillsdale, N.J.

Szeredi, P., Molnar, K. and Scatt, R., (1996) Serving Multiple HTML Clients from a Prolog Application, in *Proceedings of the 1st Workshop on Logic Programming - Tools for Internet Applications*, Bonn, Germany.

6. BIOGRAPHIES

Giovanni Adorni is a Professor of Computer Engineering at the the University of Parma and Representative of the Rector of the University of Parma for "Information and Communication Technologies". His research activities are in the area of computer vision, autonomous vehicles navigation, planning, man-machine interaction, multi-agent systems. He coordinated several national research programs on artificial intelligence, and partecipated to different european programs, including the seven years EUREKA PROMETHEUS project, where he has been the national coordinator and a member of the european steering sommittee for the PRO-ART sub-project. He received, among others, the Systems Research Foundation Award in recognition of his research on "knowledge based planning", and the ICL European Artificial Intelligence Prize on Cognitive Modelling. He has authored and coauthored over hundred scientific papers in international journals, contributed volumes, and conference proceedings. Professor Giovanni Adorni is a member of AI*IA and AAAI.

Maria Silvia Barbieri was born in 1947. She obtained a degree in Philosophy at the University of Pavia, Italy, in 1970, and a *specializzazione* in Psychology at the University of Milano, in 1974. Since 1978 she has been teaching at the University of Trieste, where presently she is full professor of Developmental Psychology. Her research interests concern cognitive development, the effects of social interaction on language and cognition, and, recently, computer mediated communication in education.

Dario Bianchi was born in 1946. He received the Dr.Ing. degree in nuclear engineering from the Polytechnic of Milano in 1971 and a *perfezionamento* in Solid State Physics at the University of Parma, in 1976. Since 1983 he is associate professor at the University of Parma. His research activity has been in solid state physics and in the usage of microcomputers in experimental physics. Presently his main interests are in the areas of natural language processing, of massively parallel systems, of genetic algorithms and fuzzy logic. He is a member of AI*IA and ACL.

Eduardo Calabrese was born in Messina, Italy on 1943. He obtained a Ph.D. degree in Physics at Lehigh University, U.S.A. in 1971. Since then, he has been employed as a professor at the University of Parma, where he has been teaching courses in Physics and Informatics. Currently, he holds a position as associate professor of Informatics at the University Engineering Department. His professional interests include educational uses of the computer which involve Internet and distance learning.

Angela Maria Sugliano was born in Genoa in 1968. She received the Laurea Degree in Philosophy of Science from the University of Genoa in 1992, and the Diploma Degree in Journalism in 1996. She is a Ph.D student in Methodology for Research in Psychology at Faculty of Psychology of the University of Genoa. Her research activities are in the area of social and psychological aspects of computer mediated communication.

GCSE project for distance evaluation of knowledge in French foreign language

R. Bedanokova and Ph. Teutsch

LIUM - Université du Maine
72085 LE MANS Cedex 9, France
E-mail : Philippe.Teutsch@lium.univ-lemans.fr

ABSTRACT

In this paper we present the GCSE project that has as its aim the creation of a system for distance evaluation of the knowledge in the French foreign language. The main objective of the system is to put at the disposal of pupils, from a distance, exam-type questions with correction and automatic evaluation. Our main interest was focused on the evaluation of the student's written response.

The design of a test environment for languages is a difficult field to manage: the modelling of the linguistic field and the treatment of language are badly understood, the learning of the language is relatively contextual. Additionally the computer creates a particular didactic situation which is unfamiliar.

We discuss the problems of putting the evaluation of student's knowledge into a computer context and present the iterative design process of the system that helps to overcome these problems.

Keywords

Automatic evaluation, Self-learning, Language-learning assessment

The Virtual Campus F. Verdejo & G. Davies (Eds.)

1. INTRODUCTION

The Interactive Learning Environments (ILE) greatly interests foreign language teachers for their capabilities to create interactive environments of learning.
What do new technologies add to the evaluation sequences of the student's knowledge? They enrich the learning environment; they offer the possibility of different forms of representation of the task-based testing material: combining text with multimedia capabilities.

Today the computer is considered to be a partner in the whole process of the learning of languages (Chanier 1991). From the trend of learner-oriented approach, the language teachers seek to put the student into a situation of real communication and to enable him to analyse his own efforts (Narcy 1990). The tools of auto-evaluation and assisted auto-orientation become in this context as important as all the others (Teutsch, Vivet 1993).

The main difficulties that we encounter in this perspective are the following:

- the use of computers as a teaching aid has had profound influence on the situation of learning but this has not been fully researched (Vivet 1991) ;
- the problems of good integration of the designed software with different teaching methods into a coherent teaching process ;
- we cannot preview the exact use that will be made of the system.

This is the context in which we have designed a GCSE server (the abbreviation of the General Certificate of Secondary Education), the system of evaluation of knowledge in a French foreign language targeted at young English people.

2. DESCRIPTION OF THE GCSE PROJECT

The aim of the GCSE project is to make available to young Anglophones the means of the preparation for the GCSE exam in a French foreign language, as a support of individualised evaluation. One of the ideas of the GCSE project is the use of new technologies to bridge the gap between students learning French and the real users of the French language, in other words, put at their disposal the means of direct contact with French tutors.

The main features of the GCSE server are: WWW-based intelligent analysis of student solutions, advanced testing and debugging facilities.

The concept of the GCSE server has been guided by MARPLE, a system of evaluation in English intended for professional training (Teutsch, 1994). The multidisciplinary team created around the MARPLE project has defined a tool for formal specification of the «Situation of Knowledge Evaluation » (Teutsch 1996, ITS). It is the meeting point between the computer specification of the system and the analysis of the didactic situation.

The context of the project

Since 1986, the diploma awarded at the end of the first cycle of secondary education in Great Britain has been GCSE: the General Certificate of Secondary Education. It is taken in various subjects including a foreign language (French, German, Spanish, Japanese, Chinese, Italian). An exam in a foreign language will become compulsory for all those beginning secondary education in 1998.

The exam can be taken in two levels: basic, obligatory for all who take a GCSE exam in a foreign language, and higher level, where the student has a choice of either passing the whole exam or only parts of it. Our system presents the user with a choice of these levels of functioning which reflects the exam options.

The aims of the project

The main functions of GCSE system are to validate certain individual skills in a foreign language - reading and listening comprehension, writing and speaking ; and to help the student realise his capabilities at the end of each session of evaluation of these skills. The role of the system is not only to validate his level, to underline his errors but also to give him a knowledge about his strong and weak points. The situation of evaluation that the student is put into by the GCSE server directly involves him in self-appraisal and self-learning. It helps them to confront and compare their capabilities with the standard.

Through exercises of the test situations and through linguistic exchanges between the system and the student the latter develops analytic abilities. He also learns how to master his mistakes, to assess and explain them, and to solve them. It is the student who is in control of the pedagogical sequence, it is he who decides what is the next step. The role of the teacher is to help the student to work in this direction and to overcome his problems. Under these conditions, the fact that the teacher has at his disposal a means of supporting his work of evaluation, he needs no longer mark papers but may become a directly accessible tutor, as the GCSE server can not replace the teacher in more individual consultation or in making decisions concerning the student's needs.

The problematic of the question

In our work we were interested in overcoming the problems that are encountered by the designers of CALL (Computer Assisted Language Learning) systems and in investigating in the following problematic:

- representation of the knowledge
- the method of the system design.

The use of the computer aid in an educational process requires the formal representation of the knowledge of the domain. But the problems that arise in attempting to comprehend the language teaching make it very difficult.

The existing systems lack expertise in the didactic situation of their use. Those systems are only oriented towards grammatical and linguistic knowledge (Yazdani 1989) and do not take into account the cognitive process developed by the student. The result is limited to dull structural exercises with limited aim (Swartz&Yazdani 1991), the analysis of responses is relatively poor.

In terms of evaluation of the system, « English Tutor » (Fum 1991) has some advantages in applying strategies of analysis: the error response activates the creation by the system of number of hypotheses on the certain knowledge of a student that are taken into account in the choice of next set of exercises.

The research work on the development of such systems (representation of the knowledge of the domain, architecture of the system, user interface) has to be built around the analysis of where the system supports the teacher in the process of evaluation and of the analysis of the aspects of its real use.

Our method is to create an interactive linguistic, cultural and didactic area, where the student is going to progress, discover for himself his abilities; the system is designed to increase his performance. We have designed the interactive environment in a style which is also characteristic of the situation of its real use. The system benefits the main guidelines of the GCSE exam: communicative approach, tolerance of mistakes, a learner-oriented approach, use of real documents. To achieve this, we have used the iterative method for the conception of the system.

One of the objectives of our work is to present the specification of the methods of conception that can be generalised and reused in other situations.

3. SITUATION OF KNOWLEDGE EVALUATION

This model consists of three main classes that describe the elements of the interaction and their features.

- The description of the teaching material (sequence of courses, grammar material, vocabulary and especially the test situations) together with the cultural topics.
- The description of the support to the process of evaluation seen from its objectives, description of the activity proposed by the test and detailed reference to the material to work on. Each question corresponds to the « Model of Analysis » which defines the anticipated student's input and the comments to his errors.
- The description of the mode of interaction as a support to the presentation (text, sound, image) and the mode of response, proposed to the user. In the evaluation of the student's output the mode of interaction has to be taken into consideration as it influences more or less the student's response.

This model of « Situation of Knowledge Evaluation » helps to adapt at the same time the design according to the principles of modular architecture and to the iterative method of designing. In the dialogue between specialists in didactic and computer sciences, the initial design hypothesis is modified by experimentation.

4. THE ITERATIVE METHOD OF THE SYSTEM DESIGN

The conception of the GCSE helped to overcome these problems by using the iterative method of conception that consists in creation of prototypes taking into consideration the objectives and constrains of activities in both fields: creating an interactive system and studying the didactic situation of evaluation (Teutsch 1994).

Cumming and Self (1990) showed that the « front approach » in the conception of ITS requires an extremely detailed representation of knowledge. As a consequence the encountered difficulties prevent the creation of usable systems.

For GSCE, the first step was to define and design the interactive environment proposed to the student, that is based on the specification of the situation of evaluation; and the second step was concerned with the studies and designing of the linguistic contents and test material.

Thus, in designing the GCSE system, we have followed the stages of:

1. Preliminary studies. Studying the user together with the context of the use of the system, the first specifications of the situation of evaluation.
2. Creation of a model of a system. Specification of the interactive environment seen from a user interface, designing the system architecture. On this stage we are concerned with aspects of interaction that are created by the situation of evaluation.
3. Development of the system. Designing the linguistic contents of the system: the specification of the linguistic knowledge; definition of the test situations , making the hypothesis of the student's responses. On this stage we are mainly concerned with adapting the test material to the peculiarities of the system usage and the difficulties that the student may encounter.
4. Experimentation. On this stage our objective is to validate the proposed situations and to learn the linguistic behaviour of the students in the situation of real use.
5. Creating a new prototype. The evaluation of results of real usage requires incorporating the design changes into a model that we test on the users again.

The use of this spiral method in designing of an interactive system allows us to propose the skeleton of the architecture of the system and then to refine gradually its functional and communicative aspects.

5. THE ENVIRONMENT OF EVALUATION

As we have mentioned earlier, the test material proposed by GCSE system is designed to follow the objectives of GCSE exam in a French language and is based on the real life situations and are supported by authentic documents (brochures, posters and signs).

The system presents all the situations of evaluation in two major axes: to enable a student to be evaluated in a certain skill in a foreign language; to enable a student to get evaluated in a foundation or higher level.

All the presented situations can be tried in two test modes:

1. Exam mode, which places the user in an exam situation with an access to the answers only at the end of the session.
2. Training mode, in which answers and explanations are given during the test.

Each of these modes gives the possibility of being evaluated in four skills: listening, speaking, reading, writing that evaluate four respective communication skills of the students. At present the software has only been developed for two: reading and listening.

Listening: the system tests listening comprehension skills using multimedia facilities to present audio material, the recorded documents specially made for the exam.

Reading and writing: the system tests these skills by evaluating in a synchronous way the answers through writing in input fields, checkbox or map-images.

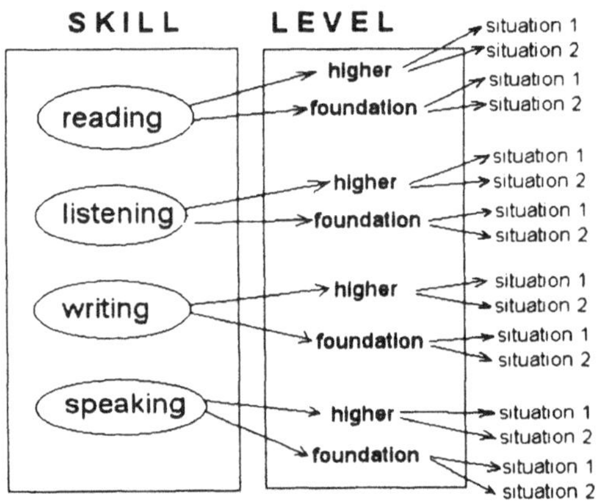

Figure 1. The elements of GCSE system.

In figure 1 we present the elements of the system. At the beginning of each session of evaluation the student is free to choose the mode of work (exam or training), the skill to be evaluated (reading, listening, writing or speaking) and, finally, the level of the competence (foundation or higher). Each situation (situation 1 or situation 2) comprises a set of questions (from 3 to 7 for each level), dealing with different subjects. For example, while travelling to France the student finds himself on the ferry, in the shop, where he has to put the fight labels to the items of clothes, at a restaurant, in the tourist office, etc.

The representations of the test material is chosen for its explicative power, communicability, simplicity and for facility of execution. The advantage of the use of such a system is that the student makes free choices in mode, skill or level over and over again, is free to control the session of evaluation. They also can modify their responses and check them again. The material is presented in a way that allows the student to progress from easier questions, some in mother tongue, at a allows the student to progress from easier questions, some in mother tongue, at a foundation level, to more difficult questions at a higher level. They plan themselves the amount of time spent on the preparation for the exam. This is not possible in a usual situation with a single available teacher for the whole group.

In the training mode, if a student would like to see the corrections to his answers, the system launches the window of comments. In the exam mode the student doesn't get the synchronous evaluation. He can have his results only at end of the session. Figure 2 represents respectively the copy of the page of one of the situations and the window of corrections. The topic of evaluation concerns the trip of one of the main characters of the GCSE situations - a French girl Sandrine.

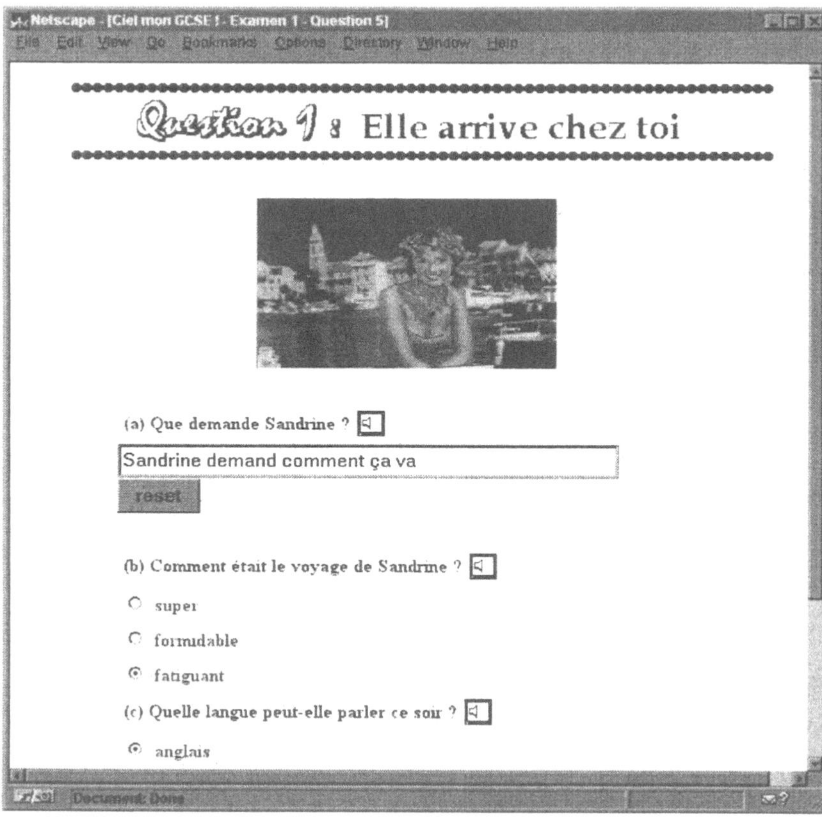

Figure 2 (a).Situation of evaluation in listening comprehension/foundation level.

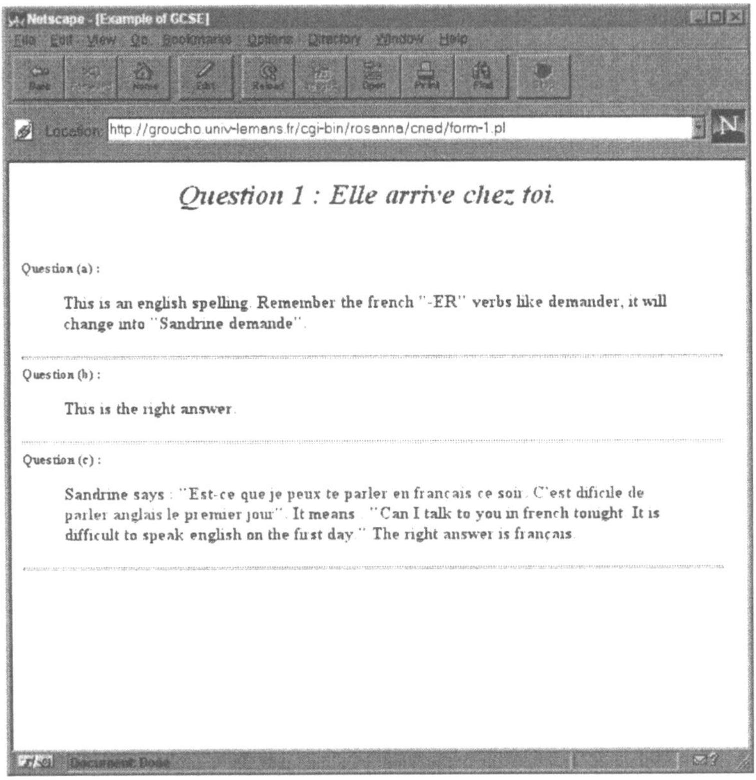

Figure 2 (b). Window of correction corresponding to student's responses.

6. EVALUATION OF STUDENT RESPONSES

In the designing of the GCSE server our interest was mainly focused on the WWW-based intelligent analysis of the student's input data, on the measuring of individual performance with a set of tasks in a specific situation. While creating the hypothesis on the student's responses, we took into consideration the frequent errors made by Anglophones in the French foreign language.

In our case we are dealing with the functional, linguistic (grammar, morphology, syntax), lexical and cultural knowledge of the student. It might contain descriptions, expressed as linguistic frames, schemes, the meanings of words and the types of the associations between the lexical units in mother-tongue and target language the student might have built. Therefore this analyser comprises many different levels of analysis.

The basis of analysis of the written response of the system is the comparison of the student's answer against the tree of possibilities foreseen by the teachers. This tree is deduced from a whole range of possible responses. Each response model describes an envisaged answer and incorporates into it correct and incorrect answers for each term. The analyser exploits permanent syntax, spelling, grammar, lists of equivalent terms as well as detectable mistakes and their type.

```
modele: {#G1 [Sandrine | [Elle | {$O-GRAPH #IL il} | {$O-GRAPH #EL %elle] ] [demande |
{$CS-TRANSF #DEMANDE demand}] [comment | {$O-GRAPH #COMMENT %comment}] [ça |
{$O-CCEDIL #CA ca}] [va | {$CS-SENS #ORDER va [bien |{$O-CONFUS #BIEN bein}] }] }
modele: {#G2 [Sandrine | [Elle | {$O-GRAPH #IL il} | {$O-GRAPH #EL %elle] ] [demande |
{$CS-TRANSF #DEMANDE demand}] si [ça | {$O-CCEDIL #CA ca}] va ([bien |{$O-CONFUS
#BIEN bein}]) }

modele: {#G3 ([Comment | {$O-GRAPH #COMMENT %comment}]) [ça | {$O-CCEDIL #CA ca}] va
}
modele: {#G4 (Si) [ça | {$O-CCEDIL #CA ca}] va ([bien |{$O-CONFUS #BIEN bein}]) }
modele: {#F-NONE NONE}

equivalence: %comment - [coment | commant | comant | comman | commen |coman ]
equivalence: %elle - [Ele | El ]

commentaire: #G1 - file://quest-2-C.html
commentaire: #G2 - file://quest-2-C.html
commentaire: #G3 - file://quest-2-C.html
commentaire: #G4 - file://quest-2-C.html
commentaire: #CA - file://ca.html

commentaire: #COMMENT - file://comment.html
commentaire: #BIEN - file://bien.html
commentaire: #DEMANDE - file://demande.html
commentaire: #ORDER - file://order.html
commentaire: #IL - file://il.html
commentaire: #EL - file://el.html
commentaire: #F-NONE - file://quest-1-NONE.html
```

Figure 3. « Analysis chart » in GCSE.

Each question corresponds to the « analysis chart » (figure 3) which consists of the response models, equivalences of various forms of words or their synonyms and comments to be shown to the student in the function of his response :

- The syntactic response model. The models present both correct and incorrect answers using the equivalences for some words or groups of words where necessary. For each type of the error a special code is used, which is also incorporated in this model. The programme refers to the list of types of errors to decode it and adds this information to the trace of the student's session.
- Equivalence is used where necessary to mark the fact of equivalence between words or phrases in the treatment of the student response.
- Comments. To each anticipated response the system can give a comment in the mother-tongue. It allows a student to be informed about his successes or errors.

For each student's answer the system compares it word by word with the response models in the corresponding « analysis chart ».

Together with the evaluation the system aims at the qualitative and quantitative improvement in foreign language competence. The comment material relies on the principle that students must « learn from their mistakes ». But also we can't forget about the fact that young English people might have problems in understanding the grammar explanations in the comments to errors as they are often not taught much about the grammar structure of their mother-tongue.

The system uses the direct remediation in most of the cases: a direct corrective statement, dealing with the knowledge that the student should have rather than the buggy knowledge he does, in fact, have. This choice is primarily made in the case of the wrong translation of words when the buggy knowledge is considered as a mere factual error which does not indicate a misconception.

For example, the error in grammar « ils parle » is corrected with the following explanation : « **-ER** verbs like *parler* change their endings for each person : je parl***e*** - I speak, tu parl***es*** - you speak, ils parl***ent*** - they speak ».

The error of the type « bon idée » is corrected with the following explanation : « **idée** is a feminine word so the adjective describing it needs to be in a feminine form too : un***e*** bon***ne*** idée ». Also the correction of errors consists of material that suggest the ways of associating the words (memo-rules). If an error is made in the spelling of the word « comment » in the phrase « Comment ça va? » (« How are you? »), the system suggests it is associated with another English word : « Think about the English word *comment,* it is just the same spelling ».

In the case where there are errors in grammar or spelling, the explanations of the rules are given. In the cases where the system cannot interpret a student's input, it informs the user that his or her response cannot be evaluated and collects these unforeseen responses that will be treated and added to « analysis chart ».

7. CONCLUSION

The GCSE server presents a system of the evaluation of student's knowledge in French and a tool for preparing for the GCSE exam. In the system design an effort was made to transfer pedagogic knowledge to the creation of a computerised environment.

A redefinition of roles takes place with the appearance of new actor - computer technology in the teacher-student relationship. How exactly does the server replace the teacher in the evaluation process? In organising the evaluation environment; in providing the language data for the learners; in providing appraising feedback to the learners. But the GCSE server does not make decisions concerning their individual needs. It is the learners who make this decision for themselves. How does the server support the learner's activity in the evaluation process? By building the conditions for their autonomous work, benefiting the gradual process of constructing knowledge about self-knowledge, by allowing them to check and govern their own output and learn from their mistakes.

The specification of the « Situation of Knowledge Evaluation » and the iterative method of the designing enabled us to create a system that meets all the requirements of its use. The flexibility of the system allows the experiment results to be incorporated in the response models at each step of this spiral process.

8. REFERENCES

Chanier Th. (1991) Perspectives de l'apport de l'EIAO dans l'apprentissage des langues étrangères. *4ème Assises de l'IA et de la Formation*, Paris.

Cumming G. and Self J.(1990) Intelligent Educational Systems: Identifying and Decoupling the Conversational Levels. *Instructional Science*, **1-17,** *n°19.*

Fum D., Giandgrandi P. and Tasso C. (1991) The Use of Explanation-based Learning for Modelling Student Behavior in Foreign Language Tutoring, in Swartz & Yazdani 1991.

Narcy J.P. (1990) Apprendre une Langue Etrangère, Les Editions d'Organisation, Paris.

Swartz and Yazdani (1991) Intelligent Tutoring Systems for Second-Language learning, the Bridge to International Communication, Springer Verlag.

Teutsch Ph. and Vivet M. (1993) Interaction Issues in Computer Assisted Language Learning Systems. *International Conference on Computers in Education*, **144-149,** Taiwan.

Teutsch Ph. (1994) Environments Interactifs et Langue Etrangères, MARPLE: système d'évaluation et de suivi de formation. Thèse de l'Université du Maine, Le Mans.

Teutsch Ph. (1996) Un modèle de Situation d'Evaluation pour le Suivi de Formation en Langue Etrangère. *ITS'96 Third International Conference on Intelligent Tutoring Systems*, **315-323,** Montréal.

Vivet M. (1991) Usage des tuteurs intelligents: prise en compte du contexte, rôle du maître. *2ème Journées EIAO*, **239-246,** Cachan.

Yazdany M. (1989) An Artificial Intelligence Approach to Second Language Teaching, *2nd ICCAL* (ed. Springer Verlag), Dallas.

9. BIOGRAPHIES

Rousanna Bedanokova is post-graduate student and **Philippe Teutsch** is researcher in computer science laboratory of the Université du Maine (LIUM, Le Mans, France). Both study the design of interactive learning environments and the use of such systems in distance learning situation, especially in the language learning domain. Their actual research focuses in the use of knowledge of language teachers to make an intelligent evaluation of language ability, and to give advice about further training.

Conceptual Learning of Sciences Supported by Java Compliant technologies

S. Divjak
Faculty of Computer and Information Science,
University of Ljubljana
Trzaska 25, 1000 Ljubljana, Slovenia
e-mail: sasa@fri.uni-lj.si

Abstract

The paper presents the concept of reusability of experiments prepared with CoLoS authoring tools and converted into a Java environment. This permits increased platform independence and a possible usage in a distributed environment. The original CoLoS experiments are running on Motif compliant platforms which are normally used on workstations with the UNIX operating system. These experiments are converted into applets which can be used as normal components of hypertext based lessons. In such a way original CoLoS authoring tools are still useful for the development of new experiments that can be used on platforms which are most popular in the schools. The concept is further extended with the possibilities offered by the local networks and the Internet. The additional tools for distance learning and distributed groupwork are developed.

Keywords

Simulation, Physics, Distance learning, Java

The Virtual Campus F. Verdejo & G. Davies (Eds.)

1. INTRODUCTION

CoLoS (COnceptual Learning Of Science) is a consortium founded in 1988, initially composed of research teams from western European universities. Today the research teams from the following universities represent CoLoS (in alphabetical order): Balearic Islands, Berlin, Cambridge, Cottbus, Delft, Edinburgh, Genova, Oxford, Kiel, Las Palmas, Ljubljana, Lyon, Madrid, Maribor, Murcia, Paris, StPetersburg. Fields of interest of various CoLoS research groups are: physics, chemistry, electrical engineering, mechanical engineering, computer science.

The major goal of this consortium is to encourage and co-ordinate the development of teaching methods to improve the knowledge and understanding of fundamental concepts with a special focus on intuitive and qualitative approaches, more particularly in the scientific and technical fields.

The general CoLoS objectives are: to enhance the teaching of science by using innovative and highly interactive software; to explore the new ways of using computer applications in scientific learning; to develop an intuitive understanding and feel for science in students.

One of the methods that has been developed by CoLos is based on the mimicry of nature and its fundamental principles instead of solving mathematical equations. The computer is used for the visualisation of molecular or atomic behaviour. The teacher or students can interact with the simulated system and in this way obtain a better understanding. From the technical point of view this is achieved through 2D or 3D visualisation of simulated world equipped with the needed control buttons, sliders and other possible interacting components.

During the first years of the CoLoS activity more than 60 applications have been developed, the common platforms being powerful workstations with the UNIX operating system and with good computational and graphical characteristics. The development of new experiments has been enabled by means of authoring tools like xdev and xyZET. Xdev is in fact a program generator that enables the creation of new applications through a user- friendly graphical interface. XyZET is both an authoring tool for the development of new experiments and a simulator for their execution. Both tools have been upgraded with the possibility for the remote control of experiments through the commands that can be included and activated in hypertext- based lessons.

The expansion of the Internet and the appearance of Java have permitted the development of platform independent applications. This technological trend has influenced the strategy of CoLoS. The need for reusability of already developed courseware demanded the development of the additional software tools which are described in this paper.

2. REUSABILITY OF EXPERIMENTS PREPARED BY XYZET

XyZET is an interactive, graphically oriented simulation tool that permits the presentation of objects and structures in 3D. The basic building elements of these objects are particles that are defined by their mass, charge, initial position and velocities. These particles can be connected with springs. In such a way more complex, non-rigid bodies can be presented. Different internal and external forces influence the particles in the system. Their behaviour can be observed during the animation. The basic phenomena from the domain of mechanics and electricity can be explored (kinematics, conservation of energy and momentum, Hook's law, gravity, charges, field lines and equipotential planes).

The conceptual learning of the particular phenomena can be achieved by incremental building of simple and then increasingly more complex bodies and structures and by experimentation with various physical parameters. The teaching scenario can be included in accompanying and interacting hypertext. In such a way complete courses in the domains of mechanics and electricity have been created. In the course of mechanics the student first achieves the understanding of the coordinate system, of constant and accelerated motion. He continues with the experiments explaining the basic mechanical laws and ends with an advanced study of various pendulums. These examples are simple but didactically well selected and explained.

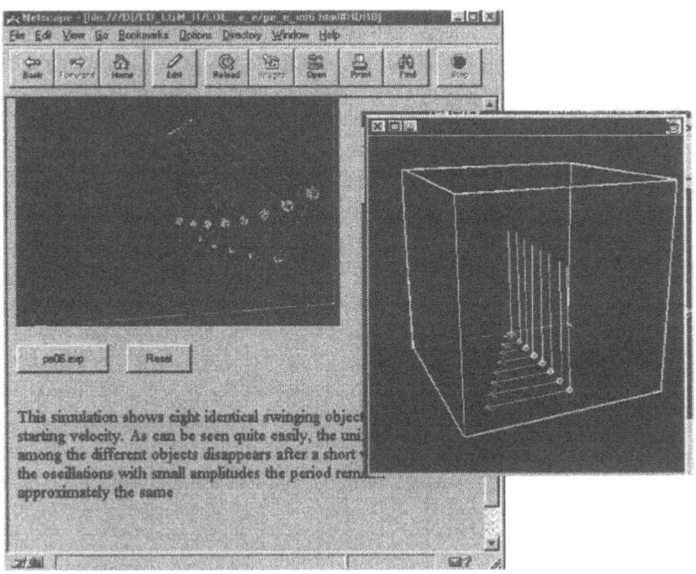

Figure 1. Screenshot with a hypertext lesson and an interacting experiment

The gallery of more than 200 experiments includes some extremelly complex examples with bodies consisting of more than 100 interconnected particles.

In order to permit a platform- independent visualisation of these experiments a viewer has been developed in the form of a Java applet. This applet is represented as a button which is integrated in the hypertext- based lessons. Activating the button, a visualized 3D world in a separate frame appears. The parameters of the experiment can be controlled by means of buttons, sliders and other controls that are located in a user-friendly way in the hypertext. Figure 1 Presents a screenshot with a simple physical experiment explaining the dependence between period and amplitude.

The simulation can be suspended, reset or restarted by activating the corresponding buttons. According to the selected mouse mode (rotate, zoom, pan) the function of the mouse changes. Dragging the mouse over the frame the viewpoint to the visualized world is changed. The user can activate numerical and graphical monitors which correspond to some observed variables. Graphical monitors permit the visualisation or better time-dependent plot of velocities, forces, accelerations and other variables of selected objects. The numerical monitors permit the modification of some significant properties of the selected objects.

3. CONVERTING EXAMPLES PREPARED WITH XDEV

Xdev is another frequently used authoring CoLoS tool. It permits the design of new experiments by means of a user friendly interface. The building components of developed experiments are widgets. The most signifficant widgets are 2D and 3D worlds which can contain the basic (graphical) primitives (normally particles, points and lines). These two types of widgets are used for the visualisation of the models of the physical experiments. Observed experiments can be controlled by the usual buttons, sliders and similar controls which are represented as widgets.

Xdev is in fact a program generator with a graphically oriented user interface. The basic xdev frame is shown on the figure 2.

A creative teacher can design new experiments by inserting and modifying the basic components in a defined frame. He can describe the behaviour of the particles and other primitives in the included 2D and 3D worlds by specifying the algorithms of the simulated experiment in a simplified C-code. The result of xdev is a Motif-compliant program. Experiments prepared with xdev can be combined with hypertext and remotely controlled as is done by xyZET.

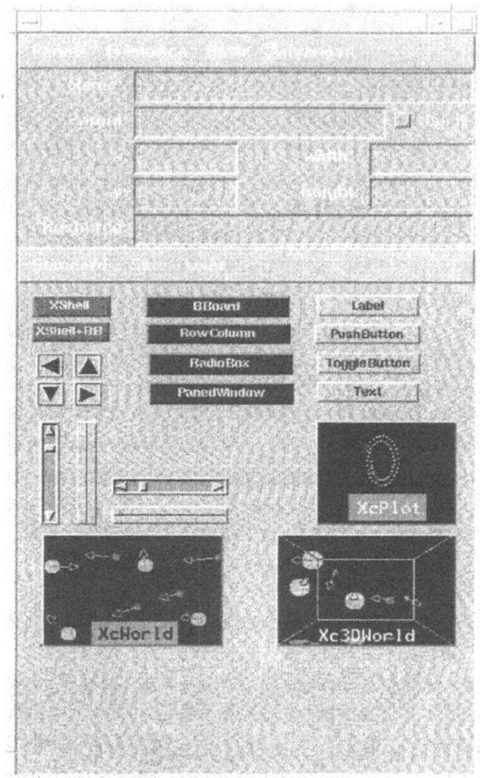

Figure 2. Basic frame of the xdev authoring tool.

An atractive tutorial concerning thermodynamics has been created and supported with xdev-based experiments. The microscopic interpretation of temperature in this course makes easier the understanding of many phenomena involving the pressure in gas and expansion in solids.

Besides this complete tutorial, several other experiments from the domain of physics have been created with xdev.

Considering the current strategy to port all software into Java, a converter (named xdj) has been developed. It reads the output files created by xdev and creates corresponding source Java files (xxx.java).

After that a normal Java compiler creates applets which can be included in hypertext based lessons. The applets use xdj package that are explained later. This conversion process is represented on the following figure.

The basic idea implemented in the converter was to create Java classes (XcWorld, Xc3DWorld) which correspond to the widget components that are implemented in xdev. The functions (callbacks) which were created for the Motif environment are converted into corresponding methods for these Java classes. All these classes are combined in the so called xdj package

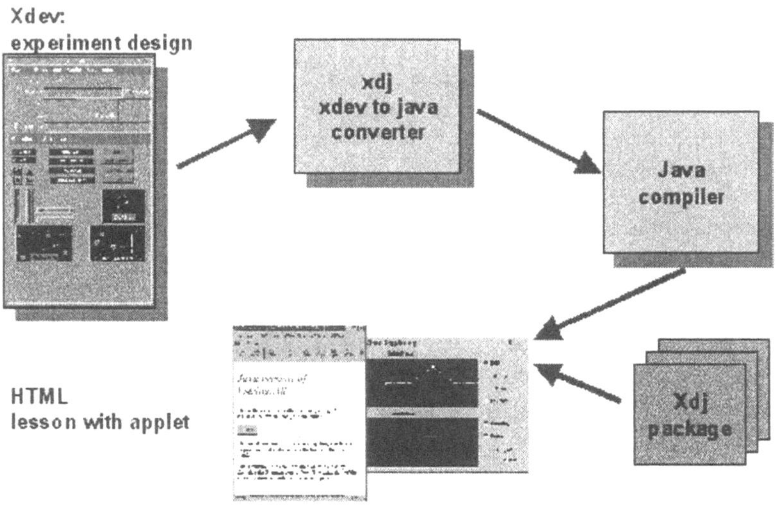

Figure 3. Conversion process of xdev-generated experiments into Java applets.

Figure 4 represents one simple experiment -a vibrating string- that has been converted into a Java applet. The applet is visualized as a pushbutton that is included in the hypertext. On activating this button a new frame with the visualized experiment appears.

The conversion process is 80% automatic, but some additional manual modifications to the created files are still needed. In any case the programmer's work is simplified and the didactic experience with existing simulation is extended to new platforms.

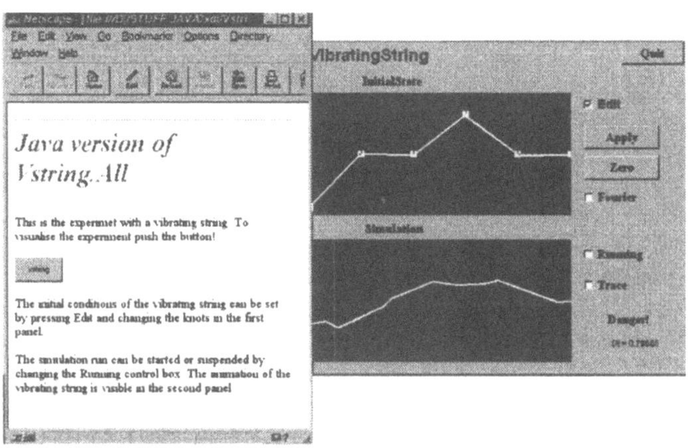

Figure 4. Converted experiment prepared with xdev

4. CURRENT DEVELOPMENT

The user interaction with experiments is achieved through buttons, menus, sliders and checkboxes that are located in the tutorial. Some of these controls have been implemented as separate applets and therefore the concept of simple inter-applet communication has been realized. The applets interact through the variables and methods that are included in a common static abstract class. This approach is simple enough but it is limited to the applets residing on the same HTML page. For the case of separate interacting tutorial pages the communication with sockets was implemented and successfully tested. In the future this interaction will be extended with additional tools which will permit the distributed cooperation of teacher and students. Currently some examples of multiple user interactions through the well-known whiteboard are being studied. For the moment, the platform in use is still JDK1.02, but the new features offered by JDK1.1 will certainly facilitate this research.

5. CONCLUSION

The conversion of physical experiments into java applets offers the required platform independence and provides the possibility of implementing didactical scenarios for virtual classrooms. However, not all simulations can be succesfully converted from the previous Motif compliant environment. First of all, the numerically intensive experiments and visualisations are still too slow. The security restrictions are a factor that inhibits some functions already present in normal applications. The development of robust and stable applications is also limited by the rapid development of new technologies that are therefore sometimes not compatible.

6. REFERENCES

Esquembre, F, Zamarro, JM, Martin,E (1992) Authoring Tool Under UNIX/X-Windows/MOTIF Oriented to Program Development for Simulation of Physics Phenomena, Computer in Physics, Vol 6, No 4

Haertel, H, Martin, E (1993) New Path for Teaching Electricity, Proc of the Int. Conf on Computer Based Learning, CBLIS 93, Wien

Divjak, S (1996) Conceptual Learning and java programming, Proc of Multimedia and Hypermedia Systems, MIPRO 96, Rijeka

Divjak, S (1996) Conceptual Learning of Sciences Supported by the Simulation of Natural Phenomena, Eurosim, Simulation News Europe, Nov. 1996, ISSN 0929-2268

7. BIOGRAPHY

Sasa Divjak received D.Sc. degree in Electrical Sciences at the Faculty of Electrical and Computer Engineering, University of Ljubljana in 1975. He is head of Chair for Software at the Faculty of Computer and Information Science, Ljubljana, head of Laboratory for Computer Graphics and Multimedia. Responsible for several projects in the field of multimedia and related technologies. Member of Program Council for computer supported education of Slovenian Ministry of Sport and Education. Senior member of IEEE.

Extending Web educational applications via SGML structuring and content-based capabilities

B. Fernandez-Manjon, A. Fernandez-Valmayor and A. Navarro

Escuela Superior de Informatica,
Universidad Complutense de Madrid, Avda. Complutense s/n,
28040, Madrid, Spain
e-mail: bfmanjon@dia.ucm.es, valmayor@fis.ucm.es,
anavarro@eucmax.sim.ucm.es

Abstract

In this paper we present an approach to the development of World Wide Web educational applications based on a deeper understanding of the role that mark-up languages play in the Web, and how they could improve Web educational applications. The paper begins with a discussion of the Web's key features that have made it so successful. Then we present and analyse different approaches to educational uses of the Web. We introduce the SGML/HTML as a tool to organise and structure information, and propose a new approach to the development of Web educational applications based on SGML extensions to the HTML language. Finally, we use our own experience in developing educational applications as an example of the new possibilities offered by this approach.

Keywords

Web applications, Mark-up languages, Educational multimedia, HTML, SGML

The Virtual Campus F. Verdejo & G. Davies (Eds.)

1 INTRODUCTION

Initially, the Word Wide Web was designed as a researchers' tool for sharing information and producing documents in a collaborative/co-operative way over the world's largest computer network, the Internet (Berners-Lee, 1994). However, the Web is now the fastest growing resource on the Internet. It is not difficult to understand why the Web is growing exponentially and why it is used by all kinds of institutions and people in all type of activities: academic, commercial, entertainment, etc. All of them find advantages in the way the Web can manipulate information, that is: simplicity of use, an attractive presentation, an easy way to relate dispersed information, low cost of creation and maintenance of the information nodes, and finally, facilities for interaction and communication. What it is maybe not so evident to Web users is that all these characteristics that make the Web so flexible and attractive are based on a mark-up language defined using a complex standard, the SGML (Standard General Mark-up Language). Browsers can interpret documents written using an application of this language: the HTML (Hypertext Mark-up Language) documents or Web pages. Therefore, it is the definition and interpretation (i.e. the syntax and semantics) of this language which set the limits of what it is possible to do in the Web, and it is SGML the main tool we should use if we want to change those limits.

From an educational point of view and due to the increase of information available (and the Web is a main contributor to this information explosion) new ideas are breaking through, and educators are reconsidering traditional approaches to education in the new light provided by the information technology. Now, viewing education as the mastery of a body of knowledge is becoming outdated. Instead, we recognise that students need more than ever to have acquired skills, such as rapid comprehensive reading, critical thinking or qualitative reasoning, along with abilities, such as the ability to find needed information and the ability to work well with others (Twigg, 1994).

Many educators (Jonassen, 1995; Trentin, 1996; Wulf, 1996; Ibrahim, 1995) consider that information technology, and specifically the Web, have to play a central role in those educational changes, driving the information explosion and making possible the construction of new learning environments. But the key to the successful use of the Web as an educational environment is a deeper understanding and clarification of its possibilities and possible roles in education. There is no doubt about the benefits the Web can bring to education: co-operative/collaborative work and the remote and egualitarian access to information are often mentioned as the benefits of networking and Internet (Collis, 1995), but to share information is not to educate and having access to information does not imply learning. At present, there are still some technical problems (e.g. the limited capacity of the communication link, slow modems access), but these problems are not our main concern because these technologies are improving all the time. The real problem is how to deal with cognitive and pedagogic situations in the Web. In part because the Web was not originally designed as an instrument to educate people problems like disorientation, lack of planning or guidance on the access to information, and information overload affect more seriously the usefulness of the Web as an educational tool (Buenaga, 1995; Nunes, 1996).

This paper is organised as follows. First we present and analyse current educational applications and proposed taxonomies on educational uses of the Web. Then we propose new approaches to Web uses in education. We also present the HTML and investigate in which way it is possible to use it or its proposed extensions as an educational tool.

2 WEB EDUCATIONAL USES: TAXONOMIES

Entering the Internet, from a computer at home or at workplace, users can access a vast amount of library catalogues, course materials, journal indexes, reference books, full text of journal articles and books, art exhibits, employment notices, discussion groups, business data, etc. Clearly, the availability of all this information offers us new opportunities for teaching and learning. Consequently, there has been a growing interest in the educational uses of the Web. Hence to better explore the potential role of the Web in education, we will start analysing some of the proposed taxonomies on these educational uses of the web.

The taxonomy offered by Wulf could be representative of those classifications that take into account the purpose of use (i.e. for what we are using the Web). Wulf (1996) identifies seven different uses of the Internet in education:

1. Electronic mail: delivery of course materials, sending in assignments, getting/giving feedback, using a course electronic discussion group.
2. Bulletin boards/newsgroups for discussion of special topics.
3. Downloading of course material or tutorials.
4. Interactive tutorials on the Web.
5. Real-time interactive conferencing using systems like Internet Relay Chat.
6. "Intranets": corporate websites protected from outside access that distributes training for employees.
7. Informatics: the use of on-line databases, library catalogues, and gopher and websites to acquire information and pursue research related to a study.

Other classifications put the stress on the way that educational applications take advantage of Web attributes like interconnectivity or the presentation and interrelation of information. In this sense, Carvin (1997) identifies four different educational uses of the Web:

1. The Web as tutor: that is, the Web as a way to provide on-line tutorials and lessons, based on its ability to present information clearly, attractively and practically.
2. The Web as publishing house, so teachers and students can create in-depth "hyper-reports" with links leading to numerous subtopics and related network connections.

3. The Web as forum for discussion of ideas and virtual debate, for example using mailing lists (listserv).
4. The Web as navigator, or as a tool to search for information all over the network.

On the contrary, other authors claim that the classification of use in education of computer networks has to be done taking into account the degree of enhancement (added value) offered by this technology and not so much by its particular uses. The main difference is between situations, or contexts, in which innovation brought to them by telematics is mainly a technological improvement and new situations that could not take place without the network. Examples of the first case, of technological improvement, is the handling of intercommunications via electronic mail or the remote access and sharing of data and educational materials. Examples of the second case, new situations, are co-operative learning with on-line interaction in virtual classrooms. That way, Trentin (1996) identifies three educational contexts:

1. Plain utilisation of the network for communication, based not so much on specific approaches, but rather on using the network to provide a powerful tool for navigation through distributed information and for interpersonal communication.
2. Using computer networks in support of educational activities that can be conducted with or without the network but which in this way are improved producing greater motivation and involvement.
3. Learning activities based on specific approaches that are strictly dependent on the use of specific characteristics of the network and could not exist without it.

Finally, it is also necessary to notice that there are too many specific applications and research projects using the Web in educational settings to be possible to do a comprehensive study. For instance, Computers & Education (Kibby, 1995), and Internet World (1995) special issues about Education and Internet present some particular uses. General discussions about the roles of telematics and new hypermedia technology in education can be found in (Jonassen, 1995; Kearsley, 1995; Davis, 1995; Laurillard, 1995; Nunes, 1996; Kerka, 1996).

3 NEW APPROACHES TO WEB EDUCATIONAL USES BASED ON WEB LANGUAGE CAPABILITIES AND SGML EXTENSIONS

At first it seems natural to think that with all these characteristics the Web can be the ultimate educational tool. Nevertheless, the first conclusion of our survey is that most applications and research analysis as those previously mentioned take for granted a positive effect when using the Web as an educational resource. However, the outcome of our survey is that even if most of the projects dealing with the educational possibilities of the web come to mainly positive conclusions, in these projects it is not clearly stated and defined which are the unique characteristics in the educational activity. Moreover, in general the requirements of the new educational frameworks that the web could help to develop are not described.

We consider that the key characteristic of the Web is its mark-up language. It is HTML that converts a document into a hyperdocument. This hyperdocuments can contain appealing multimedia information, and can be accessed remotely by browsers. Therefore, we think that a taxonomy of web educational uses have to be based on the contributions that HTML, or more generally, SGML could bring into education together with improvements in communications technology. We would try to synthesise those classifications in a comprehensive one. In the first place, we would also distinguish between the educational context where the innovation brought by the Web is mainly technological and new contexts promoted by the Web that could not exist without it (Ibrahim, 1995).

1. The Web as a technological improvement, enhancing human communication and human access/sharing of information.
   - Enhancing human to human communication in a distance learning or educational context (e.g. e-mail and list-servers).
   - Student/student.
   - Student/teacher.
   - Teacher/teacher.
   - Enhancing human access to educational objects (e.g. downloading courses and tutorials).
   - Enhancing human access to information objects in an educational context (e.g. databases, repositories).

2. New situations based on specific characteristics of Web's language that offer a new kind of learning situations to students.
   - Interacting with Web based tutorials that could need or not specialised viewers or browsers. A web-based tutorial will not only use HTML tags for hypertext and hypermedia links but will also use HTML tags to pedagogically structure the document.
   - Interactive searching of information in the Internet. That means not only that students and teachers can use search engines (e.g. Infoseek or Lycos), but also they systematically make use of previous efforts of other users reflected in well-organised personal pages.
   - Personal or collaborative building of well structured Web documents and/or Web based tutorials.
   - Virtual classes in open and more authentic contexts that promote a meaningful learning (Jonassen, 1995). The web is not merely used as an information delivery medium, but rather as an organiser of thoughts and facilitator of knowledge construction.

This double classification tries to state the singular role of the mark-up language in the Web. In the applications comprised in a) the HTML language is used to integrate different operations in a simpler and friendly interface. These operations can be done using different Internet tools like ftp, e-mail, IRC or telnet. But, the applications comprised in b) are based in a more educational approach to the possibilities offered by HTML. For example, from a web tutorial it is equally simple accessing a local document as a remote document or even to look for complementary information in a different server.

Nevertheless, we think that today most educational applications do not take full advantage of the (limited) possibilities offered by HTML. The role of the web seems to be restricted to hypertextbook type applications where the predominant model continues to focus on the production of information resources and much less on the learning processes in which the student must be engaged. Possible reasons for the present situation are:

- Current HTML definition has been done taking into account mostly the needs of the net's publishing industry requirements (i.e. mark-up for tables, styles, forms, etc.).
- There has not been a substantial development of tools, browsers and editors, specifically adapted to educational tasks.

Therefore and as a result of our analysis we conclude that there are two main lines for future work and research in order to transform the Web into a more powerful educational medium:

- First, to develop special browsers for a generalised mark-up language able to capture the logical structure of a document, beyond simple characteristics such as title or body text. These browsers could be an intermediate step between a generalised marked document and a HTML document or a full marked document browser (Burnard, 1997; Sperberg-McQueen, 1994).
- Second, to provide the specifications and requirements to develop help and instructional tools that make use of the educational possibilities of the language. Here we identify two possibilities: a) Tools that help to create and interpret Web pages specifically created with a pedagogical purpose; and b) Tools that process generic Web pages with educational purposes.

Finally, we have no doubts about the benefits and potential of the Web in educational institutions, and specifically in those providing distance education. Perhaps more than any other previous media, the Web can help to overcome the barriers of time and space in teaching and learning (Kerka, 1996). But, it is necessary to notice that the educational value of the Web is also limited. The Web will not be the solution to all educational problems. Therefore, it would be very positive to identify clearly the situations where the Web could be used to solve educational problems.

4 ORGANISING AND STRUCTURING EDUCATIONAL INFORMATION USING HTML/SGML

As previously stated, we think that most educational applications are not exploiting fully the possibilities offered by the present HTML. Web pages are structured documents which contain mark codes, that can not only be used to format documents for on-line presentation but also as a way to promote good cognitive skills in the learners. In order to obtain a really useful educational Web it would be necessary to help the learners to convert the information into knowledge avoiding problems like information overload, for instance.

The mark-up can identify portions of a document and can be a means of making explicit an interpretation of its actual content. Thus, we envisage the use of the HTML as a way to add value to the information provided in the Web. We consider the HTML language as a tool that can help to organise and structure the content of a document according to pedagogical ideas. This consideration will permit the application of pedagogical strategies in the presentation of the information making the Web a suitable tool to ease the process of learning.

The Web is written largely in HTML, which is one application of the Standard Generalised Mark-up Language (SGML). The explosive growth on the World Wide Web applications demands richer and larger sets of mark-up features in HTML. SGML introduces new concepts in information handling and exchange of information at all levels of complexity. Newer revisions of HTML will include greater numbers of SGML features. As the Web continues to grow, SGML will likely become the standard for more mark-up languages on the Internet (Colby, 1996).

4.1 Introduction to mark-up languages and their applications

The Standard Generalised Mark-up Language (SGML) is a meta-language that can be used for encoding the logical structure and content of any type of document. The goal of SGML is to standardise the definition of device-independent, system-independent methods of representing the structure and intent of a document, so the accessibility and reusability of information stored within documents can be maximised. Since 1987, SGML has been widely adopted by government, industry and academic groups world-wide.

SGML is not a set of standardised codes but a language that can be used to define precisely the elements to which a particular kind of document must conform. This definition starts by an SGML declaration, which states mandatory and optional features, used in the rest of the definition. This declaration is followed by the document type declaration (DTD) which is the formal collection of element, attribute and entity declarations that describe what mark-up to expect in this kind of documents. Finally there is the document instance, that is the document itself with the actual mark-up. The real benefit of this flow is that a computer program, a SGML parser-translator, can process the declaration and learn its rules, then process the DTD and learn the rules of the mark-up, and then process the document and determine if the document meets the rules and take the prescribed actions. This way an SGML document can be processed by different programs and with different purposes; each program can apply different processing instructions to those parts of the document instance, which are considered relevant.

Part of the possibilities of SGML are already being used in educational projects like the Text Encoding Initiative (TEI) and the International Committee for Accessible Document Design (ICADD) (SGML Open, 1996). ICADD leverages an SGML tagged document to produce multiple textbook versions from the same source document, giving print-disabled students access to the information (through Braille, large print, voice synthesis, and electronic browsing). TEI is an international effort to standardise encoding of all kinds of text in any language (mainly literary and historical texts). TEI encoded documents give researchers and students an efficient way to utilise the information contained in these texts. As these and other new initiatives evolve, more information can be handled more efficiently giving educators and students a way to manage the voluminous quantities of available information.

The web language, HTML, is an SGML application and as such its syntax is defined by the combination of the SGML declaration and the document type definition or DTD. Actually, the current HTML definition in force, HTML 3.2, places further constraints, inexpressible in the DTD, on the permitted syntax, although HTML is moving towards the larger feature set of SGML. Consequently, more SGML tools are starting to appear for the average users. For example, there is a SGML Web browser that works alongside a standard browser (e.g. Netscape) (Colby, 1996). When you encounter an SGML Web page, the program activates and enables you to browse it as easily as an HTML page.

Therefore, HTML has the potential of being a really smart use of SGML, taking advantage of SGML's flexibility without giving up a common backbone structure that any browser can readily interpret (Severson, 1995). Moreover, it is precisely this combination of simplicity and extensibility that will enable the Web to be viable for new educational applications.

4.2 A basic example of SGML application to information structuring

In this section we use a hypothetical DTD that represents a simple fax type document, along with one real fax to illustrate some of the possibilities offered by SGML. A full discussion of the SGML is out of the scope of this paper and can be obtained elsewhere (Goldfarb, 1990, Colby, 1996).

In a document we must distinguish: structure, content and format. The structure is the document's logical organisation. Content is the actual data in a document. Format consists of how the elements are visually presented and distinguished from one another within a document.

```
<!ELEMENT fax - - (to, from, date,subject?, body)>
<!ELEMENT to - - (#PCDATA)>
<!ELEMENT from - - (#PCDATA)>
<!ELEMENT date - - (#PCDATA)>
<!ELEMENT subject - -(#PCDATA)>
<!ELEMENT body - - (paragraph+)>
<!ELEMENT paragraph - - (#PCDATA)>
```

fax.dtd

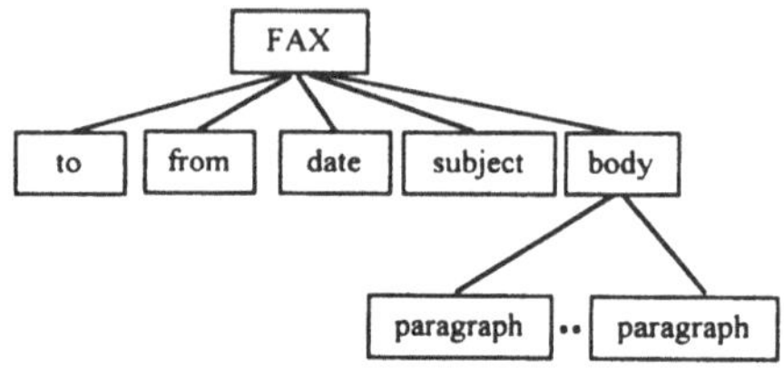

Figure 1 Fax DTD and its tree representation.

To obtain the content model or the outline structure of a fax, it is necessary to identify which are the important parts (called elements) that made up a fax. In our fax these elements are: the origin, the destination, the date, the subject of the message (that we will consider optional) and a body (the actual message) made up by one or more paragraphs. SGML captures the fax structure using a DTD and it can be visually presented as a tree (see Figure 1). We can understand a DTD as a grammar (i.e. the set of rules) to whom a document must conform. The structure defines how the document is laid out, which elements can be required or optional, if an element is repeatable or not, and in what order the elements are assembled.

In the DTD we define the tags used to mark the elements of the real document. The boundaries of an element will be given by the star-tag and end-tag. By default, SGML tag mark-up consist of the name of the element type surrounded by angle brackets (<>), with the addition of a slash (/) before the name of the end-tag. For example, the body of the message is enclosed between the tags <body> and </body>. #PCDATA means that an element contains characters.

A real fax is represented via a document instance or marked document. In the marked document we employ the DTD tags to sign the document parts. For example, for the fax instance, the mark-up would look as follows (some elements are shown on separate lines and indented with the content in bold face for ease of reading, but it is not necessary):

<!DOCTYPE fax SYSTEM "fax.dtd">
<to>**John Smith**</to>
<from>**Sam Smith**</from>
<date>**8.27.97**</date>
<subject>**Arrival**</subject>
<body> <paragraph>**I'll arrive tomorrow.**</paragraph>
<paragraph>**Your brother,**</paragraph>
<paragraph>**Sam**</paragraph></body>
</fax>

Because we have the fax represented by two parts, the DTD and a document instance, we can perform different treatments of the fax, maintaining the difference between structure, content and presentation. An important treatment is document rendering being possible to produce multiple sets of formatted output from the same document instance. But manipulations are not limited to rendering as in HTML. On the contrary, SGML also allows the automatic validation of a document checking its structural validity according to the rules of the DTD (e.g. if the fax contains the destination -element to- that is mandatory, or if at least one paragraph appears in the body). Moreover, it is possible to process and search for text based on its context, such as to search a fax containing a specific text in the subject or select those faxes that have more than 200 words in the body text. SGML also includes facilities called attributes to further describe the content of the elements and to establish cross-reference mechanisms. For instance, the fax DTD could include an attribute describing the type of the fax as personal or business.

Thus, we think SGML is the way to obtain richer mark-up languages that we needed to develop new Web educational tools. SGML is able to capture all document facets, providing us a way to design, develop and maintain new educational tools.

5 TEACHING TEXT COMPREHENSION IN A SECOND LANGUAGE: THE GALATEA PROJECT

Included in the SOCRATES/LINGUA European Union project, our group is working on the Galatea project with other European universities under the Stendhal-Grenoble III University leadership. This project is aimed at developing a set of multimedia tutorials for the written and oral comprehension of the Romance languages (see Figure 2). The pedagogical and cognitive strategies included in the set of multimedia tutorials being developed by our group are based on previous work about text comprehension done by group's members (Lopez, 1994; Fernandez-Valmayor, 1992) and also taking into account ideas of others authors (Schank, 1977; Kintsch, 1978; Adam, 1992; Grosz, 1995).

We take our work in this project as an example to describe the different roles that the Web can play in an educational application. The pedagogic scenario used in the tutorials we are producing is based on the selection of about 10 different documents written in French and in a sequence of exercises that students can make on each of these documents to improve their comprehension level of the written text. The main goal is to promote the understanding of the document content even if some words or paragraphs are initially incomprehensible. There is also a set of general-purpose tools that students can freely use: a general dictionary, a contextual dictionary, a contextual grammar and a sound tool to hear the texts. The general learning strategy is to relate the information contained in the document with information previously known by the student (Ausubel, 1963). For instance, an exercise can ask the learner questions aimed at the correct classification of the text based on external traits easy to recognise (e.g. a journalistic text, an advertising text or a fiction text). Other exercises take into account the temporal script: the prototypical sequence of events implied by the main topic of the document, (e.g. the sequence of events in a fire), or the set of words belonging to the same semantic group (e.g. words related to a fire, or words related to the family -as shown in Figure 3-). The student has the assistance of general-purpose tools, such as a dictionary and specific tools related with the specific examples appearing in the tutorial such as the contextual grammar and the contextual dictionary called "paso a paso" (see Figure 4).

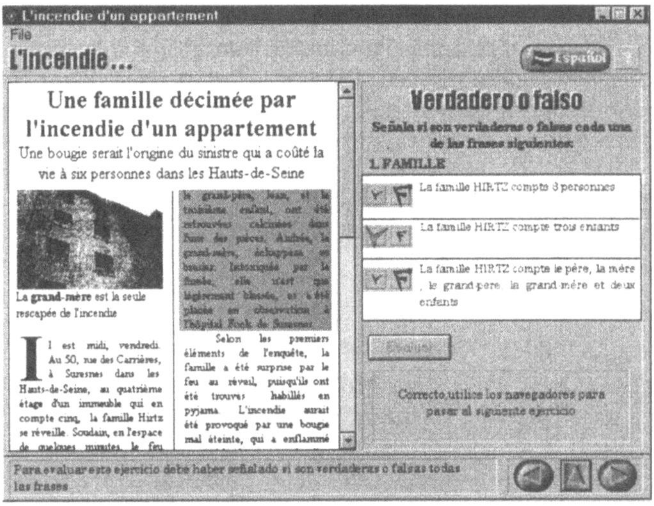

Figure 2 Screen of the Galatea current multimedia application for teaching French text comprehension.

On the one hand this kind of tutorial could be considered as a finished product that can be distributed over the network for remote execution, or for download and local execution. But on the other hand we think that there is a more promising approach making use of the same capacities on which the Web is based. This approach is to provide the documents with all the mark-up information necessary to implement general educational strategies similar to those used in our tutorial. The particular strategies used to present the information will be interpreted by a specialised browser able to understand the mark-up of those documents or, to a limited extend, these strategies could be included in a program for translating those SGML marked documents into HTML documents to be later viewed with a general browser.

Providing the mark-up documents facilitate on the creation of new educational applications because the presentation strategies of the information can be changed or adapted locally. For instance, this approach can simplify the automatic creation of a comprehensive content summary of a Web document based on its marked information. This approach can also simplify the sharing of documents and even the collaborative construction of repositories to be used in text comprehension.

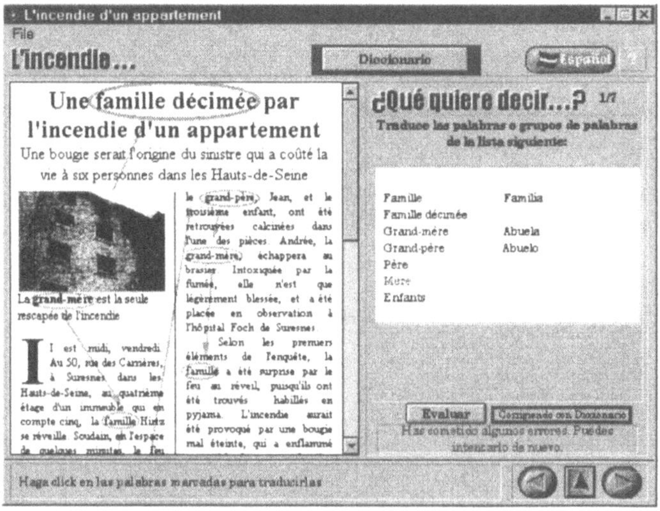

Figure 3 Exercise to improve comprehension by the translation of the set of words related to the family. After the evaluation of user's answers the user can access the dictionary to look up the meaning of the words.

Now we are shifting our approach because we realise that the use of SGML techniques is not only restricted to the mark-up of texts (i.e. to capture the information about structure and content) to be later viewed with a specialised browser (i.e. to decide the final rendering) but also they can be fully applied in the application design and maintenance steps, closing the gap between designers and programmers. This is possible because we can use a SGML DTD to capture the structure and some of the design decisions that are at the base of the educational tool under development. For example, in the texts we need to mark different kinds of information such as the keywords or several sets of related words that the user have to understand in order to get the meaning of the text. These different elements used to teach text comprehension are described in the DTD and using this DTD labels we mark the keywords or the set of families appearing in the text. Therefore the combination of the DTD plus the marked texts provided much of the design information and pedagogical decisions of the educational application.

6 CONCLUSIONS AND FUTURE WORK

The development of our educational application has showed us that the present definition of HTML is insufficient to mark-up and organise all the data contained in the documents that are relevant to our application. Thus we are now working in an extended mark-up using SGML. But in many of the current Web browser, any mark-up not recognised as supported HTML element is ignored. So this new extensions could be only interpreted with new browsers specifically designed for educational purposes or with new add-on programs (specialised parsers) for standard browsers.

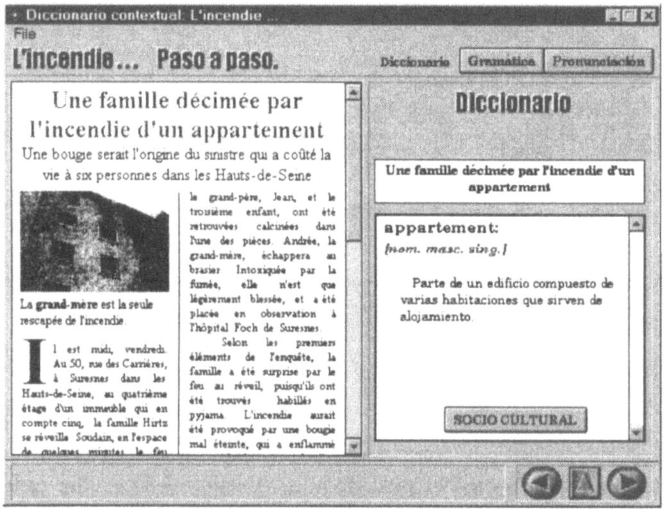

Figure 4 The user can also access a contextual dictionary where complementary information about words is provided.

We realise that a powerful communication resource like the Internet can provide new incentives and unprecedented opportunities for innovation in the field of education. The crux of the matter is to define innovative methods for designing, planning, and conducting network actions in which innovation lies not just in the mere presence of a new technology but rather in revising certain teaching processes or in creating new ones based on the new technology (Trentin, 1996). The Web is accepted internationally because its ease of use, capabilities for presentation/communication and cross-compatibility and future changes in HTML standards will make it even more powerful. It would be desirable that the future HTML standard also included capacities for educational use and not only those interesting to publishers (e.g. better tables or layouts). In other case, if we want to be able to develop and maintain complex applications extending Web educational use we should migrate to SGML or SGML/HTML browsers.

The next steps of this research will be to produce Web applications for text comprehension. At present, we are working on the final completion of the (local) multimedia educational modules for second language text comprehension (French). Currently in these modules we are using specific mark-up that we are translating to SGML format. In the future these tags will also be used for the contextual dictionary. This dictionary will consider not only the definition of words and text segments, but also its features (morphologic, syntactic and semantic) and even its use in specific text examples (see Figure 4).

Long-term objectives of the project are to obtain an educational DTD for teaching text comprehension and the use of SGML technology to simplify the design and maintenance of educational applications.

7 AKCNOWLEDGEMENTS

The EU project Galatea (TM-LD-1995-1-FR89) and the Spanish Committee of Science and Technology (TIC96-2486-CE) have supported this work.

8 REFERENCES

Adam, J.M. (1992) Les textes: types et prototypes, in *Recit, description, argumentation, explication et dialogue.* Nathan, Paris.

Ausubel D.P. (1963) The Psychology of Meaningful Verbal Learning. Grune and Stratton, New York.

Berners-Lee, T., Cailliau, R., Luotonen, A., Nielsen, H.F. and Secret, A., (1994) The World Wide Web. *Communications of the ACM*, **37**(8), 76-82.

Buenaga, M., Fernandez-Manjon, B. and Fernandez-Valmayor, A. (1995) Information Overload At The Information Age, in *Adults in Innovative Learning Situations* (eds. B. Collis and G. Davies), Elsevier Science B.V., Amsterdam.

Burnard, L. (1997) SGML on the Web: Too Little Too Soon, or Too Much Too Late. *Computers & Texts*, **15**, August.

Carvin, A. (1997) The World Wide Web in Education: A Closer Look (WWW document, URL: http://k12.cnidr.org:90/web.intro.html)

Colby, M. and Jackson D. (1996) *Special Edition Using SGML.* QUE Publisher.

Collis, B. (1995) Societal and organizational influences on integration: what about networking?. In *Integrating Information Technology into Education* (eds. D.Watson and D.Tinsley), Chapman & Hall, London.

Davis, N. (1995) Distance Education with Telematics for Distance Educators. *International Journal of Educational Telecommunications*, **1**(2/3), 199-211.

Fernandez-Valmayor, A. and Fernandez, C. (1992) Educational and Research utilisation of a Dynamic Knowledge Base. *Computers & Education.* **18**(1-3), 51-61.

Goldfarb, C.F. (1990) *The SGML Handbook.* Oxford University Press.

Grosz B.J., Joshi A.K. and Weinstein S. (1995) Centering: A Framework for Modeling the Local Coherence of Discourse. *Computational Linguistics* **21**(2), 203-225.

Ibrahim, B. and Franklin, S.D. (1995) Advanced Educational Uses of the World Wide Web. *Computer Networks and ISDN Systems*, **27**(6), 871-877.

Ide, N. and Veronis, J. (1995) *Text Encoding Initiative, Background and Context*. Kluwer Academic Publishers, Dordrecht.

Internet World (1995) The Internet in Education. *Internet World*, Special Issue, October 1995, 38-85.

Jonassen, D.H. (1995) Supporting Communities of Learners with Technology: A Vision for Integrating Technology with Learning in Schools. *Educational Technology*, July-August.

Kearsley, G., Lynch, W. and Wizer, D. (1995) The Effectiveness and Impact of Online Learning in Graduate Education. *Educational Technology*, November-December.

Kerka, S. (1996) Distance Learning, the Internet, and the World Wide Web. *ERIC (Educational Resources Information Center) Digest*, ED39521496, Columbus, Ohio.

Kibby, M.R. and Heller, R.S. (1995) Education and the Internet. Special Issue, *Computers & Education*, **34**(3).

Kintsch, W. and Van Dijk, T. A. (1978) Toward a model of text comprehension and production. *Psychological Review*, **85**, 363-394.

Laurillard, D. (1995) Multimedia and the changing experience of the learner. *British Journal of Educational Technology*, **26**(3), 179-189.

Lopez Alonso, C. (1994) Comprehension et texte: role des cadres de connaisances et du prototype. *Langages. Theorie et applications en F.L.E.*, 157-174.

Nunes, J. and Fowell, S.P (1996) Hypermedia as an experimental learning tool: a theoretical model. *Information Research New*, **6**(4), 15-27.

Schank, R.C. and Abelson R.P. (1977) *Scripts, plans, goals, and understanding.* Hillsdale, Lawrence Erlbaum Associates, NJ.

Severson, E. (1995) How SGML and HTML really fit together: The case for a scalable HTML/SGML Web. (WWW document, URL:http://www.ileaf.com/avhome/htmlscal.html)

SGML Open, (1996) SGML in Education: The TEI and ICADD Initiatives. *Computers in Libraries*, **16**(3), 26-28.

Sperberg-McQueen, C. M. and Goldstein, R. F. (1994) HTML to the Max: A Manifesto for Adding SGML Intelligence to the World Wide Web in *Proceedings of the Second World Wide Web Conference '94: Mosaic and the Web*, Chicago, IL.

Trentin, G. (1996) Internet: Does It Really Bring Added Value to Education?. *International Journal of Educational Telecommunications*, **2**(2/3), 97-106.

Twigg, C. A. (1994) The Changing Definition of Learning. Educom Review, **29**(4)

Wulf, K. (1996) Training via the Internet: Where Are We?. *Training and Development*, **50**(5), 50-55.

9 BIOGRAPHIES

Dr. **Baltasar Fernandez-Manjon** is an assistant professor in Computer Science at the Complutense University of Madrid. He received his B.S. degree in physics and his Ph.D. degree in computer science from the Complutense University of Madrid. His research interest lie in the educational uses of computers and networks (specially, user modelling, intelligent help systems and multimedia applications).

Dr. **Alfredo Fernandez-Valmayor** is a professor in Computer Science at the Complutense University of Madrid. His research interest lies in the educational uses of computers, multimedia, and automatic text processing.

Mr. **Antonio Navarro** is a researcher at the Complutense University of Madrid. He received his B.S. degree in mathematics and now he is working in his Ph.D. about educational multimedia and automatic text processing.

SimulNet: Virtual tele-laboratories over the Internet

M.Llamas, L. Anido and M.J. Fernández
Área de Ingeniería Telemática
Departamento de Tecnologías de las Comunicaciones
E.T.S.I. Telecomunicación. Universidade de Vigo
Campus Universitario 36200 Vigo. SPAIN
e-mail : {martin,lanido,manolo}@ait.uvigo.es

Abstract

Teaching and education have changed to meet the needs of the present-day working market. Because of this, professional and practical training are absolutely essential to educate good professionals, especially in the scope of Technology and Science. It is not easy to achieve this objective in distance learning environments. Our virtual tele-laboratory fills the gap between theoretical and practical teaching in a distance learning environment based on the Internet and the WWW.

SimulNet is a distributed, remote access computer based training (CBT) system. Unlike other teleteaching systems whose aim is to achieve a virtual classroom, SimulNet provides a virtual laboratory to put theoretical knowledge into practice. This is done by delivering software through the Internet which can be run on any computer. These distributed applications are simulators of those tools which can be found in a conventional laboratory. The system also provides an on-line communication channel between students and teachers to follow students' traces in their interaction with the simulator and to assist students. These features allow us to achieve a virtual laboratory where drawbacks due to geographical separation between teachers and students have overcome and advantages of telelearning and teleteaching have been gathered.

Keywords

Simulation, CBT, Teleteaching, Java, WWW, Training

The Virtual Campus F. Verdejo & G. Davies (Eds.)

1. INTRODUCTION

The ASTRO Development Team from Vigo University, has implemented a computer based training (CBT) system based on WWW* that permits supervised execution of courses, trainee evaluation and also maintains trainee state, which depends on his/her previous actions, selected navigation mode and obtained scores. ASTRO (ASTRO, Llamas 1996) allows students or trainees to follow different courses which are composed of a structured set of hypermedia documents. In this way, trainees are able to follow theoretical courses through the Internet.

The next step is to provide an approach to a virtual laboratory where the acquired knowledge can be put into practice as University or Secondary School students do in their conventional training laboratories.

SimulNet sends through the Internet applications which can be run on students' computers. So, avoiding the network overhead, students run conventional laboratory simulators interactively. The key to achieving this high level of interaction, essential in a tele-laboratory, is that SimulNet is implemented solely using Java.

Java (Abdel 1996, Java, Kramer 1996), developed by Sun Microsystems, is an object-oriented language for the Internet. Among its features, one of the most important is platform independence. Therefore, SimulNet, client and server applications, may be run on any computer, whatever its operating system or architecture.

2. WHERE AND WHY COULD WE USE SIMULNET?

Teaching and education have changed to meet the needs of present-day working market. Because of this, professional and practical training are essential to train good professionals, especially in the scope of Technology and Science. It is not easy to achieve this objective in a distance learning environment based on the Internet and the WWW.

A university, as the last step in student education, is the natural place to use a system like this. SimulNet allows students do their laboratories at home, wherever they live, and at the same time, it solves the problems related to overcrowding : restrictions due to space, allocation of resources, etc. A suitable timetable could let students go to their faculty or school only few days a week. We expect that students at Vigo University will be able to use SimulNet in several laboratories related to computer architecture subjects the following school year. Apart from a university, a virtual tele-laboratory system may be used in polytechnics and secondary schools.

---

* World Wide Web, http://www.w3.org

On the other hand, those academic institutions which have been traditionally related to distance learning, can broaden their offerings using the SimulNet system. The Internet, is an ideal way to transmit knowledge. Our system would allow students to put the acquired knowledge into practice directly and learn by teletraining.

3. OBJECTIVE: VIRTUAL TELE-LABORATORY

The Internet and the World Wide Web are distributed environments inherently. A virtual tele-laboratory over them needs a set of additional facilities to overcome the physical separation and give students and teachers the same feeling as if they were in the laboratory itself.

SimulNet provides several functions to achieve this objective:

- The simulators are interactive. There is no network overhead as the simulators run on the student's own computer.
- Trainee traces reflecting their interaction with the simulator are sent to their tutor straight away, and are stored in the SimulNet host server to be looked over afterwards.
- An on-line communication channel between teachers and students is provided. The main purpose is to tutor students in the use and aim of the laboratory's simulator. This channel can be used by the different communication facilities that SimulNet implements:
  - Text talk between a student and his/her tutor. This can be used to explain student's doubts or help students in their interaction with the simulator.
  - Multi-talk among several students and their tutor. This can be very useful to solve students' questions or teach any topic related to the current training practice.
  - Virtual blackboard shared among several students and their tutor. The blackboard's contents are displayed identically on every other blackboard. There are two operation modes : free mode, where the tutor and the students can present graphical information without any restrictions ; and master-slave mode, where the tutor uses the blackboard for his/her explanations without interference from students.
  - Electronic mail between students and tutors of SimulNet. This can be used by tutors to send training practice instructions and by students to return their results and conclusions.
- Notebooks (Lai 1995). Its purpose is to allow teachers to share notes about students and can be used to store students' grades.
- SimulNet overcomes the physical boundaries of a conventional laboratory and the time constraints of a course timetable. However, it provides the possibility of establishing a timetable which could be needed due to organisational reasons

or to occasionally restrict students' free access. SimulNet also provides facilities for substitutions among teachers or extra tutorings.

- It registers the entries and exits into and out of the system.
- Students and tutors can choose among several languages to interact with the system in every teleteaching session.

4. USER INTERACTION

For the sake of simplicity we are using from this point the masculine to refer to trainees or tutors. Of course, the reader must assume they could be men or women without distinction.

When a trainee/tutor begins a SimulNet telelearning/teleteaching session, first of all he can choose among several languages to be used in the user interface and then he must be successfully identified. After that, a list of those simulators he is allowed to access to is presented. At his point the tutor/trainee selects a simulator and the educational session starts. If he has any message stored in his mailbox it would be sent to him.

4.1 Trainee interaction

Trainees run simulators on their own computers achieving a high level of interaction. Any outstanding action from a teaching point of view would be sent to the trainee's tutor.

Trainees have on-line and off-line learning tools at their service. They are allowed to use off-line tools, like the internal e-mail, at any moment to send any question or comment to his tutor or to the system manager. On-line teaching tools, like text-talk or the virtual blackboard can be used by trainees in a more restrictive way, they are only allowed to send requests to their tutors who have the final decision to establish, for instance, a multi-talk or virtual blackboard session. From a conventional teaching point of view, students should ask to be allowed to speak before doing it.

4.2 Tutor interaction

Tutors can be connected to SimulNet without following trainees' traces or receiving trainees' questions and requests. In this way, they can look over previous trainees' traces, use the notebook facility or use the internal e-mail to send training practice instructions without interferences from trainees. At any moment they can decide to start their tutoring session and therefore receive trainees' traces and requests.

Unlike trainees, tutors can use on-line and off-line teaching tools at their service with no restriction. They can involve any trainee in any teaching tool to solve any doubt or teach any topic related to the training practices.

Moreover, they are given access to their trainees' traces as they do the training practice. So, tutors can find out the most common difficulties and help any trainee who is presumed to be in trouble.

4.3 An example

In this section we shall show an example of a SimulNet teleteaching session which gives a good indication about the environment that will be achieved.

In a computer architecture course, for instance, the use of a real computer is essential to put theoretical knowledge into practice. We can use SimulNet to obtain the same objective in a teleteaching environment.

As usual in conventional teaching, the course may be scheduled over several practical sessions. Let's follow one of them. First of all, the teacher would enter into SimulNet and, before starting the teleteaching session, he could write the training practice instructions, for instance about addressing modes, and send them to students by means of the internal e-mail. Afterwards, he would start the tutoring session and see, by means of trainees' traces functionality, how his students entered the computer simulator and read the previously sent instructions. On the other hand, students, after reading the training practice instructions, would interact with the computer simulator or use any parallel CBT course system to go through the needed theoretical knowledge to do this practice.

As students do the training practice, their tutor would receive their traces. Meanwhile, he could look over trainees' traces in previous training practices to evaluate their progress. If the tutor noticed that any of them has any problem he could use the text-talk facility to communicate with him and solve any questions related to the current training practice or to the use of the computer simulator. At the same time on students' side, any trainee in difficulty would send a request to his tutor to have a text-talk session, for instance, in order to solve his problem. The tutor would receive this request and decide, whether to start a text-talk session. During this communication, the tutor could realise that this problem could be common among his students and presume that many of them would have the same problem in the current training practice. Therefore, he would start a multi-talk session and involve every trainee in it. If necessary, they could also use the virtual blackboard to introduce some graphical information like flow charts to explain a particular addressing mode, for example.

Eventually, the trainees would complete the training practice. Then, they would send their conclusions about the training practice to the tutor by internal e-mail: what the advantages of every addressing mode are, when and where they should use every of them, etc. The tutor would grade trainees' training practices and store the grades and observations using the notebook facility.

This is just an example of the use of SimulNet in distance learning. There are many CBT systems whose aim is to teleteach which would need a way to let students undertake practice and exercises with the knowledge they have acquired. That is our main contribution to distance teaching/learning.

5. SIMULNET MANAGEMENT AND MAINTENANCE

The SimulNet management application is able to install automatically the system's server side by itself. This application provides every essential feature to manage the system: join new simulators, students or teachers to the system, shape the simulators' behaviour, disk quotas for students and tutors, test the integrity and congruence of the SimulNet's database and configuration files avoiding an undesirable system behaviour, provide user authentication, etc.

Simulators are organised in groups. So, a set up in groups of laboratories with features and interests in common is available to the system manager. This can be very useful to establish an organisation related to different University departments, research teams, or any other organisational needs because there is no interference among students and teachers from different groups.

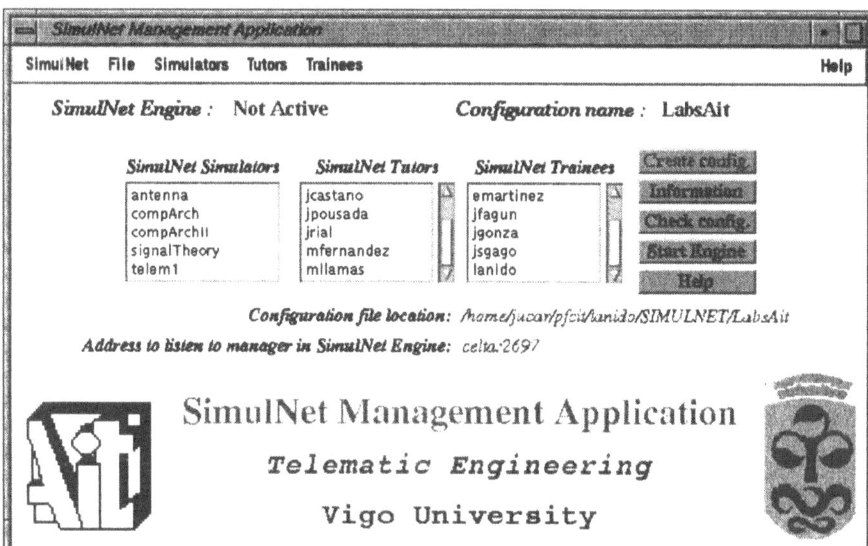

Figure 1. The SimulNet Management Application

The SimulNet management application provides an easy to use graphical user interface for the system manager to carry out his job, as shown in Figure 1. Without any knowledge about the underlying configuration files or data structures, he is able to manage the different groups of laboratories he is responsible for from the same management application.

6. ARCHITECTURE OVERVIEW

SimulNet makes use of the Internet technology to implement the needed services. The system is composed of several applications which cooperate to implement each SimulNet facility, all of them having been developed using Java, therefore platform independence, high level of interaction and easy use over the Internet is achieved. Communication among them is performed using Internet transport layer protocols (TCP/IP). This is the basis for our distributed educational environment, several Java application cooperating by means of TCP/IP communication. Moreover we have also taken advantage of other existing WWW elements: HTTP service, HTML, WWW browser and server. The interaction among the different elements of the system is outlined in Figure 2 and will be explained in the next sections.

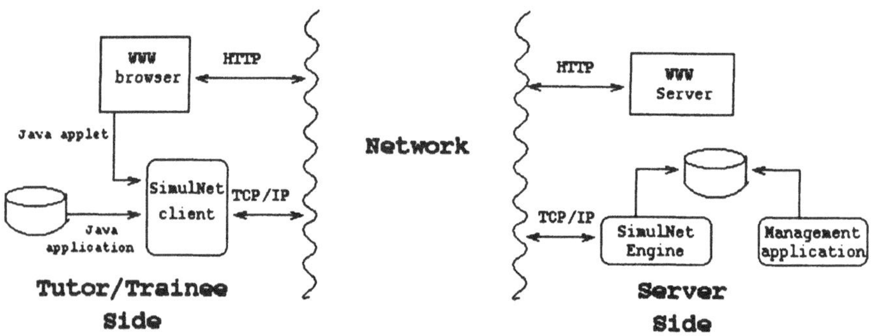

Figure 2. Module interaction.

6.1 Tutor/trainee side

Tutors and trainees can connect to SimulNet in two different ways:

1. By means of a standard WWW browser which would be used as a client browser to present an HTML document provided by the WWW server at the server side. This document contains an embedded Java applet which would launch and terminate any other Java application provided by the server side through the Internet.
2. Using a fully independent Java application stored at the tutor/trainee side. In this case, the SimulNet simulators could be used in a stand-alone way, i.e. trainees are able to practice without any help or supervision by his/her tutor. At the same time, the tutor/trainee can connect the Java application to the server side to benefit from the virtual laboratory advantages: communication channel, trainees' traces, etc.

The two previous connection modes have different advantages. The first one, which is based on Java applets, needs no additional software, apart from the browser itself, at the tutor/trainee side. Therefore, any common Internet connection supplied by usual Internet-provider companies is enough. Nevertheless, due to security restrictions in the Java's implementation, trainees/tutors could only store data in the server host machine, not at tutor/trainee side. The second one overcomes this inconvenience as it is based on Java applications. So, storage capability at tutor/trainee side is provided. The only requirement is that the trainees/tutors' computers support the Java software.

Anyway, both provide all SimulNet functionalities as explained in the previous sections, and the choice between them depends on the simulator's particular aim. They are outlined in Figure 2.

6.2 Server side

The server side functionality is implemented by three different applications.

1. WWW server. Its function is to provide HTML documents which contain the SimulNet applets and support, in this way, the first trainee/tutor connection mode, as explained before. Communication to the WWW server is based on HTTP protocol as shown in Figure 2.
2. The SimulNet Management Application. This has been implemented solely using Java and carries out every trainees/tutors management functionality and simulators' configuration, see Figure 1. Every SimulNet feature is set up using this application and is communicated to the SimulNet Engine, whose function is explained below, by means of a twofold way: using TCP/IP and sharing the same file system, as is outlined in Figure 3.

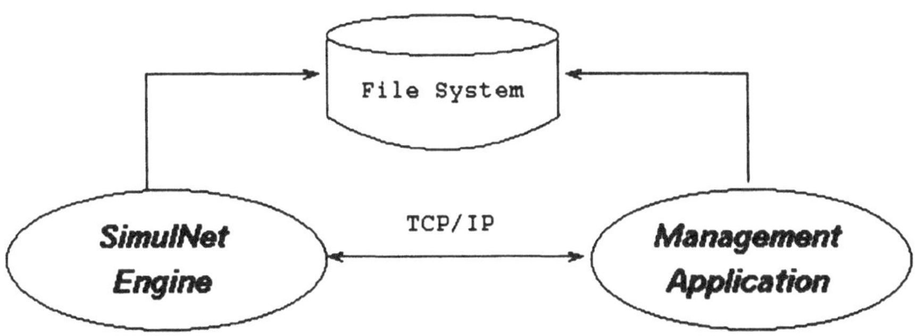

Figure 3. Communication between Engine and Management application.

3. The SimulNet Engine. This Java application supports the functionality of our system. It carries out the main system's behaviour which is set up using the management application. As shown in Figure 3, the Engine takes orders from it and performs any needed action to fit the system's behaviour to the new situation. So, new tutors or trainees could be imposed, etc, without stopping the

system. Moreover it sends information about the tutors and trainees connected to the system to the management application.

To access a SimulNet simulator, tutors/trainees have to be properly identified by the system. The aim of this identification process is twofold: reject unknown (unregistered) SimulNet users and prevent tutors/trainees accessing simulators they are not allowed to. This user authentication is also provided by the SimulNet Engine.

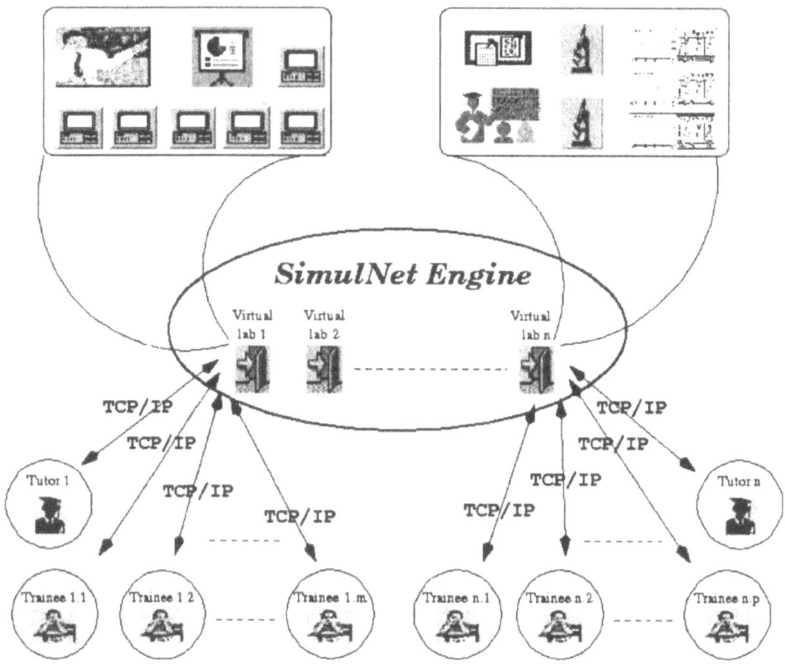

Figure 4. SimulNet architecture overview.

The SimulNet Engine provides a virtual communication channel between tutors and trainees by means of a twofold physical channel: tutor/trainee - SimulNet Engine and SimulNet Engine - trainee/tutor. Therefore, as we show in Figure 4, the TCP/IP communication between SimulNet Engine and trainees/tutors provides a virtual communication channel between them with the aim of achieving a real laboratory atmosphere as shown at the top of the figure.

This part of the server side is also responsible for managing the users' data storage and trainees' traces. At the same time that tutors and trainees are allowed to store files in the computer where the SimulNet Engine runs. The Engine itself ensures they do not exceed their disk quotas. On the other hand, trainees' traces are stored by the SimulNet Engine which sends them straight away to the tutor responsible for the trainee. So, every trainee's action can be supervised by his tutor and inspected afterwards.

Several simulators, which constitute a group of virtual laboratories, with their own trainees and tutors, can be supported by a unique SimulNet Engine. There is no interference among tutors or trainees from different simulators in their interaction with the system. This aspect is also shown in Figure 4, where several laboratories are outlined.

7. CONCLUSIONS

Java's features broaden the facilities that teleteaching/telelearning systems can provide. SimulNet has taken advantage of them and supplies a new point of view to distance learning and teaching: it allows students to do training practices in a virtual tele-laboratory. In this way, students and teachers are prevented from wasting time and money on travel.

The main objective of our system is to achieve a virtual laboratory, but despite this, it is open and flexible enough to provide different applications apart from those related to telelearning and teleteaching. This system can be used as a software on demand platform, where different applications (the simulators) are sent to the users through the Internet and where, if necessary, their execution could be supervised. Of course, every SimulNet facility could be used: use authentication, user's traces, communication channel among users, etc.

At the moment, this system is under development and we are implementing the ideas presented previously and, at the same time, we are looking for new facilities to improve the virtual laboratory atmosphere. We think this document offers a good idea of what will be achieved with the proposed framework.

This work is being partially supported by the University of Vigo in the framework of the "Apoio á innovación educativa" (support to innovation in education) program, project "ETLAO: Entorno de TeleLaboratorio para Arquitectura de Ordenadores" (Telelaboratory environment for Computer Architecture).

8. REFERENCES

Abdel, H., Kvande, B. and Nanjangud, S. (1996) *Using Java for Multimedia Collaborative Applications.* 3rd International Workshop on Protocols for Multimedia Systems (PROMS'96), Madrid.

ASTRO Course Engine Development Team. ASTRO Course Engine Public WWW Server. http://astro.ait.uvigo.es/astrodocs/main.html

Java site. http://www.javasoft.com

Kramer, D. (1996) *The Java Platform. A white paper.*

Lai, M., Chen, B. and Yuan S. (1995) *Toward a New Educational Environment.* Fourth International World Wide Web Conference. Boston

Llamas, M., Fernández, M.J., Gil, A., Rodríguez, R. and Suárez, A. (1996) *A Cost-effective Approach to WWW Education and Training.* 3rd International Workshop on Protocols for Multimedia Systems (PROMS'96), Madrid.

9. BIOGRAPHIES

Martín Llamas received the Telecommunication Engineering (1986) and Doctor in Telecommunications (1994) degrees from the Universidad Politécnica de Madrid, Spain.

Luis E. Anido has recently graduated (1997) from Universidade de Vigo, Spain with a Telecommunication Engineering degree.

Manuel J. Fernández graduated from the Universidade de Santiago de Compostela, Spain with a Telecommunication Engineering degree in 1990, and from Universidade de Vigo with a Doctor in Telecommunications degree in 1997.

They joined the Telecommunication Engineering faculty of the Universidade de Vigo. In addition to teaching, they are involved in research in the areas of Formal Description Techniques and Computer Based Training.

A distance learning application based on a digital library of courseware

M. Marolt and M. Privošnik
Faculty of Computer and Information Science,
University of Ljubljana
Traška 25, 1000 Ljubljana, Slovenia
e-mail: {matija.marolt, marko.privosnik}@fri.uni-lj.si

Abstract

This paper presents a distance learning application currently under development at the University of Ljubljana in Slovenia. The basic idea of the application is to join learning materials on various topics and written by many teachers in a digital library of courseware. Such a digital library provides a basis for creating courses on specific topics. Our application is based on the WWW and the Java programming language and can be readily used over a high bandwidth network connection. The problem is, however, that most students usually do not have high bandwidth network connections to their homes. A possible solution to this problem arose from University of Ljubljana's co-operation in the ACTS AC-018 SMASH (Storage for Multimedia Applications Systems in the Home) project. The goal of this project is to develop a mass storage device for home usage, that can hold 13 GB (or even more) of data. It uses a linear tape drive coupled with a hard disk used for caching data from tape. If the digital library were stored on such a tape, tapes could be distributed to students, and students could use the application at their homes without the need for a network connection. We are developing an interface to the mass storage device to make this possible.

Keywords

Distance learning, WWW, Courseware, Reusability of courseware, Multimedia storage, Java

The Virtual Campus F. Verdejo & G. Davies (Eds.)

1. INTRODUCTION

Recent advances in computing, especially multimedia and the Internet, offer great possibilities for educators. The World Wide Web (WWW) as a distributed hypermedia information system with capabilities that include graphics, audio and video clips, and the appearance of Java as programming language of the Internet, have given rise to a number of distance learning projects and initiatives. The educational use of computers has advanced beyond word processing and numerical calculations to include interactive tutorials with videos and learn-by-doing exercises. In fact, we could start talking about a shift from the classic lecture and textbook based teaching, which has been the way to teach for centuries, to a new level, where students are offered interactive multimedia materials with learn-by-doing examples, test questions. The teacher, of course, is still the key figure in the educational process giving lectures and guidance to students and preparing learning materials, but the way students learn can be vastly improved. Experiences show, that active "learning by doing", as opposed to "learning by seeing and hearing", can nearly double the learning effectiveness (Harger, 1996). All this shows us that these new technologies are a huge opportunity for educators.

The basic idea of distance education is "teachers are apart of learners" (Sun and Chou, 1996). In our case, distance learning is considered as a complementary process to normal learning and teaching activities, meaning that learners also have access to multimedia educational materials, when they study at home. This paper presents a distance learning application, currently under development at the University of Ljubljana in Slovenia, as an example of an educational application based on the WWW and the Java programming language. We especially address two issues we feel are very important: reusability of educational materials for different courses and dissemination of materials among students.

2. ORGANISATION OF COURSEWARE

Our goal is to develop a distance learning application, which would act as a framework for the development of different courses; thus it is not meant as an application for teaching a specific topic. The basis of each educational application is learning materials (courseware). This section describes the organisation of courseware within our application.

Materials are organised in two different ways (on two different levels). All the materials (on various topics, written by many teachers) are stored in a digital library of courseware. Within the digital library (lower level of organisation), these materials are organised in mind maps. Such an organisation connects different topics and subtopics in a tree-like structure (although cycles are allowed). Materials on four topics (3D computer graphics, image processing, virtual environments, and robotics) are currently being prepared at the University of

Ljubljana and will be joined in a digital library. When developing a course on a specific topic (higher level of organisation), a teacher specifies a linear structure similar to the organisation of chapters, subchapters... in a book. Students are very familiar with such a linear structure and it encourages them to follow the course in an orderly manner, as proposed by the teacher. Linear organisation of courses is also preferred in some other distance learning environments (see Forte, 1996).

2.1 Mind maps

Mind mapping was developed in the late 60's by Tony Buzan (Buzan, 1974), following his research into note taking techniques. A mind map typically consists of an organic chart connecting concepts of an area of information in a hierarchical inside – out manner. Concepts are presented by words or images where the most important concepts are near the centre, and less important ones at the edges, producing a growing and organised structure composed of key concepts. Every item in a map could be the centre of another map.

The structure of mind maps is two dimensional as opposed to the one dimensional list structure of a conventional text. A mind map shows the relative importance of concepts and the way that concepts relate to each other. This helps relative significance of concepts to become evident in a more meaningful way and associations to be made easily. Mind maps help organise information into a form that is easily assimilated by the brain and easily remembered. With a mind map a bigger subject can be understood and remembered much more efficiently.

Mind maps have many advantages over ordinary linear text in being visual and easily remembered, flexible and open ended, clear in themes, structure, and relative importance, compact... (Russel, 1979).

Our application uses mind maps to structure materials in the digital library. When a teacher creates learning materials, he maps every topic to a concept in a mind map, defines its parent and child concepts (topics) and, if he wishes, defines several other attributes (such as importance, colour, picture...). These mind maps are used by the application to present the structure of each topic to students (see section 3 for more details).

2.2 Creating courses

To create a course on a specific topic, a teacher uses documents from the library and creates a list of references to these documents, structured as chapters, subchapters... This list defines the structure of materials in the course. The structure is linear (as in a book) and defines the path a student should follow in order to study through all of the required materials. No changing of materials in the library is necessary in order to make a particular course, a teacher simply defines the course's documents and their order.

Such an organisation tries to solve two problems. The essence of hypertext is the ability to take a particular keyword within a document and assign it a link, which points to another document carrying more information on that keyword. This is a very fine concept, but can introduce a lot of confusion if not used properly. Hypertext nodes may be linked together in a manner that can leave students confused as to whether or not they made through all of the material they should have read (Mengel, 1996). Such a system of links must therefore be carefully designed. Courses made with our application have a linear chapter-by-chapter organisation. A linear organisation can be easily followed by students and does not lead to confusion as can be the case in a network of hyperlinks. This does not mean, however, that documents in the library may not contain hyperlinks! These can still exist, they are just treated differently by the application (see the next section for more details).

The use of hyperlinks to bind the materials together into a course (linking various topics using hyperlinks), can lead to difficulties when a teacher wants to prepare a new course by using materials from an existing course. If nothing else, he has to correct all the links within various documents to point to new materials. In our application, the structure of materials in a course is not directly related to materials in the library (it is specified separately). Therefore, materials can be reused very easily and no correction of hyperlinks, is necessary.

3. DISTANCE LEARNING APPLICATION

3.1 Creating Materials and Courses

As mentioned in the previous section, all of the materials are stored in the digital library. The process of creating materials for the digital library and individual courses is illustrated in Figure 1.

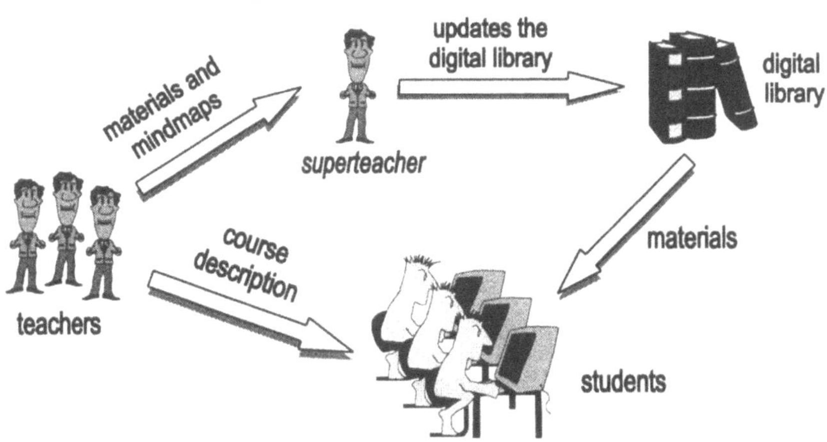

Figure 1 Creating materials and courses.

Each teacher that wants to contribute new materials is given a set of guidelines for their preparation in order for all of the materials to have a "common look and feel". Materials are HTML documents and teachers are encouraged to use a lot of multimedia and interactive features, such as video clips, VRML files, Java applets, Tests for students, such as multiple-choice questions or learn-by-doing etc. Tests for students, such as multiple-choice questions or learn-by-doing examples should also be provided. Teachers have to organise their materials into mind maps. Each topic is represented by a concept in a mind map. Concepts are linked together and may have many additional attributes, such as importance, shape, colour, URL, position... A teacher should define the concepts and their relations in a special *mind map file*.

When a teacher prepares his materials and the mind map file, he sends them to a so-called "*superteacher*". Superteacher is a person, whose task is to organise the materials and mind map files provided by teachers and to integrate them into the digital library.

Each teacher that wishes to use the materials in the library to create a course gets a list of all the available materials and can browse the library to find the documents he wishes to include in his course. These documents can be written by the teacher himself or by another teacher. A course is then described as a list of references to documents in the digital library, organised into a sequence of chapters, subchapters, sections, subsections, etc. A teacher can also specify the level of difficulty of each topic (easy to learn, hard to learn,...). This sequence of references is specified in a special *course file*. When a teacher wants his students to study for a particular course, he only has to give them the course file and if students have access to the digital library, they can start with their studies.

3.2 The Application

Students can access the digital library with a WWW browser (e.g. Netscape) that supports Java. The distance learning application is written in the Java programming language and handles student's interactions with educational materials. A view of an early prototype of the application can be seen in Figure 2.

The user interface is divided into 4 sections.

On the left side, students see the chapter-based linear structure of learning materials (as provided by the teacher in the course file). This includes the title of the topic (chapter) a student is currently studying and its subtopics. Special tags will also be used to mark the level of difficulty of each topic.

The upper left part of the window contains a type of a map (only text in the current implementation) that shows how students got to the topic they are currently studying.

The toolbar includes navigation buttons for moving to the next/previous subtopic or up to the title topic in a linear manner. Other buttons will also be included, such as a "help" button, "send e-mail" button, or "start a teleconference" button (the latter if the student's computer is connected to a network providing enough bandwidth for teleconferencing).

The main part of the application's window contains mind maps of learning materials or learning materials themselves. Mind maps are drawn according to the organisation of materials in the digital library. The title of the topic a student is currently studying is displayed as the central concept of the mind map with its related subconcepts positioned around the centre. Note that these subconcepts do not necessarily correspond exactly with the subtopics of the main topic as displayed on the left part of the screen (they are usually a superset of subtopics). The subconcepts that do correspond are marked with a special tag. When mind maps are not displayed, this window displays the actual learning materials (as can be seen in Figure 2).

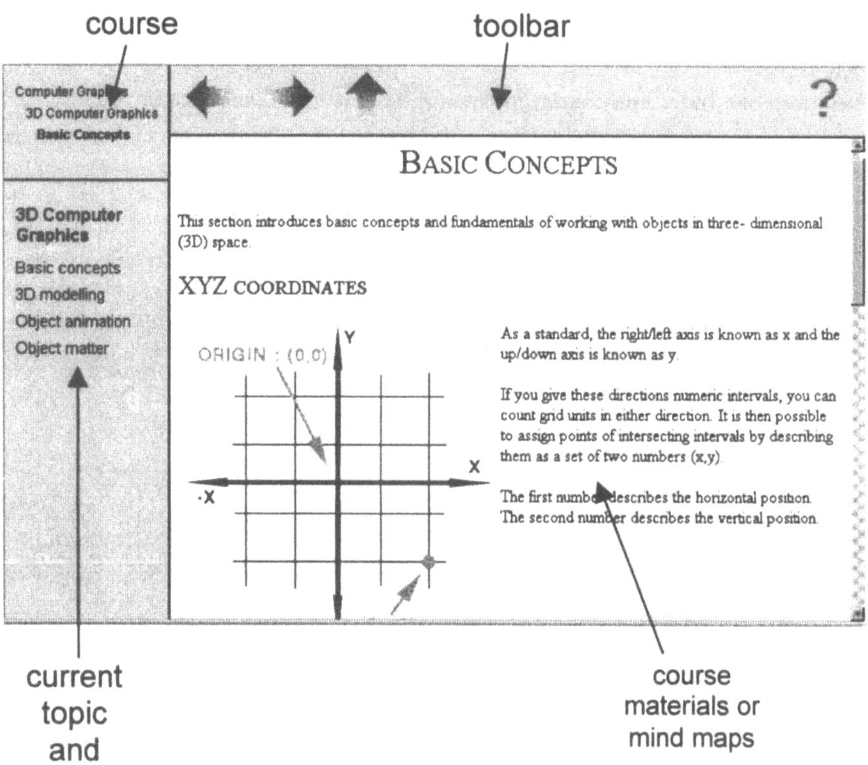

Figure 2. Application's user interface

Students can navigate through a course in various ways:

- by clicking on the next/previous buttons, students can browse the materials in a linear manner, as recommended by the teacher. When navigating in this way, students can be sure that they have studied all of the required materials.

- when mind maps are displayed, students can browse the materials by clicking on concepts within mind maps. As noted before, it is not necessary for a topic and its subtopics, defined by a teacher as required materials a student should study (and displayed on the left side of the window) to directly correspond to the mind map of that particular topic. The mind map usually includes more items for a particular topic than students are required to learn for a course. Such organisation of materials encourages students to explore new topics, which are related to a particular topic, but are not considered as required knowledge. When students choose a topic that is not part of a designed course, the topic opens up in a new window (containing only the hypertext and mind maps; without the toolbar and the list of chapters). Students are then free to explore that topic. When they finish, they simply close the window and continue where they left off (somewhere in the middle of materials they are required to study). This ensures that when students wander away, exploring new materials and following hyperlinks, they always come back to the topic in the required part of materials, they last studied.
- when materials are displayed, students can navigate by clicking on hypertext links within the materials. As when exploring non-required topics through mind maps, a new window opens up with the contents of the hyperlink. When students finish with browsing, they close the window and return to the topic, they last studied.

In addition to all the features described, we plan to add the possibility of displaying lists of particular types of materials to students. For example: students might need a list of all the test questions in the course (multiple-choice questions or learn-by-doing examples), a list of all the movies or animations or a list of topics of a particular difficulty level. Such a list would then be displayed and students could quickly browse its content.

4. MAKING THE APPLICATION AVAILABLE TO STUDENTS

If we want students to be able to use our distance learning application at home, we have to provide them with access to the digital library. The application itself is based on the WWW and Java, which are two Internet concepts and is therefore suited for use over the Internet. The idea of a large digital library, which would reside on a server somewhere on the network, further emphasises such a concept. If a good network infrastructure is available, the application can be readily used over the network.

The only problem is, that most students do not have high bandwidth network connections to their homes or at the campus. What they usually have is a modem connection or perhaps a basic-rate ISDN connection, but since learning takes time, these are far too expensive, and also don't have enough bandwidth for transfer of good quality video materials, which are an essential part of courses. Making CD-ROMs and distributing them among students might seem like a good solution, but

CD-ROMs could be only be used for distribution of a single course or just a part of a course to students. The concept of a digital library containing not only the materials a student has to learn, but also other useful materials could not be supported using CD-ROMs, since they do not contain enough storage space.

A possible solution to this problem arose from University of Ljubljana's co-operation in the ACTS AC-018 SMASH (Storage for Multimedia Applications Systems in the Home) project. The goal of this project is to develop a mass storage device for home usage, that can store 13 GB (or even more) of data. The device consists of a linear tape drive, coupled with a hard disk used for caching data from tape (this gives it near-random access to data). The storage device's main purpose is to record cable-TV MPEG-2 digital video streams, but it can also be connected to a computer and used as a mass storage device.
This means that the whole digital library could be stored on a single tape. Each student would then obtain a copy of such a tape and (provided he has the mass storage device at home) could run our application at home without the need for a constant high bandwidth network connection. We are developing an interface towards the mass storage device to make this possible.

5. CONCLUSION

The motivation behind the development of our distance learning application is to increase the interest of teachers in the development of interactive multimedia materials and also to encourage co-operation among teachers when developing such materials and courses. We feel that our idea of a digital library of courseware provides a good basis for such co-operation. It allows materials in the digital library to be used and reused very easily and also encourages students to explore new topics as they study through the required path of a course.

On the other hand, we are trying hard to make this application accessible to students everywhere, not just at the university, where a good network infrastructure is present, but also at home. We hope, that our involvement in the ACTS project will make this possible.

Currently, our application is still in the implementation phase. We have an early application prototype, which already works as described in the paper, but the user on interface and display of mind maps still need to be improved. We are also working on the interface towards the SMASH storage device, which should be completed soon, and are also preparing courseware on four different topics (computer graphics, computer vision, digital signal processing and robotics). The courseware will be integrated in the digital library and will be used for undergraduate studies of computer science and electrical engineering at the University of Ljubljana.

6. ACKNOWLEDGEMENTS

The authors thank all the members of University of Ljubljana SMASH group, especially prof. Saša Divjak, prof. Jure Tasi, dr. Aleš Leonardis, dr. Jasna Maver, dr. Marjan Leban, Urban Burnik and Andrej Košir.

7. REFERENCES

ACTS AC-018 SMASH project Deliverable #5, a0018/tud/it/ds/p/ 005/b1, 1996.

Buzan, T. (1974) Use your Head. BBC Publications, London.

Harger, R.O. (1996) Teaching in a Computer Classroom with a Hyperlinked Interactive Book. IEEE Transanctions on Education., **39-1**, 327-335.

Mengel, S.A. (1996) The Need for a Hypertext Instructional Design Methodology. IEEE Transactions on Education, **39-1**, 375-380.

Russel, P. (1979) The Brain Book. RKP, London.

Sun, C.T. and Chou, C. (1996) Experiencing CORAL: Design and Implementation of Distant Cooperative Learning. IEEE Transactions on Education, **39-1**, 357-366.

Wentland Forte, M., McMurray E. and Simillon, F. (1996) Teaching Informatics with ARIANE: An Experimental Internet-Based Pedagogical Environment. Proceedings of Computer Aided Learning and Instruction in Science and Engineering, CALISCE'96, San Sebastian, Spain.

8. BIOGRAPHIES

Matija Marolt is a young researcher at the Faculty of Computer and Information Science, University of Ljubljana, Slovenia. His research interests include computer music, virtual reality and hypermedia. He received his diploma in computer science from University of Ljubljana in 1995. He is currently a PhD student at the Faculty of Computer and Information Science, University of Ljubljana.

Marko Privošnik is a teaching assistant at the Faculty of Computer and Information Science, University of Ljubljana, Slovenia. His research interests include cognitive science, human-computer interaction, intelligent user interfaces and hypermedia. He received his diploma and MS degree in computer science from University of Ljubljana in 1992 and 1997, respectively. He is currently a PhD student at the Faculty of Computer and Information Science, University of Ljubljana.

Authoring tools for network-based training

E. McDaid, G. Row, W. O'Brien and A. Hashim
School of Computing, Information Systems and Mathematics, South Bank University
103 Borough Road, London, SE1 0AA, UK
E-mail: mcdaideg@sbu.ac.uk

M. McCool
INCORE
University of Ulster, Magee College, Londonderry, BT48 7JL, UK

Abstract

This paper presents an overview of the TALENT toolkit--a software architecture and set of software tools designed for producing and delivering multimedia training material over computer networks. The toolkit addresses many current problems relating to multimedia development and delivery including conversion of existing materials, reusability, internationalisation, customisation, intellectual property right tracking, support for multiple developers and abstraction neutrality. Organisational and commercial requirements are also addressed. The toolkit has been designed from the outset to be network-centric and the development tools themselves can operate over a network. Issues relating to the design and implementation of the toolkit are discussed. A simple model of multimedia systems is presented and the main components of the toolkit are described. The toolkit would appear to represent a significant advance in our ability to develop and deploy multimedia training over networks.

Keywords

Training, WWW, Courseware, Java, Authoring, Interactive multimedia

The Virtual Campus F. Verdejo & G. Davies (Eds.)

1. INTRODUCTION

Recent advances in computer technology such as improvements in the multimedia capabilities of personal computers, the World-Wide Web and its wide range of associated technologies together with faster computer networks have made network-based training a technologically viable option. These factors, in conjunction with the increasing adoption of the Internet and corporate intranets by commercial organisations, have led to significant interest in the use of network-based training as a cost-effective mechanism for training delivery.

Given the size of the training industry, let alone education in general, and the huge investment in existing training materials these developments represent a significant opportunity as well as a threat to those organisations currently engaged in training. The opportunity lies in the possibility of exploiting wider markets and new business areas while the threat lies in any failure to make effective use of these opportunities.

The TALENT project (Training and Learning Environment with Networked Tutoring) which is funded under the ESPRIT IV programme of the European Commission has the goal of providing a complete software environment for training development and delivery as well as network-tutoring in order to support a distributed virtual training centre. In addition, the environment will support the supply chain issues of the network-based training industry of the future.

The TALENT consortium is composed of representatives of each part of the training supply chain from courseware developers through training providers, localisers, resellers and consumers as well as training technology developers.

This paper is concerned with Phase I of the TALENT project which is nearing completion. This has included the development and use of a prototype software toolkit for producing and delivering multimedia network-based training. We will describe the design and development of the toolkit together with it's associated software architecture but first we will discuss some of the issues which the toolkit addresses.

2. INTERACTIVE MULTIMEDIA

Many of the potential benefits claimed for network-based training have been cited in the past for more traditional forms of interactive multimedia training such as that delivered using Interactive videodisc, CD-I and CD-ROM technologies (Fletcher, 1996). It is argued that interactive multimedia enhances the learning process through engaging the student while the use of multiple simultaneous media improves information transfer and retention. In addition, there are potential economic benefits for the organisation through reduction in the requirement to travel and lower costs associated with self-paced learning. While there is evidence to support these claims (Fletcher, 1996), the widespread adoption of interactive multimedia in training which was predicted has failed to materialise for a number of reasons.

A major hurdle to the adoption of multimedia training has been the high costs associated with the production of multimedia titles. Estimates vary but guidelines for multimedia development indicate that it can require between 50 to 600 hours of development time to produce one hour of multimedia training (Golas, 1993). This is in contrast to conventional tutor-led training which may require 6 to 20 hours of preparation time for a one hour training session. Other factors include multimedia development skills which are in short supply and demand a premium. The expense of acquiring and supporting specialist multimedia development software and hardware is another significant obstacle. For these reasons, embarking on a first multimedia development project can present a daunting prospect to many organisations particularly from the perspective of cost.

Existing authoring systems used for multimedia development can require considerable expertise in order to be used effectively. This is due to the fact that they are, in the main, general purpose multimedia development tools rather than being geared specifically to a particular problem. As such, authoring systems contain many features both in their scripting languages as well as in their developer environment which are seldom or never used by the majority of developers. These features do, however, add significantly to the learning-curve for the package as a whole. For example, the majority of authoring systems have internal tools for painting. These are seldom used by professional developers who prefer to use specialised painting tools even though they are external to the authoring environment.

The majority of existing authoring systems are intended for used by a single developer. This is a major drawback and in some ways quite surprising as multimedia development is often a team effort due to the size, complexity and required skills set of many multimedia projects. Single user development tools represent a significant bottleneck as they prevent the efficient use of workflow methodologies and may require additional integration phases in order that the efforts of individuals may be brought together to form a unified system. Such integration may be complicated in some authoring systems because of the paradigms which they employ. In any case, extensive use of stubs during development and glue during integration may be required.

Interchange of information or assets between different authoring systems is currently poorly supported. A variety of standards exist for individual media types such as text, sound, image and video data--indeed, several standards exist for most media types. A number of multimedia document standards have been proposed or are under development (Newcomb, Kipp and Newton, 1991, Kretz and Colaïtis, 1992), however, none are in widespread use at this time. As a result it can be difficult for information in one multimedia title to be reused in another unless the same authoring system is used. Even then this process may require significant integration effort as mentioned above.

In addition to development skills it may also be necessary for the multimedia author to possess a certain degree of creative ability if titles are to embody professional design or exhibit high production values. By analogy, it is possible for anyone to buy a paintbrush but that does not mean that they will produce a masterpiece. Few individuals are talented in both technical and creative areas. As a result it is often necessary for multimedia productions to require teams of specialists such as programmers, designers and various creative types.

Cross-platform compatibility issues have been a major problem for multimedia development. While some tools provide support for multiple platforms it is rarely a straightforward process to develop cross-platform titles or to port from one platform to another after development. Problems often arise because the versions of the same authoring tool on different platforms are not completely compatible with each other. Also, there are often underlying technical problems such as the different ways in which colour is handled for example which can present traps for the inexperienced or unwary developer.

Another problem with traditional multimedia training material has been the requirement for specialised platforms for its delivery. Videodisc and CD-I machines have never been commonplace in the majority of commercial environments and even now multimedia PCs are not the normal specification for desktop workstations. In addition, some organisations discourage the purchase of computers with CD-ROM drives as these are often perceived as being used by employees solely for listening to music while they work.

Finally, interactive multimedia courseware despite its high development costs may become obsolete soon after production. This is due to the fact that optical disks which are used for distribution are not generally rewritable and there are significant overheads in the production of the various sorts of disks employed for delivery. Optical disks are still the only viable physical medium for the distribution of multimedia due to the large quantities of data involved. Mass production reduces the cost per unit but exacerbates the problem of changing a title to reflect changes in the course due to the additional mastering and pressing costs. This is, of course, on top of any additional authoring costs incurred.

Most of the problems we have just mentioned are applicable to all authoring systems. Many are to do with the way in which information is assembled and stored within the authoring environment or distributed to the consumer. Network-based training may succeed in delivering on the promises of interactive multimedia training if it can overcome these and other problems.

3. REQUIREMENTS

The fundamental requirements of the TALENT toolkit were that it be capable of supporting the development and delivery of multimedia training over networks. From the above discussion it is clear that a number of other important requirements should be addressed if the toolkit was to be successful. Prime among these is the need to bring down the development costs associated with the production of multimedia courseware. Within the TALENT project we refer to this as 'moving from the Hollywood model to the newsroom model'. Costs can be reduced in a number of ways--many of which relate to the problems described above.

Network delivery of training in itself addresses issues of specialised platform requirements, cross-platform compatibility and obsolescence through physical distribution media. The increasing importance of networks is helping to break down compatibility barriers between different platforms through the use of standard network protocols--network delivery can therefore help to overcome cross-platform development problems. It also reduces the hardware requirements for the delivery platform. Indeed, low specification platforms such as the low-cost Network Computers which are currently under development are capable of use as network-based training delivery platforms. The problems of obsolescence associated with optical disks can be reduced through the use of hybrid technologies which enhance content on disks with live links to updated information on the network. There will probably be a requirement for disk based distribution for some time due to the limited bandwidths of many users network connections.

Ease of use is of crucial importance. The toolkit should be usable by individuals with little or no experience of multimedia development. This will ease the entry of organisations into multimedia development as they can use their existing staff without the need to reskill or replace them. Also, users will have less of a learning curve if usability is greater. The issues of design or creative ability can be addressed through the use of templates and through the inherent support provided by the network approach for a multi-user, multi-disciplinary team.

It is important to provide support for multiple developers and to improve the productivity of developers in general. Support for multiple developers could be achieved through using client-server technology for the toolkit itself. Improving productivity would be addressed through focusing the toolkit on the particular domain of multimedia training as opposed to trying to produce a general purpose authoring tool. Productivity could also be improved through better design of the tools such that they focus the efforts of the developer on the task of courseware development--particularly on the information necessary for the process.

Information interchange is a significant requirement for multimedia courseware. It is often necessary for assets or parts of courses to be reused in other courses either in an unmodified or modified form. It is also envisaged that there is the potential for increased traffic in assets and courseware between training organisations in the future training business marketplace. It is important to be able to track the use of assets for IPR purposes such as royalty payment and it may also be a requirement to support the watermarking of assets for the purpose of copyright identification.

In the absence of widespread standards for multimedia document interchange it was decided to take an open, abstraction neutral approach to information storage and organisation. This approach is equally applicable to card, script or time-line based paradigms.

In addition to requirements indicated by existing authoring systems and their use a number of additional requirements were determined through surveys conducted by the consortium.

In order to protect investment in existing training materials a major requirement of the TALENT toolkit was that it provide support for the conversion of these materials most of which exist as paper-based or computer-based documents in a variety of formats. Obviously it is not possible to produce an interesting multimedia system from solely from a word-processor document. However, it is necessary to provide a means of reusing the text, image and other assets from which they are composed. In addition, much of this material is the result of extensive pedagogic design so it would also be useful for the resulting multimedia system to retain this instructional design in some way.

Support for internationalisation is increasingly important--particularly with the trend toward globalisation. Markets such as Europe and Asia are comprised of many linguistic, national and cultural groups so the ability to easily localise products such as training materials can have a significant impact on the size of their potential market. Therefore, it is important to provide facilities which support localisation such as the isolation of language sensitive information or the provision of support for different character sets.

In addition to the above, mostly technical, requirements a number of commercial requirements were identified including access control, logging and reporting, registration of students and enrollment for courses and so on. Such business services provide a realistic starting point for the integration of the toolkit in to a commercial training environment.

These requirements indicated that the TALENT toolkit would be significantly different from existing multimedia authoring systems as well as presenting an interesting set of technical challenges. In order to determine the best way to proceed we investigated the nature of multimedia systems and arrived at a simple yet useful model.

4. A SIMPLE MODEL OF MULTIMEDIA

Multimedia systems are fundamentally composed of atomic objects or assets which correspond to information in one of a number of formats such as text, audio, image, video and so on. While it may be possible to subdivide assets, for example, decompose a text string into characters or a video sequence into frames, it makes no sense as far as the holistic nature of the system is concerned to do so.

Assets are organised within a multimedia system in space and time such that, for example, a video may appear at a certain location on the screen at a particular time while being synchronised with an audio sound track that begins and ends at the same time as the video.

A number of abstractions are in common use which are intended to assist the developer as well as the user in the process of forming mental models of the multimedia system. These include timeline, card and script based abstractions as well as a number of others (Vaughan, 1996). Abstractions also serve to support the dialogue structure of the system in terms of differentiating and grouping screens, forming navigational structures and reinforcing spatial cues which assist in the formulation of cognitive maps.

However, ultimately all multimedia systems can be reduced to state based descriptions in which objects appear on the screen at a certain point in time, possibly move around, perhaps in response to user interaction and subsequently disappear from the screen at a later time. Accompanying phenomena such as audio can be treated in exactly the same way.

This abstraction neutral view of multimedia has the potential for supporting a certain level of multimedia document interchange between different authoring packages. As an illustration, it is possible to simulate a card-based metaphor in a timeline-based authoring system and vise versa. Abstraction neutrality was a central concept in the ScriptX system (Pinheiro, 1994). However, the advent of Java led to the demise of the ScriptX project.

Such a reductionist view leads us to a simple model of multimedia systems which focuses on the information which they contain. We see multimedia systems as being composed of three elements:

1.Content;

2.Structure;

3.Presentation.

The first point is simple--multimedia systems contain a set of assets from which they are composed. The structure is the way in which these assets are organised within the system and this can be made to reflect any abstraction which can be imagined. Structure is different from presentation in the sense that the structure specifies which objects occur on a particular screen but the presentation may describe where they are, what size and what color.

Using this model it is possible for us to develop systems in which content, structure and presentation may be treated separately. This has a number of important advantages. For example, it is possible to apply different structures to the same content in order to impose different pedagogic principles on a particular course. It is also possible to apply different presentation templates to a given set of structure and content for the purpose of tailoring a title to a particular organisation or audience. A major advantage lies simply in the ability to work on each element in isolation while the approach itself greatly encourages the reuse of assets and structure components.

This simple model which is similar in some respects to that used in the Open Document Architecture standard (Appelt, 1991) greatly simplifies the authoring process and has the potential to greatly reduce the effort and costs associated with multimedia courseware development.

5. CONTENT

The content of a multimedia system is the set of assets from which it is composed. As we have seen assets can be pieces of text, images, sounds, video, music and so on. The TALENT toolkit must allow developers to store, browse, search for and update assets in any of these forms. This requires the storage of assets as well as information relating to these assets such as name, owner, description, creation date and so on.

As the system may contain a large number of assets it is important to provide mechanisms for finding and organising assets according to user defined criteria. In order to encourage reuse and to support multiple developers it is important that all assets are available to each developer. However, the concept of ownership is important so that one developer does not remove or modify assets that belong to someone else. This protects the integrity of each developers work.

6. STRUCTURE

The structure of a multimedia document describes how the assets are combined and presented to the user. It is the structure which specifies both the makeup of the individual screens, windows, cards or whatever and the navigational paths which allow the user to move between them.

The TALENT toolkit takes an abstraction neutral approach to structure by allowing for the creation and storage of arbitrarily complex structures within the system. These structures can be created and manipulated through the use of tools. It is possible to provide a range of tools each of which is optimised for a specific kind of structure -for example, trees graphs, tables, lists and so on. Because a single internal representation is used it is possible to add new tools in order to support new kinds of structures and thus to extend the toolkit without introducing incompatibilities.

Three basic kinds of structures are central to the current implementation of the toolkit. These are: a tree based hierarchy which reflects the overall organisational structure of a piece of courseware; a graph based navigational structure which is driven by pre-requisites in order to implement a pedagogic model; and a list based content structure which maps assets onto particular screens. This last structure is also used to map assets onto templates which, as we shall now see, can change the way in which they are presented.

7. PRESENTATION

Templates provide a useful means of changing the presentation of information while keeping the content the same. Presentation graphics packages such as Powerpoint use templates to provide different layouts, backgrounds, colour schemes and typography while the information in the presentation remains the same.

TALENT templates are more complex as the number, order and format of the assets which go to make up screens can vary. For this reason, TALENT templates are really families of templates with each asset in a particular screen having a template type. The template type then maps on to a range of particular template instances corresponding to media formats for which that template type is valid. In addition there are template types for complete screens as well as for structures of assets such as lists and tables. At this time templates are not created by the user but a range of templates are provided.

TALENT templates are complex but the underlying principle is simple. The developer can change how an asset is rendered by specifying a given template for that asset. A complete description of TALENT templates is beyond the scope of this paper.

8. ARCHITECTURE

The TALENT toolkit takes an information-centred view of multimedia and the software architecture which was developed to support the toolkit reflects this. Central to the architecture is a database in which all assets, as well as structures, templates and other information are stored. The software tools act as an interface between the developer and the database for the purpose of inserting, modifying and accessing the various kinds of information. Figure 1 shows an overview of the TALENT architecture.

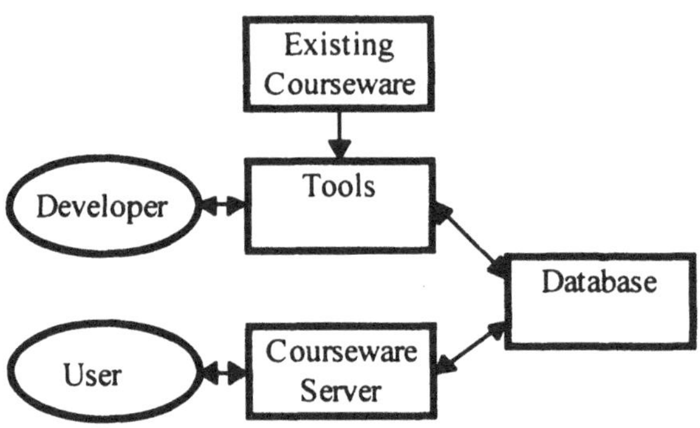

Figure 1. Overview of TALENT Architecture.

The World Wide Web is used as a development environment and delivery vehicle for the toolkit as well as the courseware which is produced using it. This affords considerable flexibility as both developers and students can access the courseware via a network.

The majority of the toolkit has been developed using Java and it is currently implemented as a set of Java Applets. This goes a long way towards making the toolkit cross-platform as it can be accessed from any machine that supports a Java enabled WWW browser.

The database is a modified version of Msql which is a light weight database server implementing a useful subset of ANSI SQL. This has been extended to cope with binary large object (BLOB) data in order to be able to store assets such as images and sounds. It should be an easy matter to modify the toolkit in order for it to work with commercially available database products such as those produced by companies like Oracle.

The database is capable of storing many courses or versions of courses simultaneously. As these courses may share assets and structures it encourages reuse in an efficient manner. It also makes it easy to localise a course simply by providing replacements for language sensitive assets.

The courseware server is currently a CGI extension to a WWW server and courseware appears to the users as a series of WWW pages. The WWW pages are created dynamically using assets, structure and templates extracted from the database.

In addition to courseware, the database is also used to store a wide range of administrative and housekeeping information including student records and registration.

The database is also used to implement a virtual file system which allows multiple developers to store and organise information in ways that can be shared and which encourage the reuse of assets and sections of courses.

The TALENT toolkit consists of a number of major components:

1. Courseware converter;
2. Asset manager;
3. Filing system;
4. Structure editors;
5. Template editor;
6. Integrity checker;
7. Courseware server.

The courseware conversion tools are described elsewhere (McDaid et al, 1997). Additional tools provide support for administrative and tutoring functions but these will not be discussed here. We will now look at a few of these tools in more detail.

9. TOOLS

Figure 2 shows the asset tool which is central to the management and organisation of content. This is divided into two parts: the left side relating to assets and the right side interfacing to the virtual file system.

The list on the left presents a subset of all of the assets in the database. The contents of this list are modified using the asset filter dialogue (see below). An asset in this list may be selected for viewing, displaying information or editing as appropriate. New assets may be uploaded into the database using a separate dialogue. This allows the developer to select a file on their desktop computer which is then uploaded through the HTTP protocol. A set of format conversion filters can be applied to convert the format of a particular asset to a standard format at this stage. The current filter set supports many popular image and sound formats.

The virtual file system implements a hierarchy of folders within the database which provide user space for each developer. The option button (top right) displays the path within the file system and is one of the ways in which the user can change directory. The list below shows the assets and folders within a given folder. Assets are not physically copied into folders but rather references to them so the folder system imposes a low overhead on the database. Also it is not possible to delete an asset simply by removing all of its folder entries. The copy button allows assets to be copied into folders while the buttons at the bottom allow folders to be created, deleted and permits the user to change directory. A separate folder tool (not shown) permits users to copy and move folders and assets around the file system.

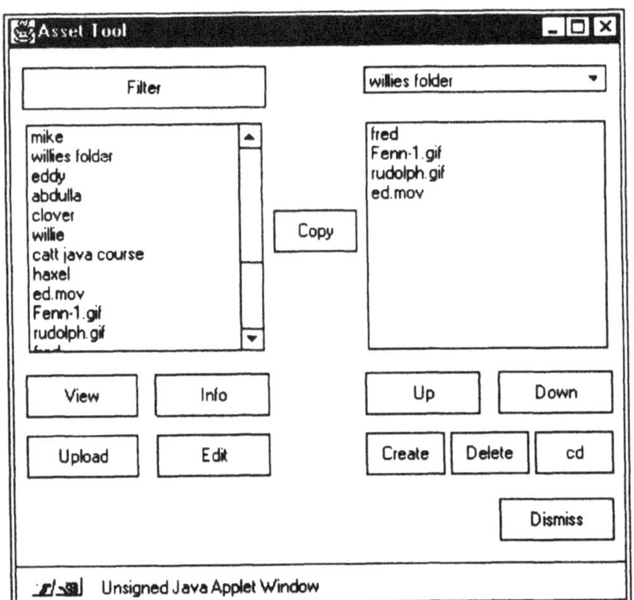

Figure 2. Asset Tool.

The asset filter is shown in figure 3. This allows the developer to select a subset of assets from the database for use within the asset tool. This dialogue allows the user to construct a query filter based on a variety of criteria. The results of this query are displayed in the left hand field of the asset tool.

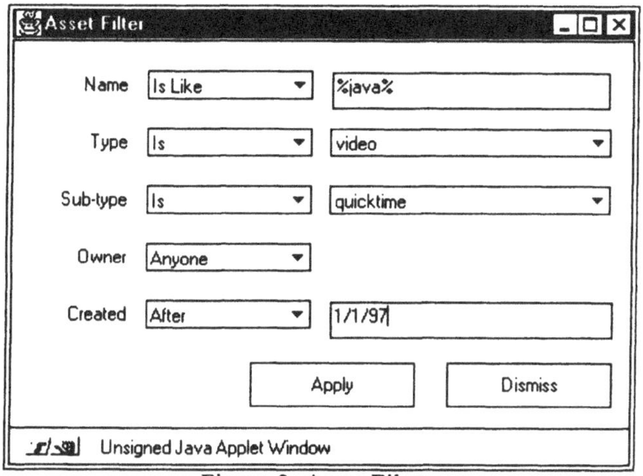

Figure 3. Asset Filter.

A number of tools allow the developer to create and manipulate the various structures within the database. Figure 4 shows the structure editor which displays the overall structure of a piece of courseware as a tree.

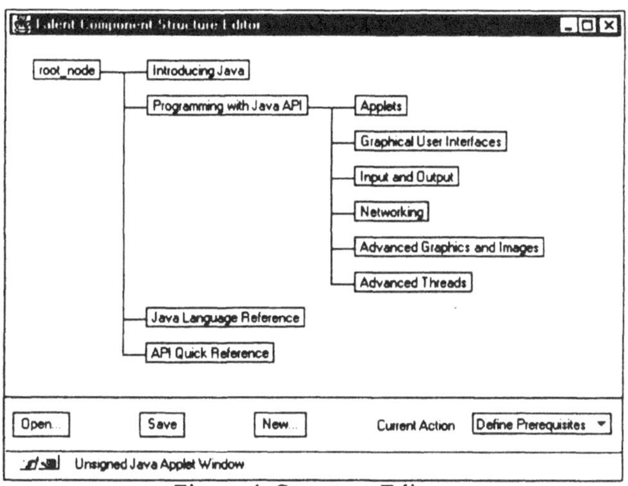

Figure 4. Structure Editor.

This has all of the usual features associated with tree editors including the ability to move nodes around within the hierarchy as well as the ability to fold and expand branches. Nodes can be added, deleted or modified.

Hierarchies can be created from new or are produced when an existing piece of courseware is converted. It is possible to copy some or all of a hierarchy for inclusion into a different course. Such a copy may simply be a reference in which case it cannot be changed or the hierarchy may be cloned and the cloned copy can then be edited. Audit trails record the provenance of such structures to prevent undesirable conditions such as referenced hierarchies being edited or deleted. Similar measures are taken to prevent assets being deleted if they are being used in any course.

The hierarchy diagram presents one aspect of the navigational structure of a course. Fine control over the pedagogic structure is expressed through the graph tool (Figure 5).

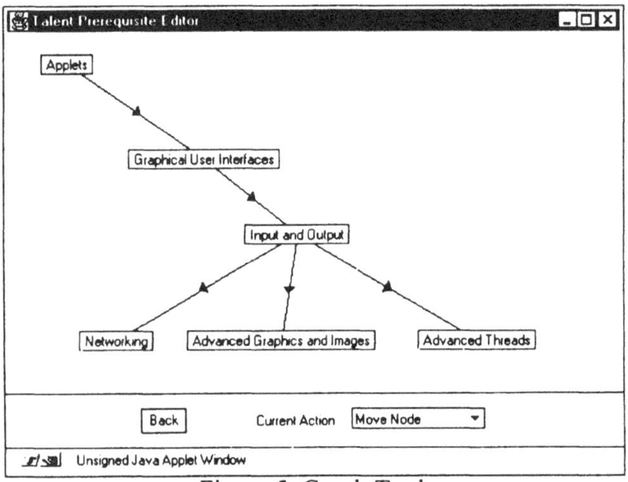

Figure 5. Graph Tool.

The graph tool allows the developer to describe the pre-requisites which apply within a course by specifying which nodes must be completed before a particular node may be attempted. The concept is similar to that of a PERT diagram as used in project management tools.

The nodes within the graph tool are the same nodes that occur in the hierarchy tool and together they allow the designer to specify the possible navigational structures in abstract terms. Thus, it is not necessary for each possible path through the system to be explicitly defined as any path which meets the criteria is possible. This allows the student to access the courseware in a flexible way which can be tailored by the student or developer to meet particular interests or needs. The dialogue structures are enforced by the courseware server which provides the necessary additional navigational controls to permit the student to navigate the course.

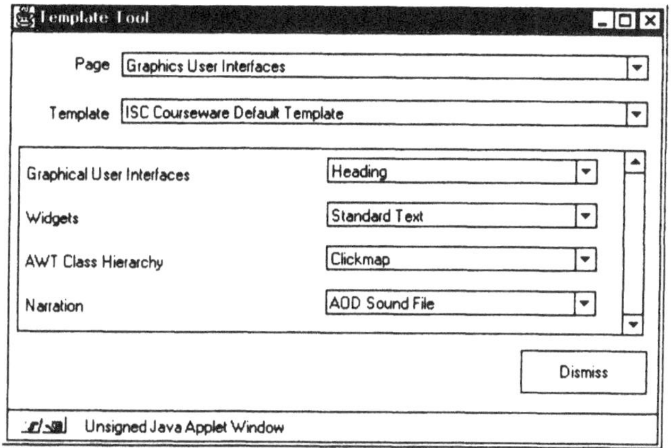

Figure 6. Template Tool.

The template tool (Figure 6) permits the designer to change the way in which the assets which go to make up a particular page are presented. The page template specifies a set of templates which can be applied to each of the asset types present. It also controls reordering and layout of components on a page as well as specifying global variables which in turn effect the individual asset templates. Each asset type has an associated set of templates including a default template which is used if no template type is specified. In simple terms templates can be thought of as HTML wrappers which change the way in which assets are rendered onto WWW pages. However, the implementation is more complicated.

This brief overview is intended to provide a flavour rather than an in depth description of the tools. The toolkit contains a large number of other tools and interested readers may wish to refer to the TALENT toolkit user guide for a more detailed description of the software (McDaid, 1997).

10. DISCUSSION

The TALENT toolkit has been implemented and used within the consortium to produce a number of courseware modules. Some of these have been converted from existing courses while others have been produced from new. It has also been used to localise some of these courses into different European languages.

It is apparent that the implementation is still a prototype and considerable refinement would be required before this software could be turned into a commercial product. However, the approach would appear to be promising. In particular, the use of the Web as an authoring environment has significant benefits including cross-platform delivery, support for multiple developers, reusability and internationalisation. The information-centric model is interesting in its ability to overcome the current lack of multimedia document standards. Compatibility with emerging standards can be easily provided and a certain degree of interoperability with conventional authoring systems is also possible.

The TOOLKIT will continue to develop throughout the project in response to feedback from users as well as advances in its underlying technologies. The next phase of the TALENT project will see the addition of tutoring facilities based on text-based chat and video-conferencing. It is likely at this stage that the delivery mechanism will evolve beyond HTML to a more advanced and interactive software layer but it is too early to predict how the technologies that this will be based on will develop. Later development of the toolkit will focus on the supply chain and organisational functions supported by the tools. However, it is envisaged that technological enhancement will continue throughout the project.

11. CONCLUSIONS

The TALENT toolkit addresses a number of important problems in the development of network-based multimedia courseware. By adopting a network-based architecture it provides improved support for cross-platform development and for multiple developers. The model overcomes a number of problems in conventional authoring systems particularly in the interchange, reuse and internationalisation of courses and assets. The toolkit is simple and easily extended and as such could provide the basis for important future work in this field.

12. REFERENCES

Appelt, W. (1991) Document Architecture in Open Systems, The ODA Standard. Springer-Verlag, New York.

Fletcher, J.D. (1996) Does This Stuff Work? Some Findings from Applications of Technology to Education and Training. Proceedings of Conference on Teacher Education and the Use of Technology Based Learning Systems. Warrenton, VA: Society for Applied Learning Technology.

Golas, K.C. (1993) Estimating Time To Develop Interactive Courseware In The 1990s, Proceedings of the 15th Interservice/Industry Training Systems and Education Conference, Orlando, Florida, November 29-December 2, 1993.

Kretz, F. and Colaïtis, F. (1992) Standardizing Hypermedia Information Objects, IEEE Communications Magazine, p60, May 1992.

McDaid, E., Row, G., McCool, M, Hashim, A. and O'Brien, W. (1997) Converting existing training materials to multimedia. Proceedings of Multimedia and Hypermedia Systems 97, Opatija, Croatia, 19-23 May, 1997.

McDaid, E. (1997) The TALENT Toolkit User Guide. TALENT Consortium Document 05R0010A, Interactive Systems Centre, South Bank University.

Newcomb, S., Kipp, N. and Newton V. (1991) The HyTime Hypermedia/Time-based Document Structuring Language, Communications of the ACM, p67, November 1991.

Pinheiro, E.J. (1994) New Tools for Multimedia Development: ScriptX. 1994 CAUSE Annual Conference. Orlando, Florida, November 29-December 2, 1994.

Vaughan, T. (1996) Multimedia: Making It Work, 3nd Ed., McGraw-Hill, New York.

13. BIOGRAPHY

Eddy McDaid is a computer scientist who has been involved in human-computer interaction research since 1983. During that time he has worked at various centres of excellence in the UK on research and consultancy projects addressing HCI, KBS, multimedia and distributed systems. Current interests include Java, visual programming, multimedia authoring tools and Web exploration technology.

Using telematics to overcome educational constraints: teaching differential equations using the world-wide-web and multimedia technology

G. P. Tsironis
Physics Department, University of Crete, and
Foundation of Research and Technology - Hellas (FORTH)
P.O.Box 2208, 71003 Herakleion, Crete, GREECE
e-mail: gts@physics.uch.gr

G. Neofotistos
Lambrakis Research Foundation
Paparigopoulou 3, 10561, Athens, GREECE
e-mail: georgen@www.lrf.gr

Abstract

A university course to introduce sophomore (second-year) physics university students to differential equations with the help of the world-wide-web and interactive multimedia technology is currently being designed and implemented at the Physics Department of the University of Crete. On-line differential equation solvers, interactive multimedia demonstrations, lecture notes and a set of worked examples on contemporary physics and real-life applications (chosen to reveal similarities between subfields of physics or between physics and other sciences,) and student term-projects on modern science developments, aim at improving the conceptual understanding and the problem-solving ability of the physics majors.

Keywords

Tools for distance education, Web applications, Interactive multimedia, Differential equations, Physics

The Virtual Campus F. Verdejo & G. Davies (Eds.)

1. INTRODUCTION

The physics curriculum, as presently taught, was developed over thirty years ago (Redish and Wilson, 1993). Although physics has changed a lot during these years, the curriculum has not changed very much. Thus, the introductory college student rarely gets any hint of modern developments or of the excitement of doing physics and learning new things about the world that no one has known before. Another shortcoming is that, although standard instruction introduces students to the basic content of physics, it provides almost no activities that illustrate how research is done. To professional physicists, much of the pleasure of doing physics is associated with satisfying curiosity and learning surprising relationships and analogies of structure. Very little of this joy of the profession is present in the traditional introductory physics courses. Furthermore, research on student conceptual understanding has shown that many physics students entering college today have been trained to associate learning physics with memorization and application of memorized laws in narrowly defined situations. The traditional introductory courses do little to counter them on these views. An additional obstacle is the limited mathematical ability of the introductory student. Creative and open-ended problems require a level of mathematical sophistication (using analytical tools) usually not obtained by students until their third year of college.

The recent immense growth in the power and availability of computer tools and technology can help overcome the above mentioned constraints that have kept the physics curriculum from introducing more creative science at an early educational stage. The power of present-day computational environments can enable students to solve more interesting problems in the introductory course with relatively little training (Mestre et al., 1993.) In this paper, we will describe such a computational environment which we have designed and implemented in the context of the "Introduction to Differential Equations" course taught to sophomore physics majors at the Physics Department of the University of Crete. It comprises an environment where the students can access (in the course's web-site) course-notes and homework assignments, on-line differential equation solvers, animated interactive demonstrations, solved problems on contemporary physics and real-life applications, and the term-project reports (on modern science problems) of students. Shortly, a stand-alone interactive multimedia CD-ROM will be handed-in. Our objective is to instill the excitement, curiosity, and creativity of doing physics in the physics majors and develop their conceptual understanding and problem-solving skills.

2. THE PERCEIVED EDUCATIONAL NEEDS OF PHYSICS STUDENTS

Research on student conceptual understanding over the past decade has shown that many students are not developing a satisfactory conceptual understanding of basic physics (Goldberg and Bendall, 1995). Many of these studies have documented the difficulties students have making connections between various representations (graphs, diagrams, equations), basic concepts and principles, and real world phenomena (McDermott et al., 1987.) What has become apparent is that many decisions students make about the behaviour of physical systems seem to be driven more by prior knowledge and beliefs than by interpretations and applications of formal physics principles (Johansson et al., 1985.) Other studies have shown that students' knowledge often seems to consist of separate facts, formulas, and equations organized poorly for retention and use (Van Heuvelen, 1991.) A study by Hammer (1994) suggests that students may hold the belief that physics is just a collection of symbols, formulas, and the rules of manipulating them

Teaching differential equations should focus on improving the knowledge structure and the problem-solving ability of physics majors; this will be discussed in the following section. This objective can be achieved by immersing the student in an educational environment where he or she will integrate principles, concepts, and procedures. The main intent is to highlight the role of concepts and procedures in problem solving and in doing so to counter novices' tendency to rely on formulaic problem-solving approaches.

3. TEACHING DIFFERENTIAL EQUATIONS: THE EDUCATIONAL OBJECTIVE

In physics alone, most physical phenomena, whether in the domain of fluid dynamics, electricity, magnetism, mechanics, optics, or heat flow, can be described in general by differential equations; in fact, most of mathematical physics is differential equations.

Differential equations provide an extremely fertile ground to 'tie' similar phenomena together (wherever they may appear - either between subfields of physics such as in mechanics, acoustics, optics, electricity, heat, and theoretical physics, or between physics and allied scientific disciplines - see also, Shive and Weber, 1982.) Focusing on such similarities, students develop a more comprehensive view of nature and achieve confidence in dealing with new ideas, whether encountered in textbook problems or in real life situations. In addition to this aspect, the philosophy behind putting "Introduction to Differential Equations" in the Web is to make mathematics more useful, enjoyable, and readily available for all students. The basic technique is to engage students in situations so that they are motivated to "explore" phenomena and problems in physics and allied disciplines, and make use of the solvers and/or the computer when appropriate.

Our approach to the use of the computational tools is based on the following three principles (Redish and Wilson, 1993):

- It is not enough to use the computer to illustrate examples from the current curriculum. We must rethink the curriculum from the ground up, now assuming the availability of the computer. What can we teach now, with the help of current computer technology, that we couldn't teach before?

- The computer should not replace anything in the current educational environment: not the textbook, not the teacher, not the laboratory.
- The student should run the computer, not the other way round.

4. DESIGNING AND IMPLEMENTING A WEB-BASED COURSE

With the above mentioned goals in mind, we have designed and implemented a course in which emphasis has been put on skills related to the use of software rather than on programming skills. A major factor in the decision not to focus on programming is the availability of other means by which students can become proficient in programming languages. Students who wish to learn programming or to become more proficient than they already are can take a variety of courses offered by the Physics Department.

The content of the "Introduction to Differential Equations" course, which is offered to the sophomore physics majors in the Fall Semester, covers ordinary differential equations, power series solutions, systems of linear differential equations, formal theories of linear differential equations, and the Laplace Transform. It lasts 12 weeks and has an attendance of about 70 students. At the end of every week, concise lecture notes are posted in the course's web-site. The web-site related activities constitute an aspect of the course which can be done without. If the student decides that he/she wants a 'traditional' coursework, the student can proceed as he/she wishes; class lectures, tutoring, homework assignments, final exams take place 'as usual'. Above all, what the student interest and involvement indicated (see Table 2 for students' opinions), was their *voluntary* interest and involvement to learning through the new technologies. The web-site comprises lecture notes, solved problems (applications of differential equations to physics and real-life problems,) homework assignments, animated interactive demonstrations, and the on-line (web-based) differential equation solvers (in which the student assign numerical values to the parameters of the differential equations,) which solve and visualize the solution. The assigned problems are similar to the problems that appear in the new generation of introductory books on differential equations, i.e., Lomen and Lovelock (1996), Borrelli and Coleman (1996), Rice and Strange (1994), Braun (4th edition; 1993), and Strogatz (1997), as well as in the somewhat "older" ones, i.e. Shive and Weber (1982).

1. Predator-prey problems; shark population in the Mediterranean Sea during WWII
2. War in the Balkans (an interactive application of Lanchester's combat model)
3. Stability of a floating body
4. Non-linear energy transfer in organic systems
5. Ocean-atmosphere dynamic coupling in the Tropics
6. Evolution of a star
7. Richardson's model of conflict
8. Population dynamics of bugs
9. Earth's population dynamics
10. Greece's population dynamics
11. Authenticity of paintings
12. Epidemiology
13. High-altitude free fall
14. Water-leaking buckets
15. Internet-users population dynamics
16. An atomic waste disposal problem
17. The battle of Iwo Jima
18. Using mathematics to understand HIV immune dynamics
19. Euler's three body problem
20. Applications of the logistics equation
21. Two-dimensional motion with air resistance quadratic in the speed
22. Tacoma-Narrows bridge failure
23. A simple non-linear oscillator
24. A simple model for the detection of diabetes

Table 1: student projects

For the term-projects, students can select, voluntarily, problems of interest to them. The projects are of sufficient difficulty that it required more than a simple homework solution. One project involved the combination of a multimedia authoring tool with a programming language in order to create an interactive game (on-line). Table 1 presents the projects taken by the students during the Fall '96 Semester. The reports of these projects have been posted on the course's web-site (in greek; at http://www.physics.uch.gr/~diffeq.) These web-based reports enrich the course material for the students to come as well as the continuing education of the practicing high school teachers who can remotely access the course's web-site.

It should be noted that the students can access the materials by logging-in remotely or through one of the computers available for student use in the computational laboratory of the Physics Department (20 in total). The class of '97 statistics and the students' opinions (as registered in a questionnaire which was distributed to them during the final exam) are presented in Table 2:

ENROLLMENT: 68 students (43 passed, 25 failed)
NUMBER OF STUDENTS TAKING PROJECTS (VOLUNTARILY): 40
(of these students, 32 passed, 8 failed)
DID STUDENTS CONSIDER THE WEB-BASED MATERIAL USEFUL?
Yes: 41
No: 16
No answer: 5
DID STUDENTS CONSIDER PROJECTS HELPFUL TO THEIR UNDERSTANDING?
Yes: 66%
No: 21%
So-and-so: 5%
No answer: 8%
STUDENTS LIKED:
Interdisciplinary problems: 47%
Student collaboration: 29%
Posting the project report to the web-site: 16%
Opportunity to research: 50%

Table 2: Class Statistics and Students' Opinions

We are currently in the process of creating a CD-ROM, on the course's material, as a stand-alone educational tool (which will be handed to the students in the beginning of the semester) to enable the student to be an active participant to his or her own learning. We have designed four *Rooms* (the *Classroom,* the *Library,* the *Applications Room,* and the *Computer Room,*) where the student can navigate through and "explore" differential equations from different points of view.

5. CONCLUSION

Teaching differential equations should focus on improving the knowledge structure and the problem-solving ability of physics. This objective can be achieved by immersing the student in an educational environment where he or she will integrate principles, concepts, and procedures. The main intent of our educational effort at the Physics Department of the University of Crete, is to highlight the role of concepts and procedures in problem solving and in doing so to counter students' tendency to rely on formulaic problem-solving approaches.

6. REFERENCES

Borrelli, R.L. and Coleman, C.S. (1996) Differential Equations, a modeling perspective; preliminary edition. John Wiley & Sons, Inc., New York.

Braun, M. (1993) Differential Equations and their Applications, 4th edition Springer Verlag, New York.

Goldberg, F. and Bendall, S. (1995) "Making the invisible visible: a teaching/learning environment that builds on a new view of the physics learner," *American Journal of Physics*, **63**, 978.

Hammer, D. (1994) "Epistemological beliefs in introductory physics," *Cognitive Instruments*, **12**,151.

Johansson, B., Marton, F. and Svensson, L. (1985) "An approach to describing learning as change between qualitatively different conceptions", in *Cognitive Structure and Conceptual Change*, ed. by L. West and A. Pines, Academic Press, New York.

Lomen, D. and Lovelock, D. (1996) Exploring Differential Equations via Graphics and Data, preliminary edition. John Wiley & Sons, Inc., New York.

McDermott, L., Rosenquist, M.L. and Van Zee, E.H. (1987) "Student difficulties in connecting graphs and physics: Examples from kinematics," *American Journal of Physics*, **55**, 503.

Mestre, J.P., Dufresne, R.J., Gerace, W.J. and Hardiman, P.T. (1993) "Promoting skilled problem-solving behavior among beginning physics students," *Journal of Research in Science Teaching*, **30**, 303.

Redish, E.F. and Wilson, J.M. (1993) "Student programming in the introductory physics course: M.U.P.P.E.T.," *American Journal of Physics*, **61**, 222.

Rice, B.J. and Strange, J.D. (1994) Ordinary Differential Equations with Applications. Brooks/Cole Publishing Company, Pacific Grove, California.

Shive, J.N. and Weber, R.L. (1982) Similarities in Physics. Adam Hilger Ltd, Bristol.

Van Heuvelen, A. (1991) "Overview, case study physics," *American Journal of Physics*, **59**, 898.

West, B., Stogatz, S., McDill, J.M. and Cantwell, J. (1997) Interactive Differential Equations, Addison Wesley Interactive.

7. BIOGRAPHIES

George P. Tsironis was born in Athens, Greece, on October 12, 1958. He studied physics at the University of Athens (where he received his B.Sc. degree in 1981) and University of Rochester (Rochester, NY, USA) where he received his Ph.D. degree in 1986. He worked as research associate at the University of California at San Diego (1986-1989) and the Fermi National Accelerator Laboratory (1989-1991). During 1991-1995 he was assistant professor of physics at the University of North Texas (Denton, TX, USA). Since 1994 he has been associate professor of physics at the University of Crete, Greece. His main interests are in the areas of nonlinear dynamics, statistical physics, and the study of chaos. He has also been experimenting with new modes of physics instruction including multimedia and the world-wide-web.

George Neofotistos has recently joined the Lambrakis Research Foundation (LRF; in Athens, Greece) where he is managing, as assistant manager, the ESPRIT MENON Project (the European multimedia support network for education.) Before joining LRF, he was with the Physics Department of the University of Crete (1996-1997), the Greek Army R&D Center (1994-1996), the Florida Institute of Technology (1991-1994; Melbourne, FL, USA; assistant professor of physics), and Temple University (1990-1991; visiting professor of physics). He got his Ph.D. degree in physics from Temple University in 1989 and joined the Electrical Engineering Department of Purdue University as a postdoctoral research associate (1989-1990).

INDEX OF CONTRIBUTORS

KEYWORD INDEX

SPRINGER NATURE

GPSR Compliance

The European Union's (EU) General Product Safety Regulation (GPSR) is a set of rules that requires consumer products to be safe and our obligations to ensure this.

If you have any concerns about our products, you can contact us on ProductSafety@springernature.com

In case Publisher is established outside the EU, the EU authorized representative is:

Springer Nature Customer Service Center GmbH
Europaplatz 3
69115 Heidelberg, Germany

FSC
www.fsc.org
MIX
Papier | Fördert gute Waldnutzung
FSC® C083411

Kolibri 360 GmbH
Ferdinand-Jühlke-Straße 7
99095 Erfurt, Deutschland
produktsicherheit@kolibri360.de